D1766355

USES OF FORCE AND WILSONIAN FOREIGN POLICY

USES OF
force

and Wilsonian Foreign Policy

FREDERICK S. CALHOUN

The Kent State University Press

Kent, Ohio, and London, England

© 1993 by The Kent State University Press, Kent, Ohio 44242

All rights reserved

Library of Congress Catalog Card Number 92-31632

ISBN 0-87338-464-4

Manufactured in the United States of America

Library of Congress Cataloging-in-Publication Data

Calhoun, Frederick S.

    Uses of force and Wilsonian foreign policy / Frederick S. Calhoun.

      p. cm. — (American diplomatic history)

    Includes bibliographical references and index.

    ISBN 0-87338-464-4 (pbk. : alk. paper) ∞

    1. United States—Foreign relations—1913–1921. 2. Wilson,

Woodrow, 1856–1924—Views on intervention. 3. Intervention

(International law) I. Title. II. Series.

E768.C354 1993

327.73—dc20   92–31632

                                            CIP

British Library Cataloging-in-Publication data are available.

To Ken and Holly Hargreaves
À la recherche du temps perdu

CONTENTS

ACKNOWLEDGMENTS

This book has been a dozen years in the making, not because the ideas were so difficult nor the research so overwhelming nor even the writing so terribly hard. Thanks to the faith and support of my good friend John T. Hubbell at The Kent State University Press, even publishing it went reasonably smoothly. Other tasks and diversions simply intervened to keep me from it. I first developed the idea for a vocabulary of force based on Woodrow Wilson's multiple resorts to force as the subject of my doctoral dissertation in the late 1970s. At the time it seemed a good idea to provide a general history of each of Wilson's seven military interventions before defining the various uses of force on which he relied.

So I set about to write that general history, thinking always of it as Part One of some larger study defining the uses of force. As I finished each chapter, I dutifully sent it off to my adviser. When I finally got through the twin interventions in northern Russia and Siberia, I put the chapters in the mail with a note indicating that Part One was now complete. I vowed to begin Part Two.

By return mail my adviser advised me that enough was enough; Part One was sufficient for a dissertation and, ultimately, for a book of its own. For that wise counsel, I am grateful for the kind intercession of Akira Iriye. He insisted that I divide into more easily digestible pieces my theories of Woodrow Wilson, his power and principles, and his uses of force. Iriye not only guided my graduate studies, delivering me to some level of maturity as a historian, but also has continued over the years to offer me the benefit of his guidance. I know of no greater historian.

Once my dissertation was complete, it was then of course necessary to earn a living and begin supporting my family. In 1984 Stanley E. Morris hired me to write a history of the United States Marshals. My work on *The Lawmen: United States Marshals and Their Deputies, 1789–1989* (Smithsonian Institution Press, 1990) again kept me from finishing Part Two. Curiously, though, the marshals complemented my work on Wilson. In *Power and Principle*, I studied the government's application of power internationally; in *The Lawmen*, I studied its domestic application.

For the past seven years, I have worked with a group of men and women who use force professionally. Seeing it expressed at that primal level has given me a considerably different perspective on force. Reading eighty-year-old letters and reports of Wilsonian interventions is one thing; watching (from a distance) a deputy marshal, weapon to hand, kick in the door of a wanted felon's house is quite another. I am grateful to all those deputies, and there are a large number of them now, who suffered my curiosity—and kept me from harm—as they risked their lives chasing fugitives, protecting judges, escorting prisoners, or executing the orders of the courts.

Over the years a number of good friends have debated my ideas with me, challenging me to think more thoroughly than I am accustomed to doing. I am grateful to Steve Wheatley and Jack Michel, Deborah Gough and Nancy Protheroe, Barry Karl and Friedrich Katz, and David Trask and Jonathan Utley. Lloyd Ambrosius read the manuscript and offered many useful suggestions and critiques. I also imposed upon a number of friends to read it. Jeff Miller and Roger Archega, Michael McShane and Ana-Marie Sullivan, and Akira Iriye and Cynthia G. Fox each gave invaluable comments on the early drafts of this book. They improved it considerably, though I am afraid that my native Southern intransigence may have kept those improvements to a minimum.

As always, my parents, Jim and Eleanor Calhoun, sustained me beyond the point of parental support or filial recompense. Their faith in me and my future has always been the brightest beacon guiding me.

Ken and Holly Hargreaves, more than anyone else outside my family, have suffered with me the writing of three histories. Their influence has been immeasurable, their friendship irreplaceable.

My wife Leslie has occasionally been able to remind me that there is life beyond Wilson and the United States Marshals. She and our children, Austin and Emily, have enriched that life with their love.

And to Amy Blake Calhoun, who was born just as I finished reviewing the final page proofs to this book, I can only repeat what I once wrote her older brother and sister. I hope that she will grow up in a world where the subject of this book will be an archaic curiosity. The first step to achieving that is understanding. I have—again—tried to take that step.

The ideas, conclusions, interpretations, and errors in this study are purely my own and do not represent the views of the many friends and advisers who helped me with it. Nor are they the views or interpretations of any of my employers, past or present.

USES OF FORCE AND WILSONIAN FOREIGN POLICY

1 The Uses of FORCE in Wilsonian Diplomacy

Force achieves many international goals. Nations turn to arms to defend their territories or to steal more; to protect their citizens or to punish others; to exert their independence or to subdue it in others; to resolve disputes or to impose their views. Wars have been fought over God and women, gold and land, glory and status. The Greeks fought for a decade to rescue Helen of Troy; the crusaders battled for two centuries to reclaim the Holy Land. Throughout history, national leaders have accepted force as a convenient method to express their will, whether toward their own peoples or toward the peoples of foreign lands.

In a previous book, I suggested that international power assumes many forms—diplomatic, economic, moral, military (the threat of force), and armed power (the actual use of force). To examine the subject of power, the study used force as the example, policy as the theme. The presidency of Woodrow Wilson provided the setting. Wilson repeatedly relied on force to implement his foreign policies. Between April 1914 and July 1918, he embarked on seven armed interventions, a record unsurpassed by any other American president. Wilson dispatched military expeditions twice into Mexico, into Haiti, the Dominican Republic, the battlefields of World War I, northern Russia, and Siberia. In Wilsonian foreign policy, force was an adjunct to diplomacy.

After analyzing each of Wilson's military interventions, I concluded that Wilson turned to force to promote American ideology, enforce international law, encourage international cooperation, and effect collective security. During each intervention, Wilson maintained strict command over the military to ensure that his policies—and his alone—were implemented. In the Wilsonian way of war, civilian control over the military was the method used to employ force. American democratic ideology defined the goals for armed power, international law described the rationale, and cooperation among nations provided the conceptual framework for international relations.[1]

Force was ancillary to Wilsonian internationalism. Wilson insisted that the same principles and moral scruples that shaped his internationalism also guided his use of armed power. "The force of America is the force of moral principle," Wilson proclaimed to the graduating class of the U.S. Naval Academy shortly after the navy occupied Veracruz, Mexico, in 1914. "Is that not something to be proud of," he asked the new graduates, "that you know how to use force like men of conscience and like gentlemen, serving your fellow men and not trying to overcome them?" America was unique, Wilson argued, because it directed its power toward the greater good of mankind, not toward aggrandizement and oppression.[2]

In investing American power with internationalism and ideology, Wilson insisted on absolute control over armed power. He imposed stringent limitations on his uses of force and the men who implemented them. Wilson depended on the American military to determine the tactical approach to occupying a city or country or engaging in a war (provided those tactics closely coincided with his policies), but he gave the military little say about the strategy and policies behind his interventions. That determination was his. The president jealously guarded his prerogative to establish the goals and define the objectives for using force.

Wilson limited his first intervention to the occupation of Veracruz, Mexico, despite the military's dire warnings that invading the city would lead to war. In taking the port, Wilson originally intended to punish the government of Victoriano Huerta, the Mexican dictator who offended Wilson's concept of democracy. In the spring of 1914, soldiers loyal to Huerta arrested a handful of U.S. sailors in Tampico, forcing them at gunpoint from a whaleboat flying the American flag fore and aft, then parading them through the city streets. This insult outraged Wilson and his military advisers. After the navy took Veracruz, however, Wilson saw an opportunity to initiate negotiations with all the parties to the Mexican Revolution. During the subsequent conference, the insult was forgotten; instead, Wilson sought not merely to rid Mexico of Huerta, but to solve the social, political, and economic problems causing the revolution. His strategy depended on limiting the intervention to the occupation of Veracruz.[3]

Two years later, Wilson dispatched the Punitive Expedition across the border to punish the Mexican marauders who had attacked Columbus, New Mexico. He again ignored the military's contention that the chase would result in war. As he had during the occupation of Veracruz, Wilson used the presence of American forces on Mexican soil to open discussions with Mexican authorities on ending the revolution. Once again, he believed that the negotiations depended on limiting the intervention, not expanding it. As a direct result of the intervention, American officials conferred with representatives of the Mexican government, but neither Wilson's force nor his persuasion proved effective in resolving the Mexican Revolution.[4]

In 1915 Wilson ordered the navy to take over Haiti and, a year later, to impose a military government on the Dominican Republic. The chronic breakdown of organized government in Haiti convinced him to protect foreign residents and to prevent some other nation—France or Germany in particular—from acting first. When, a year later, the Dominican Republic seemed to slip into Haitian-style chaos, Wilson again ordered the navy to take over the country. Throughout each occupation, the president insisted that the navy carefully restrict itself to the minimum force necessary. He intended to teach the Haitians and Dominicans American principles of democracy and self-government.[5]

Wilson timed America's entry into World War I, even to the extent of discouraging the military from preparing for it until the last moment. German transgressions on American neutral rights convinced Wilson of the necessity of war. Once he committed the country to the fight, however, Wilson hoped to reorganize international relations to avoid future wars. The reorganization depended on cooperation among nations. Throughout the war, Wilson generally allowed the military to fight as it thought best, but he reserved all authority to address the political issues of the war's resolution.[6]

Later Wilson, again overruling the military, agreed to the joint Allied interventions in Siberia and northern Russia in mid-1918. Although he concurred with his military subordinates that the interventions would offer little of military value, Wilson saw in each a way to underscore his commitment to collective action with those nations allied against Germany. In Wilson's mind, the interventions portended a future international system in which collective security would protect the peace and solve international problems. The twin interventions in Russia were the test cases for Wilson's commitment to collective action.[7]

The military never understood. "There seems to be almost a determination to deny the fact that the military ingredient exists in our national and international life," Rear Admiral Bradley Fiske, the aide for operations to the secretary of the navy, complained privately in the fall of 1914 at the conclusion of the occupation of Veracruz. Five years later, General William S. Graves, who commanded the American military expedition into Siberia—the last of Wilson's interventions—admitted that he had "never been able to come to any satisfactory conclusion as to why the United States ever engaged in such intervention." During the interventions that took place between Veracruz and Siberia, other soldiers expressed strikingly similar confusion over Wilson's policies and plans.[8]

Tasker H. Bliss, one of the few military men whose judgement Wilson respected, eventually came to share his colleagues' disillusionment with the Wilsonian approach. Bliss prayed that World War I would lead to the complete destruction of militarism and the disarmament of all nations. "It is European militarism, world militarism, that is the curse of the world," he declared firmly in October 1918. His solution to the war was to dump all armaments into the sea. "The cause," he wrote of the war, "was good because we believed that we were forever putting an end to the cruel business." Unfortunately, the Paris Peace Conference convinced him that Wilson and the other diplomats had failed to destroy militarism.[9]

As a member of the American commission to the peace conference, Bliss embraced the Wilsonian vision, even as he witnessed first hand its failure. By midpoint in the negotiations, he retained little hope that the peace settlement would achieve the Wilsonian goals. As he wrote his wife on 25 March 1919:

> Things here seem to me to grow blacker and blacker every day. Two months ago I offered to bet . . . that the Peace Conference would end in nothing. Now I am ready to bet more. To me there does not seem to be any honesty or common sense in political men over here. I don't wonder that the world is going Bolshevik. It is the last despairing cry of people who have lost all faith in their government.

"Civilization," Bliss wrote a friend, "cannot endure such another war." Unfortunately, the terms of the Versailles peace treaty, and the subsequent unwillingness of the victorious nations, including the United States, to disarm, convinced him that another war was unavoidable.[10]

Yet Admiral Fiske and his uniformed colleagues were wrong. Far from denying the importance of the military ingredient, Wilson understood it all too well. Wilson instead vehemently denied the importance of generals and admirals in determining when and why to use force, what to achieve, and when and why to quit. Wilson sought the military's advice only on how best to achieve goals that he defined. To the bitter disappointment of the leading soldiers of the day, he wanted nothing more of them.

Nor did Wilson believe, as Bliss did, that war could be eradicated simply by disarming nations and relying on international cooperation or comity. Rather, armed power undergirded the Wilsonian international system. Wilson sought limited disarmament and collective security to dissuade nations from turning to arms, but collective security meant, ultimately, collective, forceful action against renegade nations. "Armed force is in the background in this program," Wilson readily admitted about the League of Nations, "but it *is* in the background, and if the moral force of the world will not suffice, the physical force of the world shall. But that is the last resort, because this is intended as a constitution of peace, not as a league of war."[11]

Indeed, despite his reputation as a man of peace, Wilson never decried the resort to arms, only those selfish purposes over which other nations too often went to war. If the cause was right and the purposes enlightened, Wilson readily enlisted in the battle. "There is nothing noble or admirable in war itself," he maintained, "but there is something very noble and admirable occasionally in the causes for which war is undertaken." Americans, Wilson repeatedly asserted, were "the champions of free government and national sovereignty." As he explained in January 1916:

> There is something that the American people love better than they love peace. They love the principles upon which their political life is founded. They are ready at any time to fight for the vindication of their character and of their honor. . . . there is one thing that the individual ought to fight for, and that the Nation ought to fight for, it is the integrity of its own convictions. We can not surrender our convictions.

Although force was a "clumsy and brutal method," Wilson refused to advocate its abolishment until just wars were no longer necessary. "I will not cry 'peace,' " he proclaimed in 1911, "so long as there is sin and wrong in the world."[12]

In a speech to the National Press Club in May 1916, Wilson admitted that, "If I cannot retain my moral influence over a man except by occasionally knocking him down, if that is the only basis upon which he will respect me, then for the sake of his soul I have got occasionally to knock him down. If a man will not listen to you quietly in a seat, sit on his neck and make him listen." The power of America, Wilson believed, was "the might of righteous purpose and of a sincere love for the freedom of mankind." Force, for Wilson, was not inherently wrong or evil, it was the motives, purposes, and goals of force that were either wrong or laudable.[13]

In fact, Wilson promised that America "would lend her moral influence not only, but her physical force, if other nations will join her, to see to it that no nation and no group of nations tries to take advantage of another nation or group of nations, and that the only thing ever fought for is the common rights of humanity." To accomplish this, Wilson pledged "the full force of this nation, moral and physical, to a league of nations which shall see to it that nobody disturbs the peace of the world without submitting his case first to the opinion of mankind."[14]

Because he so strongly believed that force took its morality from the policies that controlled it, Wilson as president held firmly to his authority as commander in chief to control the military. He brooked neither quarrels nor interference from his uniformed subordinates. Nor did he allow them much control over any of the interventions conducted during his administration. By protecting his authority, Wilson ensured that each intervention, each resort to force, was confined to the purposes and policies he embraced.[15]

In the Wilsonian way of war, the limits of force were equal in importance to the power of force.

Consequently, the interventions undertaken by Wilson bore his stamp more than anyone else's. In the Wilsonian way of war, Wilson was the principal warrior. For this reason, studying his seven military interventions revealed much about Wilson, his policies, and his purposes. Those I analyzed in *Power and Principle: Armed Intervention in Wilsonian Foreign Policy.* But Wilson's reliance on armed power also illustrated how force could be used to achieve international goals. As I examined each intervention, it became clear that the general policies Wilson pursued—fostering American ideology, sustaining international law and cooperation, and establishing collective security—compelled him to alter, even during the course of a single intervention, the ways in which he applied force. Circumstances, too, changed, which also required Wilson to refocus the immediate purpose of the intervention on new or different objectives. The cumulative effect of studying all the interventions was to derive specific definitions or categories of how force was applied during each intervention. For my purposes, I called these applications *uses of force.*

Originally, for example, Wilson intended the occupation of Veracruz as a punishment for an insult to the American flag. As Wilson and his military advisers plotted this punishment, however, they learned that a large shipment of arms consigned to Huerta was due to arrive at Veracruz. These arms posed a serious threat to the American naval troops about to land in Mexico. Wilson hastened the intervention in order to intercept the munitions. Immediately after the occupation of Veracruz, Wilson privately arranged for the governments of Argentina, Brazil, and Chile to offer to mediate the dispute between the United States and Mexico. Wilson used that mediation to discuss the far broader issue of ending the Mexican Revolution. Months later, as he prepared to withdraw American forces from Veracruz, Wilson delayed the evacuation until the new Mexican government promised not to harm those Mexicans who had helped the American military administer the city.

Thus within the single intervention at Veracruz, Wilson changed the tactical purposes for employing force four times. The strategical goal of settling the Mexican Revolution along democratic lines remained essentially the same throughout Wilson's eight years as president. But during the course of the occupation of Veracruz, as with the Punitive Expedition two years later, the direct or immediate objectives he sought with force changed a number of times. Wilson moved quickly from punishing the Mexican government to protecting American forces from the shipment of arms, to proposing solutions for the Mexican Revolution, to protecting Mexican citizens. As I examined the other interventions, it became readily apparent that Wilson's flexibility in applying force was not restricted to Veracruz.

In the Wilsonian way of war, force responded to the needs of the moment, adeptly shifting course as events changed and new problems or concerns arose. I began to see, not a pattern, but certain characteristics as common threads. Specific uses of force reappeared in different interventions, if only temporarily. As with Veracruz, the Punitive Expedition began as an act of punishment, but during its course Wilson again arranged negotiations with Mexican authorities to discuss the Mexican Revolution. Similarly, Wilson went to war against Germany to punish its transgressions against international law. His ultimate objective was the creation of a new international system. In the Wilsonian way of war, force was a tactic of diplomacy, its uses intimately tied to foreign policy.

Other interventions contained different uses of force. The occupation of Haiti began as an effort to protect foreign interests in the strife-torn island, but it was subsequently used to impose an American solution on Haiti's presumed inability to govern itself. A similar chain of events obtained a year later in the Dominican Republic. The twin interventions in northern Russia and Siberia began as efforts to cement Allied cooperation under the publicly proclaimed excuse of protecting Allied war supplies in the north and Czechoslovakian troops in Siberia. Both interventions were quickly, though unsuccessfully, used to compel a peaceful, non-Bolshevik resolution of the Russian Revolution. In the Wilsonian way of war, force was flexible, its uses responding to new conditions, new policies, and new goals.

In thinking about the common threads running in various ways through the interventions, I developed a vocabulary to describe them. The idea for such a vocabulary was borrowed from international law, which uses such terms as *reprisal, force short of war, police action, limited intervention,* and *war* to discuss the various ways force is used among nations. The concept of defining different types of force is a sound one because it provides a convenient way to discuss complex events. The legal vocabulary of force permits international lawyers to justify, compare, and contrast armed interventions across time and among different nations. In other words, international law has developed an authoritative language for discussing force.

Their particular terms, however, are better suited to the demands of the law, not to the needs of historians. The terms are defined in broad generalities meant to cover myriad possibilities. Lawyers use them to describe an entire intervention at once, thereby compressing into one definition the changing purposes and circumstances that beset most resorts to armed power. Because the purpose of each term is to assess the legality of the action, the vocabulary implicitly contains a moral judgement. National leaders throw them about quite freely to justify their actions, to cover their misconduct, or to rationalize their decisions, thus making the vocabulary of international law too encumbered to be of much use to the historian.

I defined my own terms. The new vocabulary offers three principal advantages. First, the terms provide a convenient shorthand for describing the shifting course of events. They help clarify what happened during each intervention by tracking the changes that Wilsonian policy underwent. After isolating the various ways in which Wilson applied force, it was relatively simple to plot the changes during each intervention. The picture that developed showed that Wilson was reasonably capable of responding to changing circumstances. By defining the uses of force, a clear image of an enforced flexibility inherent in Wilsonian foreign policy emerged. Far from being a rigid idealist, Wilson was strikingly adept at fashioning his policies to the circumstances of the moment.

The new vocabulary provides a concise description of each intervention.

Second, the new terms allow comparisons among the seven interventions. By defining specific uses of force, it is possible to discuss how Wilson applied force in similar ways during different interventions. The occupation of Veracruz in 1914, the Punitive Expedition in 1916, and America's entry into World War I in 1917 each contained an application of force to punish those who had transgressed against the United States. By defining a particular use of force as a punishment, I was able to study how Wilson used it during at least three interventions. Identifying other uses of force allowed me to analyze the other elements of the several interventions. The terms establish criteria for assessing each intervention and for comparing the several interventions to one another. These comparisons help clarify what happened during each intervention.

The new vocabulary provides comparative terms for analyzing each intervention within an overall context.

Third, the new terms promise the potential for analyzing force across time and place. If Wilson used force in a particular way, then perhaps his successors and his predecessors also might have used it in similar ways. By defining that use, it should be possible to search for similar applications in other eras, under different leaders, and even by different nations. The new vocabulary allows force to become the subject, not the example.

Defining individual uses of force simply means understanding the use of force.

A use of force, then, is the application of armed power for a specific, definitive purpose. It is a historical judgement, not a contemporary rationalization, which describes the motive behind the resort to arms at any particular moment. Because conditions change, policies evolve, and new circumstances develop, the uses of force frequently change during the course of any intervention. Although an individual use of force is a static, identifiable—and therefore definable—entity, interventions are dynamic. Within the course of a single intervention, one or dozens of uses of force can obtain, their applications shifting in response to changing conditions.

Although Woodrow Wilson did not resort to all conceivable uses of force in his interventions, he relied on five different applications of armed power. Each of these five uses of force is detailed in subsequent chapters.

The use of force for protection is a government's resort to armed power in response to specific threats, real or simply perceived. It results from the belief that another government or organized group operating in a foreign country is about to take some action injurious to the intervening government's interests, ideals, or way of life. In short, it is an international act of defense.

The use of force for retribution is a government's resort to armed power to chastise another government or organized group operating within another country. It usually results from specific grievances over the attitude or behavior of the other government or organized group. In short, it is an international punishment.

The use of force for solution is a government's resort to armed power to resolve a problem with another government or organized group operating in a foreign country. It usually results from the belief that the intervening government can dispose of a problem with a foreign government or group by imposing its solution with military action. In short, it is an international consummation of will.

The use of force for introduction is a government's resort to armed power to compel or inaugurate negotiations with another government or organized group operating in a foreign country. It usually results from the belief that a military response will justify the intervening government's participation in negotiations. In short, it is an enforced invitation to discussion.

The use of force for association is a government's resort to armed power to ally itself with specific governments or groups, or in response to demands from its allies. It usually results from the belief that a military response will cement or maintain collective international action. The associates may be motivated by different uses of force. In short, it is an international act of cooperation.

In defining the uses of force, I do not claim that they are Wilson's terms, nor even that he would have understood, much less described, his actions in precisely this way. I am imposing on Wilson's actions my own concepts, drawing them broadly enough to apply them to other interventions by other national leaders. By categorizing Wilson's actions, I am trying to elucidate how force is used by isolating its elements into discrete parts. In doing so, I well understand that the process of categorization imposes arbitrary boundaries on the flow of events. Were I writing a history of that flow, I should be loathe to interrupt it. Because I am dissecting action into elemental parts, I am wholly dependent on the interruptions. They are the dissections. My purpose is not to describe Wilsonian interventions, but to define them.

I am offering a theory of force, not a history of Wilsonian interventions. The new terms describe Wilson's actions accurately, but more important, they provide a conceptual framework, deriving general descriptions from specific events. As we emerge from the Cold War era—when wars that were not quite wars were fought with distressing regularity, when military excursions were commonplace, and when governments were toppled by subterfuge and espionage, not to mention flat-out interventions—a vocabulary of different types of force should be useful to any history of the period. It provides a schema to describe the varied ways nations exert their will forcefully.

The Wilsonian way of war helps define our understanding of force, its uses, and its abuses.

2 FORCE
for Protection

. . . a government's resort to armed power in response to specific threats, real or simply perceived. It results from the belief that another government or organized group operating in a foreign country is about to take some action injurious to the intervening government's interests, ideals, or way of life. In short, it is an international act of defense.

In the Wilsonian way of war, the umbrella of protection extended beyond the national interest to cover the fundamental principles of a righteous morality. Included were objectives such as the defense of U.S. territory and peoples, and subjectives such as American ideals and beliefs. Wilson protected the defenseless and the indefensible, peoples and panacean ideals, property and principles. He was as ready to make the world safe for democracy as he was to defend America's borders; he was as prepared to uphold the freedom of the seas and the rights of neutrals as he was to safeguard the lives of Americans. Wilson protected Haitians, Dominicans, and Mexicans from themselves as willingly as he guarded U.S. citizens from the turmoil of Latin American rebellions. Under Wilson the ideals of America equaled in importance the lives of Americans; principles were as worthy of protection as peoples or property.

Protection was an elementary aspect of the way Wilson used—and excused—force. It appeared in each of the seven interventions. Wilson extended the occupation of Veracruz in 1914 to compel Constitutionalist Venustiano Carranza to give assurances that those Mexicans who had assisted the U.S military government would not be punished. The longer the Punitive Expedition stayed in Mexico in 1916, the more frequently Wilson claimed it was there to protect the American border. The navy landed in Haiti in 1915 because revolution threatened the lives and interests of foreigners. A year later, a similar situation developed in neighboring Santo Domingo. Wilson's battle cry during World War I was "to make the world safe for democracy." The twin interventions in northern Russia and Siberia were justified by claiming the necessity of safeguarding Allied war supplies from Germany and protecting fifty thousand Czechoslovakian troops from the Bolsheviks. Even the basic premise of the League of Nations, collective security, promised protection.

In part, the similarity among the several interventions was a result of the fundamental ordinariness of protection. Protection was the most frequently used force because there was so much that needed safeguarding and because it was so readily accepted as an appropriate justification. Self-defense has always been the most legitimate of explanations. By claiming that an intervention was intended to protect American interests, citizens, or ideals, Wilson was grasping for the legitimacy implicit in the assertion. Although protection was a convenient, widely recognized explanation, it was not always Wilson's dominant motive.

Determining when the use of force for protection was a primary or a secondary motive is difficult, at times well-nigh impossible. Wilson claimed it sometimes because he meant it and sometimes because he expected the world would accept it. It was both reason and rationale, motive and excuse. Take, for example, the events that culminated in the occupation of Veracruz in April 1914. From the moment that Wilson took office in March 1913, he had fretted about Mexico, its military dictator, and its revolution. Chagrined by the help the U.S. ambassador had extended General Victoriano Huerta during the February 1913 coup against Francisco Madero and anxious to calm the subsequent turmoil, Wilson sought to assist Mexico in achieving a democratic alternative to revolution. He wanted to teach the Mexicans to elect good men by resolving their differences along the American model.

Throughout his first year in office, Wilson tried repeatedly, and unsuccessfully, to negotiate an end to the bloody reign of Huerta and the Constitutionalist rebellion against it led by Carranza and Francisco ("Pancho") Villa. Angered by a string of Huerta's broken promises, Wilson even contemplated using force, but he had no legitimate reason to intervene. By the spring of 1914, his diplomacy had stalled. He had no alternate plans. [1]

Then, on 9 April 1914, Huertista soldiers in Tampico arrested a handful of U.S. sailors, removing them at gunpoint from a whaleboat flying American flags fore and aft. The arrest was a clear insult to American honor. Wilson immediately demanded a twenty-one-gun salute to the flag as an apology. Huerta refused. His refusal opened the way for the United States to make a reprisal—an act of force sanctioned by international law. On the evening of 20 April 1914, Wilson appeared before Congress to ask its approval for taking forceful action. At this time, it was not clear where the reprisal would take place. Although Tampico was the scene of the insult, the military's meticulously prepared war plans all specified the port of Veracruz, which had a direct rail link to Mexico City, as the logical site for landing troops in Mexico. [2]

To this point the intervention Wilson contemplated fell within the definition of a use of force for retribution. On the surface, Wilson intended to punish Huerta for the insulting behavior of his soldiers. At a deeper level, he also hoped to use the intervention to introduce himself into a negotiated settlement of the Constitutionalist revolution. The Huertista insult, petty as it seemed, gave him the legitimacy he needed to go beyond diplomacy to impose himself on Mexico's turmoil.

As Wilson and his advisers planned their reprisal, news came from Veracruz indicating that Huerta was about to receive substantial quantities of munitions. The news, which took several days to reach its way up the bureaucracy to Wilson, complicated his plans. Wilson had already decided to punish Huerta when he learned of the imminent arrival of the munitions. No one in the administration dared risk allowing Huerta to restock his arsenal moments before American forces landed. The arrival of the munitions threatened the troops Wilson intended to deploy. "The thing that determined the action," Secretary of the Navy Josephus Daniels wrote, "was the feeling that if the ammunition was landed it would strengthen the usurping president and increase the loss of life in Mexico, and that the guns might later be turned upon American youths. 'There is no alternative but to land,' said the President." Wilson immediately incorporated protecting U.S. troops into his plans to punish Huerta.[3]

On 18 April, the American consul at Veracruz, William Canada, had routinely reported the arrival of the SS *Mexico*, a freighter of American registry in the Ward Line fleet. The ship carried one thousand cases of ammunition purchased by Huerta. Another steamer, which Canada incorrectly identified as the "Irpanga," was due on 21 April with two hundred machine guns and fifteen million cartridges—a quantity Canada later described as the largest ever consigned to Veracruz.[4]

The next day, 19 April, Henry Breckinridge, the assistant secretary of war, learned "quite casually" of the Ward Line's *Mexico*. He was astounded at the unruffled attitude State Department officials were taking to the news of the ship's arrival. Secretary of State William Jennings Bryan merely proposed sending his assistant, Boaz Long, to New York to convince the owners not to unload the *Mexico*'s munitions. Breckinridge feared that this would take too much time. At a meeting with Daniels, he insisted on the "necessity of taking every means to stop the landing of this ammunition . . . if necessary by arms." Daniels, though, hesitated recommending such drastic action.[5]

The State Department instead conferred by wire with the managers of the Ward Line. Daniels ordered Admiral Frank F. Fletcher, the senior U.S. commander in Mexican waters, to charter the *Mexico* and buy its war supplies.

Although the company pledged its cooperation, the two departments, as Breckinridge feared, had acted too slowly. The *Mexico*'s cargo was well on its way to Huerta by the time Fletcher received his orders. Yet Breckinridge had sensitized both Daniels and Bryan to the danger of Huerta obtaining large consignments of munitions. The *Mexico* taught them the urgency of action.[6]

Attention therefore focused on the second ship. At first the Navy Department ordered Fletcher to dissuade the captain from unloading the munitions. Before the admiral could do so, however, the administration realized that Canada had misspelled the name of the German-owned *Ypiranga*. Without a declaration of war, the United States had no legal right to interfere with the movements of a foreign vessel, nor could it legitimately prevent the delivery of its cargo.[7]

When Wilson returned from addressing Congress on the evening of 20 April, he and his top civilian and military advisers debated the best way to make a reprisal against Huerta. When the president learned of the *Ypiranga*, he immediately ordered a landing at Veracruz. General Leonard Wood, the army's chief of staff, noted in his diary that "it was finally decided that Tampico was to be left until tomorrow after hearing from Fletcher, but that the custom house at Vera Cruz must be occupied because a German ship carrying 15,000,000 rounds of ammunition and 260 machine guns is due to arrive tomorrow morning." Wilson and his advisers knew they could control the destination of the cargo only by taking the customhouse before the captain of the ship unloaded its hold.[8]

The *Ypiranga* complicated the situation by compelling Wilson to adopt two separate but interrelated policies. The first was to punish Huerta; the second was to protect American forces from the deadly cargo. Under the convenient legal pretext of reprisal, Wilson took over the customs facilities at Veracruz. His immediate goal was to prevent delivery of the arms and ammunition. Wilson did not want to see the Huerta regime reinvigorated by a massive infusion of war supplies at a time when he was preparing to dispatch American forces to punish the Mexican dictator. The landing also fulfilled his intent to carry out a reprisal.

The excuse of reprisal only went so far, however, and the eventual delivery of the *Ypiranga*'s munitions to Huerta showed that Wilson clearly understood the limits of force. The German government, which took control of the ship on 24 April, declined to unload the cargo at Veracruz. It ordered the ship to sail to Puerto México, where it delivered the munitions to Huerta at the end of May. The United States made no attempt to stop the delivery because Wilson lacked both the excuse of reprisal and the powers of blockade derived from a state of war. Nor had Wilson any desire to expand his use of force to chase after the *Ypiranga* wherever it might sail. By the time the ship delivered the supplies, the situation at Veracruz had settled into a routine. An American military government administered the city while the Argentinean, Brazilian, and Chilean ambassadors to the United States mediated Wilson's dispute with Huerta. The danger that the munitions might be turned against an invading force from the United States had lessened considerably. There was no further need for the use of force for protection.[9]

The occupation of Veracruz is a perfect illustration of the complicated nature of force. It also shows the uncommon role that protection played in Wilson's decisions to resort to force. Both policies, retribution and protection, were carried out concurrently, but can be described as separate uses of force. Defining those uses helps illuminate what happened as American troops fanned out across the city.

Given the ubiquitous nature of the use of force for protection in the Wilsonian way of war, it is important to distinguish when protection was a motive from when it was simply an excuse. Although it played a dominant role during several of the interventions, during others its role was recessive. Nonetheless, Wilson frequently claimed that he was acting to protect American interests or ideals in order to enshroud the interventions in a cloak of self-defense. Determining the true purposes guiding his resorts to force helps describe the relative roles of the several uses of force.

PROTECTION DOMINANT: VERACRUZ

During the seven months that the United States occupied Veracruz, the military government established there relied on over two hundred Mexican citizens to assist in managing the city. Most of them had been employed by the city government before the occupation. By encouraging the Mexicans to resume their former jobs, General Frederick Funston, the military governor, hoped to alleviate the harshness of foreign rule and increase its efficiency. His policy was eminently practical because Mexican law, not U.S. law, provided the rule of government.

Because Mexican law also made it a criminal offense to aid an enemy of the republic, Admiral Frank F. Fletcher, who commanded the landing forces; Robert Kerr, who served briefly as civil governor; and General Funston promised protection to any Mexican who returned to his government post. Funston admitted that he felt "personally responsible" for the employees. Secretary of War Lindley Garrison finally agreed that "they all believe our good faith was pledged." In September, the pledges came due.[10]

The American administrators also feared that the customs duties they imposed on imports would be collected again by Mexican authorities. Secretary of State Bryan recognized the possibility and gave the following assurance to Garrison on 8 June:

> It appears to me that justice requires the protection of importers at Vera Cruz from the imposition of double duties. To this end it would seem desirable that before the American forces are withdrawn from Veracruz, a declaration should be obtained from the *de facto* Government of Mexico at that time to the effect that articles imported at the port of Vera Cruz during the American occupation, upon which duties have been paid to American authorities, should not be liable to any further imposition of duties by the Mexican government or the importers subject to any penalties or charges on account of such importations.

In September, this pledge, too, came due.[11]

Wilson decided on 15 September 1914, to withdraw the American forces from Veracruz. Huerta had fled the country the previous July, which meant that the occupation had achieved its primary purpose. In addition, the Constitutionalist forces of Venustiano Carranza and Pancho Villa, despite some basic disagreements, had now joined to form a new government. Carranza was first chief. By September Wilson had reason to believe that his policies fostering democracy in Mexico had finally born fruit. It was time to let the Constitutionalists settle the revolution by themselves. Wilson ordered Funston's command home.[12]

Funston suggested 10 October as the earliest date for an orderly withdrawal, but he also wanted the State Department to obtain Carranza's promise that no Mexican citizen who had worked for the Americans would be punished. Within days of the decision to withdraw, however, Funston knew that the promise would be long in coming. A "large number of secret agents of Carranza government now here preparing lists of persons who have to be dealt with," Funston reported on 20 September. "These will probably include all those who served us in the police, schools, customs house, sanitary work, and other branches of municipal government." Mexican law, he advised Garrison, imposed an eighteen-year prison term on those who "served a foreign invader." Funston had no doubt that Carranza intended to enforce this law. The first chief had designated the Constitutionalist governor of the state of Veracruz, General Candido Aguilar, who was well known for his "senseless cruelty," to arrange the restoration of Mexican control over the city of Veracruz.[13]

At first Garrison seemed more concerned about the imposition of double import duties than about the protection of Mexicans. He asked Bryan to take up with the Constitutionalist first chief the import issue and, if possible, to extract Carranza's promise not to punish anyone. Nonetheless, Garrison was not sure that the United States had any responsibility toward the Mexicans. They were, he told Wilson, citizens of Mexico and therefore subject to its protection and laws. The United States had no way to protect them from their own government and no authority to evacuate them from Veracruz.[14]

But Garrison reached that rather cold-hearted conclusion before he knew of the promises made by Fletcher, Kerr, and Funston. As soon as he learned of the pledges, he immediately changed his mind, and so informed Wilson. On 22 September, acting secretary of state Robert Lansing cabled Cardoso De Olivera, the Brazilian minister in Mexico City who represented American interests, asking him to obtain from Carranza "specific assurances" that both importers and Mexicans would be protected. "You will please intimate to General Carranza," Lansing added, "the advisability of giving these assurances in definite form and as soon as possible in order that there may be no delay in carrying out the proposed evacuation of Vera Cruz by the American forces." For the first time, the evacuation was tied to the protection of importers and Mexicans. Veracruz was still a hostage, but now to the use of force for protection.[15]

Despite Wilson's keen desire that "we ought not to linger in our departing," American forces remained in control of Veracruz for six weeks beyond Funston's originally scheduled withdrawal. Throughout September and into October, De Olivera repeatedly approached Carranza, seeking assurances about the double duties and the Mexican employees. The first chief, whose stubbornness nearly matched Wilson's, refused even to reply. In the meantime, the political situation collapsed. Villa went into open rebellion against Carranza over the triumphant revolution's program. Other factions led by Emiliano Zapata in the south, José Maria Maytorena in Sonora, and other smaller groups throughout Mexico also turned against the first chief.[16]

Even as Wilson struggled to hold the Constitutionalists together, he pressed Carranza for the promises. The pressure seemingly had little effect. Frustrated by Carranza's unwillingness to cooperate, American officials discussed alternate ways to protect the importers and the Mexican employees. Funston suggested registering each of the Mexicans at the American consulate, then notifying the Mexican government "in terms that could not be misunderstood that the United States would tolerate no punishment of them for having served us." Once "under the protection of the United States," he felt sure that they would be safe.[17]

Still, the negotiations dragged on, a test of who was more obstinate, Wilson or Carranza. In early November, General W. W. Wotherspoon, the chief of staff, advised General Tasker Bliss, who commanded the army along the Mexican border, that "things around Vera Cruz are not by any means improving. . . . We do not know who to turn the dirty place over to and we cannot get guarantees from anyone." The United States, Lansing informed Carranza, "feels morally bound to comply with its promises" to Mexican citizens and importers. The bind ultimately proved stronger than Carranza's pride. In late October, in a face-saving measure, Carranza posed the issue to the constitutional convention then meeting in Aguascalientes. The conventioneers proclaimed the necessary assurances for both those who had helped administer the city and those who had paid the import duties. In separate notes dated 9 and 10 November, Carranza finally gave his promise.[18]

Thus assured that the Mexican citizens and importers were now adequately protected, Wilson again ordered Funston to evacuate. On 23 November, six weeks after he originally intended to withdraw, Funston and his command boarded navy transports and steamed away from Veracruz. They left their Mexican employees to find their fates under the new regime, but took with them a wooden chest and an ordinary field safe containing a total of 1,604,905.26 pesos collected by the military government in import duties.[19]

PROTECTION DOMINANT: HAITI

By extending the occupation of Veracruz, Wilson showed how strongly he embraced the duty to protect foreign citizens, even sparing them from their own government and laws. During his second intervention, the occupation of Haiti in July 1915, Wilson resolved to protect the Haitian people from the chronic pattern of rebellion into which they had fallen. The intervention epitomized the Wilsonian use of force for protection. He was much less concerned about protecting U.S. interests in the country than he was determined to protect the Haitians from their own habitual revolutions. Wilson knew that accomplishing the latter assured the former.

For two and a half years, Wilson tried to arrange U.S. oversight of Haiti's finances, particularly its customs revenues. By managing the money, he could control the Haitian government. His model was the 1907 customs receivership that the United States had established over Haiti's neighbor, the Dominican Republic. Unfortunately, and to Wilson's increasing frustration, no government remained in power long enough to accede to the arrangement, even if any had been particularly willing to surrender such control. Generations of Haitians had evolved a revolutionary system of government—literally. Presidents were changed by the simple expedient of revolt. To facilitate the frequent transitions, the Haitian constitution allowed a national assembly to select the president, who was almost always the victor of the most recent revolution. Popular elections were unknown and unnecessary.[20]

The rebels were generally recruited from among the *cacos*, bandits who infested the northern hills. Most rebellions thus started in the north, then advanced down the coast. Traditionally, the rebels first captured Cape Haitian. The president, usually too indebted by his own revolt to rehire the cacos, fled the country. The national assembly quickly confirmed the new victor, who established himself in the presidential palace at Port-au-Prince. Soon after, some other enterprising individual hired his own cacos to launch his own insurrection. Revolutions were relatively bloodless, primarily because the cacos were mercenaries, not ideologues. They very much intended to live to fight again. The result, however, was constant turmoil.[21]

Most U.S. officials—junior and senior, civilian and military—thought of Haiti in the language of protection. "Only one President of Haiti has served out the regular term of office, seven years," Boaz Long, the chief of the Division of Latin American Affairs, observed early in 1914. "The political system which obtains throughout the country constitutes a certain form of slavery for the masses, and no helping hand has been stretched out to the common people in an effort to improve their condition." Lemuel W. Livingston, the American consul at Cape Haitian, complained in late 1914 that "if something is not done to put an end to this intolerable situation, the same business stagnation, suffering, pillaging, burning, and assassination . . . will most probably continue indefinitely."[22]

Navy officers unanimously believed that conditions in Haiti were chaotic and that force would be needed to protect American and foreign interests. The officers of the cruiser squadron under the command of Admiral William B. Caperton arrived in Haitian waters in January 1915 assuming that "conditions in Haiti are chaotic. The present government is without funds. Some action on our part will be demanded in the immediate future." Campaign Order Number 1 for the USS *Wheeling* specified that the ship would "operate to protect the lives and property of *Americans* and other *foreigners*." In the final report on the occupation, Caperton used the language of protection to describe his attitude:

> Haiti had witnessed the most kaleidoscopic political changes in history and we were of the opinion that only a government superimposed by the firm hand and supervised by the watchful eye of the United States, as a friend and well wisher, could ever rescue that unhappy republic from her beastly national sins. I was much interested in the fate of the Republic of Haiti. The history of the Island, its wealth and its commercial importance, justified our most intelligent and constructive assistance.

The navy's orders embraced the same logic. "Use force only on principles of humanity in protecting any actual or impending attack on the persons of foreign[ers] or their personal bona fide property or any other foreign properties in their possession," Caperton instructed his squadron commanders. [23]

Wilson concurred with the views of his subordinates. His policy, simply put, was "to bring some order out of the chaos." He wanted "to assist, in a friendly way, the establishment of order and the administration of a government which will safeguard the rights of the people of Haiti as well as protect the rights of foreigners doing business in Haiti." As Wilson once explained to Bryan, "The United States cannot consent to stand by and permit revolutionary conditions constantly to exist there." Motivated by a compelling ethnocentric humanitarianism—the desire to help other nations achieve the blessings the U.S. enjoyed, whether they wanted them or not—Wilson simply wanted to teach Haitians the American method of democratic self-government. But first it would take the use of force to protect the Haitians from themselves. [24]

Other factors, geopolitical and financial, also motivated American involvement in Haiti. There was much to protect. After the Spanish-American War, the American empire burgeoned. The addition of new possessions in Cuba, Puerto Rico, and the Panama Canal made Haiti essential to the defense of the United States. As the nineteenth century closed, Admiral George Dewey, the hero of the Battle of Manila Bay, described the geopolitical importance of Haiti:

> From the moment that we occupied Porto Rico, on one side, and eastern Cuba, on the other, the intervening Republics of Hayti and San Domingo became an essential factor in any war situation which we can conceive as likely to exist in the future. Our tenure of control is threatened with an instant collapse in Porto Rico and Eastern Cuba if any enemy seizes Hayti and occupies it strongly with land and sea forces.
>
> The consideration of an Isthmian Canal will in the future give to Hayti and San Domingo still weightier bearing upon the West Indian situation both in peace and war.

Admiral Caperton accepted Dewey's wisdom. Testifying before a Senate inquiry into the occupation, Caperton explained that because of Haiti's "vital strategic importance to the Navy in future operations in this our most threatened area, and the complications that might arise with foreign powers growing out of its chaotic conditions, I had devoted myself to especial care in all operations in that vicinity." Similarly, Secretary of State Bryan, whose understanding of geopolitics can, at its best, be described as primitive, confirmed that Haiti now assumed an "increased importance" because of the Panama Canal. [25]

Bryan was particularly interested in obtaining control of the Mole St. Nicholas, a "very desirable harbor" on the west coast of Haiti, across the Windward Passage from Cuba's Guantánamo Bay. Although navy officials were not enthusiastic about the Mole as a coaling base—they already had Guantanamo—they were adamant that it be kept out of foreign hands. After the start of World War I, they were particularly concerned with preventing Germany from establishing a submarine base on the island. Bryan negotiated with Haitian authorities for the purchase of the Mole, but the Haitian constitution prohibited the sale of national territory. The secretary had to settle for a promise not to allow any other government use of the harbor. Once the United States controlled Haiti, navy officials moved quickly to ensure that the Mole and other ports remained out of foreign hands.[26]

U.S. officials also feared the expanding financial interests of foreigners, particularly the Germans and, to a lesser extent, the French. "If our Government desires to eliminate the ever present danger of German control, which is today apparently more of a menace because Haiti's tragic political situation affords a favorable opportunity," Long wrote in May 1914, "let us now seize this moment to send a special emissary there to endeavor to bring her to a reasonable basis of financial administration." In January 1914, French and German troops landed to protect their embassies from yet another revolution. U.S. Marines also landed to defend the American legation. The experience convinced Wilson and his advisers that henceforth the United States would have to assume the full burden of protecting foreign interests in Haiti. They determined to avoid future landings by any forces except American.[27]

Yet American investments there, according to one historian, were "of limited scope." In 1913, U.S. investors had only about $4 million in Haiti, most of it tied up in the railroads and the national bank. By comparison, American investments in Cuba came to $220 million; in Mexico, they approached $800 million. Protecting American investments in Haiti was far less important to Wilson and Bryan than setting it on a straight course toward prosperity. Although Roger Farnham, who had significant investments in the National Bank of Haiti, was one of the State Department's closest advisers on Haitian affairs, Bryan seemed oblivious to Farnham's obvious conflict of interest. The secretary assumed that, like any good American, Farnham simply wanted to help.[28]

Nor was the Wilson administration particularly keen on compelling the Haitians to expand financial opportunities for Americans. In December 1914, a new president of Haiti, fresh from his own triumphant revolution, offered American investors special trade concessions in exchange for diplomatic recognition. Bryan was infuriated. "It is so evidently an attempt to negotiate for concessions that I think it is well for us to let them distinctly understand that this Government is not disposed to make a bargain of that kind," he wrote Wilson. The offer was especially insulting because the United States "was actuated wholly by a disinterested desire to render assistance." As Bryan once advised the German ambassador to the United States, the Wilson administration considered the United States the "nearest friend and natural champion" of countries like Haiti. It had no self-interest to promote, but would extend to all nations the advantages it enjoyed.[29]

Neither Bryan nor Wilson had other than humanitarian motives toward Haiti. Unfortunately, their humanitarianism was tainted by ethnocentrism. "While we desire to encourage in every proper way American investments in Haiti we believe that this can be better done by contributing to stability and order than by favoring special concessions to Americans," Bryan wrote the American minister to Haiti. The secretary was confident that once order was established, American investors would rush to the island. American policy was "actuated wholly by a disinterested desire to render assistance." Because U.S. officials attributed Haiti's chronic instability to bad finances, Wilson and Bryan proposed an American financial adviser to supervise Haitian customs as the best way to provide for the "tranquility, security and prosperity of the Republic."[30]

The French and Germans, Bryan believed, were not so generous. Although he found the idea of "forcible interference on purely business grounds" distasteful, Bryan proposed in April 1915 to use force to compel American supervision of customs. In this way, the United States could thwart the insidious effects of foreign influence. He advised Wilson that

> as long as the [Haitian] Government is under French or German influence American interests are going to be discriminated against there as they are discriminated against now. I have been reluctant to favor anything that would require an exercise of force there but there are some things that lead me to believe it may be necessary for us to use as much force as may be necessary to compel a supervision [of the customs] which will be effective . . . we have as much reason to object to the control of a Latin-American Government by foreign financiers as by a foreign government, and there is no doubt that the foreign financiers have been a controlling interest in the politics of Haiti.

Wilson agreed in principle with Bryan, though he was not yet ready to turn to force to combat foreign investments. As early as March 1914, he specifically determined that he would allow no outside influence other than his own in the finances of the Haitian government. To prohibit such interference, it was necessary to protect those interests. In July 1914, as yet another rebellion began, Bryan asked Daniels to station warships close to the island. Navy commanders were instructed to "afford protection to foreign property in Haiti." Within the year, U.S. commanders were assuring their French and German counterparts that the United States would protect the interests of their citizens.[31]

And the revolutions followed with disconcerting regularity. Michael Oreste survived as president of Haiti from May 1913 to February 1914 when the brothers Oreste and Charles Zamor overthrew him. That spring, Davilmar Théodore launched his revolution against the Zamor brothers, chasing them from Port-au-Prince the following fall. Theodore barely had time to enjoy his victory before Vilbrun Guillaume Sam organized a rebellion in December 1914. Once victorious, Sam was challenged by Dr. Rosalvo Bobo in May 1915. By the end of July, Bobo had captured Cape Haitian, the traditional signal that he had won.

Then Sam changed the rules of Haitian revolutions. As Bobo's mercenaries moved toward Port-au-Prince, Sam ordered the arrest of 240 of his political opponents. Secretly, he instructed the jailer to execute the prisoners if Bobo's rebellion succeeded. The arrests were an unprecedented outrage. In response, a mob attacked the presidential palace on 27 July. Sam fled to the French legation and the executions began. As news of the murders spread across the city on 28 July, another mob formed outside the French legation. Clamoring for Sam's head, the mob broke through the gates and rushed into the building. Sam was dragged outside, his body cut to pieces, and the pieces paraded through the streets of Port-au-Prince.

The flagship *Washington* steamed into the harbor just as the parade began. Admiral Caperton watched the gruesome victory march from the bridge. "I decided," Caperton later recalled, "to land American forces for the purpose of preventing further rioting and for the protection of the lives and property of foreigners and to preserve order." As soon as the cruiser docked, two companies of marines and three companies of seamen deployed ashore. The original landing, which Lansing subsequently endorsed, was for the immediate purpose of stopping the riot. Caperton's orders specified that the landing was "for the prevention of further rioting, for the protection of foreign life and property, and for the preservation of law and order ashore." He moved quickly, so "there would be as little excuse as possible for the French to disembark." The marines and sailors accomplished their mission easily. By nightfall, the bloodied mob had exhausted itself; the American forces controlled the city.[32]

But then what? Most administration officials agreed that Caperton had acted correctly in landing forces to protect foreigners and restore order.

Wilson wrote Daniels that he was counting on him "to do everything that is necessary to maintain peace and order and protect the embassies." He wanted Daniels and Lansing "to quiet the fears of the French and other embassies at Washington so that there may be no confusion of ships and interferences at Port-au-Prince." Other than that, though, no one in the administration quite knew what to do next.[33]

Having used force to protect the Haitians from themselves, it was inconceivable to members of the administration that the navy should withdraw and allow Haiti to collapse again into chaos. Yet the United States had no legitimate justification to keep its forces in Haiti. Stopping a riot, particularly one that had violated a foreign embassy, was one thing; it was an altogether different matter to extend or to expand the intervention once the riot was quelled. The use of force for protection only went so far. It could meet the immediate threat by subduing a mob of Haitians, but it could not legitimately go much beyond that. Once the mob dispersed and order was restored, the need for protection ended. Consequently, Wilson and Lansing grappled their way toward another use of force to solve the Haitian problem.

"The situation in Haiti is distressing and very perplexing," Lansing advised Wilson on 3 August, "I am not at all sure what we ought to do or what we can legally do." Wilson agreed. "My own judgment is as much perplexed as yours," he confessed to Lansing. "I fear we have not the legal authority to do what we apparently ought to do," he added, but "there is nothing for it but to take the bull by the horns and restore order." Wilson instructed Lansing to arrange with Daniels to send a sufficient force to Haiti to control Port-au-Prince and the surrounding countryside. The Haitian congress should know that the United States would protect it, but "we will not recognize any action on its part which does not put men in charge of affairs whom we can trust to handle and put an end to revolution." Finally, the United States would now insist on constitutional government there, even if it had to "take charge of elections and see that a real government is selected which we can support."[34]

But this plan went well beyond protecting American and foreign interests from the chaos that was Haiti. Years later Lansing explained that Wilson's policy in Haiti was dominated by two purposes:

> 1. To terminate the appalling conditions of anarchy, savagery, and oppression which had been prevalent in Haiti for decades, and to undertake the establishment of domestic peace in the Republic in order that the great bulk of the population, who had been downtrodden by dictators and the innocent victims of repeated revolutions, should enjoy a prosperity and an economic and industrial development to which every people of an American nation are entitled.

2. A desire to forestall any attempt by a foreign power to obtain a foothold on the territory of an American nation which, if a seizure of customs control by such a power had occurred, or if a grant of a coaling station or naval base had been obtained, would have most certainly been a menace to the peace of the Western Hemisphere, and in flagrant defiance of the Monroe Doctrine.

Yet the use of force for protection could not help Wilson achieve these more ambitious policies. Protection had justified the original landing, but in itself it could not effectively resolve Haiti's root problems. Once order was restored and the riot quelled, a semblance of peace returned to Haiti. Neither American nor foreign interests, nor even the Haitians themselves, were immediately threatened. Bobo was on the outskirts of Port-au-Prince, ready to occupy the presidential palace. After a few days, the navy easily could have withdrawn, though doing so most assuredly would have allowed Haiti to slip quickly back into its traditional pattern of revolution.[35]

Wilson decided to maintain American forces in Haiti to compel the Haitians to follow his direction. Although still intent on protecting the Haitians from themselves, he had determined that the only way to do that was to impose—if necessary, by force—American control. Wilson set about to teach the Haitians to elect good men by posting armed marines throughout the country. Caperton and his troops ceased protecting and began creating a new government for the country. The intervention expanded from controlling the city of Port-au-Prince to occupying all of Haiti. Caperton selected a new president for the country and wrote a new treaty for him to sign. In taking these steps, Wilson changed the use of force from protection to solution.[36]

PROTECTION DOMINANT: THE DOMINICAN REPUBLIC

The occupation of Haiti provided the cleanest example of the way in which Wilson used force for protection. The constant turmoil and chronic revolutions so close to the American doorstep were intolerable. After a frustratingly long, unsuccessful process of diplomatic and financial pressure, Wilson finally surrendered to the necessity of intervention to spare the Haitians from themselves. He followed a similar pattern of pressure culminating in intervention with Haiti's island neighbor, the Dominican Republic.

Unlike relations with Haiti, the United States enjoyed a formalized say in the finances, and therefore in the affairs, of the Dominican Republic. Under a customs receivership imposed by Teddy Roosevelt in 1905 and legitimized by a convention in 1907, the War Department's Bureau of Insular Affairs (BIA) administered Dominican customs duties, doling out an allowance for government operating expenses and applying the rest to retiring the large

Dominican debt. The relationship gave the United States a vested interest in Dominican affairs. U.S. customs receivers were stationed throughout the country, which meant that they needed to be protected. More importantly, the collection of customs required the preservation of a stable, constitutional government. The debt could not be paid if no revenues were raised and revenues were threatened by revolution. Thus protecting the customs receivership meant ending the chronic revolts.

As with U.S. policy toward Haiti, Wilson determined to support constitutional government in the Dominican Republic, if necessary by force. "Our experience in San Domingo and Haiti convinces me that we can render no more neighborly service than to rid them of constant revolutions which impoverish the country at large and enrich only a few ambitious chieftains," Secretary Bryan advised Wilson in July 1914. The president fully concurred. When the Dominican government faced yet another of its interminable revolutions, Wilson defined American policy:

> The government of the United States desires nothing for itself from the Dominican Republic and no concessions or advantages for its citizens which are not accorded citizens of other countries. It desires only to prove its sincere and disinterested friendship for the republic and its people and to fulfill its responsibilities as the friend to whom in such crises as the present all the world looks to guide San Domingo out of its difficulties.

As with Wilson's policy toward Haiti, rendering that assistance ultimately required the use of force for protection. [37]

In March 1913, just after Wilson took office, the Dominican Republic endured its own leadership transition. It went not nearly as smoothly. Ill health compelled the resignation of Monsignor Adolpho A. Nouell, the American-sponsored president. José Bordas Valdés won the election as provisional president to serve out the year remaining in Nouell's term. Over the next several months, Bordas's dispensation of patronage and government contracts managed to offend his supporters and his opponents. By September 1913 the small republic was in turmoil. Several political factions rose up against Bordas to claim by rebellion what he had denied them. The uprisings continued, with occasional respites, through two more presidents and two and a half years until Wilson dispatched U.S. forces to salvage what they could of Dominican democracy.

Wilson and his secretaries of state, Bryan then Lansing, consistently described U.S. policy toward the Dominican Republic as assisting "in the establishment of justice, in the remedying of abuses, and in the promotion of the welfare of the people." The best way to achieve these goals, they decided, was to protect constitutional government. In practice this meant installing a government "chosen by the people" and then ensuring that "changes in law and in personnel of the Government should be by constitutional methods and not by revolutions." As each new uprising was put down, U.S. officials chorused the Bryanesque refrain: "The day of revolutions has passed."[38]

Yet making sure the sun had truly set on Dominican chaos proved considerably more difficult than pronouncing it so. The search for a solution inexorably sucked the United States deeper into the Dominican morass. In December 1913, under an arrangement negotiated by the American minister, James M. Sullivan, thirty-three U.S. observers supervised the election of delegates to a constitutional convention. Bordas's candidates suffered an overwhelming defeat, which sent Bordas on a frantic search for some way to keep himself in office beyond the April expiration of his term.

Wilson and Bryan continued their blind support of Bordas. He had, after all, been chosen by a proper election and, for that, personified constitutional govenment in the Dominican Republic. In a spirit of benign friendship, the Wilson administration pressed on Bordas numerous suggestions for political and financial reforms, including the appointment of an American comptroller to handle government expenditures. Bordas placated the Americans, all the while hoping that they would support his overriding ambition to stay in power. He was a democratic imposter.[39]

Bordas, however, had not counted on the strength of Wilson's commitment to constitutional government. In April Bordas postponed the presidential election, finally, and clumsily, rigging his own reelection the following June. A Dominican revolt greeted the postponement; an American solution resulted from the fraudulent reelection. "Conditions are becoming intolerable," Lansing declared in May. Bryan announced that the United States "cannot remain passive any longer in the face of the unsettled state of affairs which is devastating the Republic of Santo Domingo." Unmasked as a constitutional fraud, Bordas lost the support of the United States. On 2 July, Bryan proposed to Wilson that they "insist upon the setting up of a provisional government and the holding of a fair election with the understanding that we will then prevent insurrections." Wilson adopted the idea as his own. In August 1914, as his wife lay dying and Europe marched to war, he devised a plan to protect the Dominicans from themselves.[40]

The Wilson Plan depended on the ouster of Bordas, the selection of a transitional president agreeable to the several contending political factions, and the holding of elections under U.S. supervision. Revolutions would cease; future changes in government would be by peaceful means. "By no other course can the Government of the United States fulfill its treaty obligations with San Domingo or its tacitly conceded obligations as the nearest friend of San Domingo," Wilson concluded. He dispatched a special commission to ensure that the plan was implemented. Under Wilson's threat—backed by U.S. gunships—that he would "not brook refusal, change of purpose, or unreasonable delay," the commission reported "full acceptance" of the plan in late August.[41]

On 27 August, Ramón Báez was sworn in as provisional president. Two months later, with American gunships stationed offshore with orders to "safeguard the lives and property of all foreign residents" and to assist "in preserving law and order," Báez dutifully held elections. On 5 December, he surrendered his office to the new president of the Dominican Republic, Don Juan Jiménez. "The period of revolutions is passed," Bryan again crowed, "law and order will be supported."[42]

The success of the Wilson Plan further entangled the United States in Dominican affairs. Having helped install a new government, it was necessary to ensure that it survived. "The entire principle that control of customs in turbulent countries preclude the possibility of revolution is now at stake," J. W. Wright of the Division of Latin American Affairs later argued, "and should it fail it will have, I fear, a far reaching effect upon the countries of Central America and particularly upon our present relations with Haiti." General Frank McIntyre, chief of the Bureau of Insular Affairs, advised Walter Vick, the general receiver in Santo Domingo, that "we are in a position somewhat different from our position in the past; that is, we are going to do more for this government than we ever promised any Dominican government." Succinctly stated, McIntyre wrote Vick that "the United States proposed to suppress any revolution against the Jiménez government." Like the old Chinese proverb, having saved constitutional government in the Dominican Republic, Wilson was now responsible for it.[43]

Bryan, with Wilson's blessing, described that responsibility in the language of protection. "This Government would furnish whatever force was necessary to help the President maintain order," the secretary wrote in January 1915. On 12 January he instructed Sullivan:

> You may say to President Jimenez that this government will support him to the fullest extent in the suppression of any insurrection against his Government. The election having been held and a Government chosen by the people having been established no more revolutions will be permitted. . . . The people of Santo Domingo will be given an opportunity to develop the resources of their country in peace. . . . A naval force will be sent whenever necessary.

Henceforth, Bryan wrote a month later, "reforms must be secured by constitutional methods." The United States promised to use all necessary force "to suppress insurrection and preserve orderly government." Jiménez was "entitled to and will receive from this government any assistance that will be necessary to compel respect for his administration." The United States, Bryan declared in April, "meant what it said . . . that it would tolerate no more insurrections in Santo Domingo and it will furnish whatever force may be necessary to put down insurrections." This litany of protection led ultimately—inexorably—to the use of force for protection.[44]

In spite of American support, which offended Dominican chauvinism more than it calmed its chaos, Jiménez governed the country, albeit uneasily, for well over a year. At the same time, Jiménez faced considerable pressure from the United States. Wilson and his advisers continued to press on the Dominican government various financial and political reforms, including the acceptance of U.S. advisers. The Americans, convinced of the purity of their own motives, failed to understand that accepting the suggestions would have solidified Dominican opposition against Jiménez.[45]

By the fall of 1915, as continued, occasionally violent, opposition to Jiménez disrupted constitutional government and the collection of customs dues, Wilson's policy began to shift. It had, in fact, been slowly changing since he formulated the Wilson Plan a year earlier. The United States grew less interested in protecting the customs convention and constitutional government from Dominican chaos and increasingly more concerned with protecting the Dominicans from themselves. After Sullivan resigned in disgrace over the private financial arrangements he had made with the Bordas regime, Chargé d'Affaires Stewart Johnson represented American interests in the Dominican Republic. By September 1915 Johnson was urging the State Department to prepare for a "comprehensive occupation." The Jiménez government was a failure; American intervention was the only realistic solution.[46]

The instructions issued to the new U.S. Minister, William W. Russell, reflected the transition in Wilson's policies. Wilson urged Russell to "exercise a real guiding influence in affairs in San Domingo." Russell's formal instructions, which were prepared in September 1915, specified that he was to add five amendments to the 1907 customs convention. The additions ranged the spectrum of interference in Dominican affairs, including the appointment of an American financial adviser, the establishment of a Dominican constabulary supervised by Americans, a protocol for settling financial claims, improvements in tax collections, and permission for the United States "to intervene in the Dominican Republic for the maintenance of a Government adequate to protect life, property and individual liberty." Only the Dominicans thought this was a bit much to ask.[47]

Strenuous, widespread opposition within the Dominican Republic defeated Russell's initial efforts. At the same time, the suggestion of greater interference on the part of the United States further weakened the Jiménez regime. By November U.S. policy was defined as awaiting the opportune moment when the Jiménez government would collapse so that American troops could take possession of the republic and impose a new convention incorporating the goals set forth in Russell's instructions. Short of that, the United States would not recognize any new government "until the rights necessary to the preservation of a permanent peace in the Dominican Republic are fully established."[48]

Secretary of State Lansing looked to the brighter side of Dominican opposition. "If President Jiménez should resign, or a revolution break out for any cause," he advised Wilson on 24 November, 1915, "we should be justified in landing forces to prevent bloodshed and to give the Dominican Congress an opportunity to ratify an amended convention." Although Russell was asked to "discreetly inform" Jiménez's opponents that the United States intended "to maintain the present constituted authorities, to support them in their efforts to secure peace and prosperity for their country, and to prevent the recurrence of bloodshed and anarchy," the Wilson administration was actually waiting for the Jiménez government to collapse.[49]

To everyone's surprise, they waited a frustratingly long six months. Other issues—the war in Europe, the struggle between Carranza and Villa—distracted Wilson's attention, but the lack of real resolution for the Dominican Republic festered. Jiménez had effectively blocked Wilson's efforts to help, but had not succeeded as well in solidifying his control over the country. In February 1916, the Dominican congress began impeachment proceedings against Jiménez. Desiderio Arias, who had long been the principal troublemaker in Santo Domingo, launched a revolution in April. Lansing again arranged for the navy to protect "constituted authority" in the republic. On 30 April, the USS *Prairie*, Commander W. S. Crosley commanding, steamed to Santo Domingo.[50]

When the *Prairie* arrived, Crosley found that Arias controlled the capital, though Jiménez and a force of loyal Dominicans were encamped on the outskirts. On 5 May Crosley landed three hundred marines and bluejackets to protect the U.S. legation. The troops made no effort to overwhelm Arias. From Haiti, Admiral Caperton, "perturbed and exercised" over Dominican events, sailed toward Santo Domingo with three more steamships. Crosley decided to warn Arias that he would bombard the capital if Arias did not lay down his arms.[51]

The next day, 6 May, Jiménez finally asked for help. Russell welcomed the opportunity to intervene by advising the department that "it should be for ultimate occupation and not for Jiménez." Crosley spent the morning preparing his forces. As he did so, Jiménez had second thoughts; that afternoon, he withdrew his request for help, then resigned the presidency. Crosley, floundering with no legitimate reason to intervene, cancelled the invasion. Caperton turned his fleet back toward Haiti.[52]

But Lansing and Wilson had had quite enough. Seizing on Jiménez's desperate request for help and ignoring his subsequent withdrawal of it, they determined that the "President be upheld in every possible and proper means." The fact that Jiménez had resigned was somewhat irritating, but not reason enough to keep the United States from protecting his government. Caperton again headed his fleet toward the Dominican Republic.[53]

The marines and bluejackets landed in force on 15 May. They quickly controlled the capital, then moved across the country. Caperton's campaign orders specified that the troops were there "supporting the constituted government, maintaining peace and order, and protecting life and property ashore." American officials continued to insist that they were there at the invitation of the Dominican government. Russell later wrote that the marines, "at the request of President Jiménez, had landed on May 15, 1916 to preserve law and order . . . and to protect the lawfully constituted government against the unwarranted and senseless rebellion."[54]

The Dominicans refused to cooperate in their own salvation. During the summer of 1916, Caperton extended American control throughout the country, subduing recalcitrant Dominican patriots and establishing law and order in the republic. The Dominican congress meanwhile chose Federico Henríquez y Carvajal to replace Jiménez as president. The choice was unacceptable to the United States. Wilson refused to recognize the new government. At this point, as he had with Haiti, he switched his use of force. Having landed to protect the Dominicans from themselves, by the fall of 1916 Wilson determined that it was necessary to use force to solve the republic's problems. In late November the United States imposed a military government composed of U.S. Navy officers on the Dominican Republic. No longer using force for protection, the imposition of an American military government signaled the beginnings of the use of force for solution.

PROTECTION RECESSIVE

During Wilson's several other resorts to force—the Punitive Expedition, World War I, and the interventions in northern Russia and Siberia—the claim of protection was also invoked. In those instances, though, protection as a motive seemed not nearly as important (or dominant) as it was at the end of the occupation of Veracruz, or at the beginnings of the occupations of

Haiti and the Dominican Republic. Although it can not be entirely discounted—the great battle cry of World War I was to make the world safe for democracy—other motives resulting in other uses of force dominated. In the Wilsonian way of war, the net of protection spread widely.

In March 1916 Pancho Villa, angered by Wilson's de facto recognition of Carranza, yet still hoping to unite the Mexican people behind his banner, raided Columbus, New Mexico. Wilson responded with the Punitive Expedition, which, as its name implied, was a use of force for retribution. Unfortunately, General John J. Pershing and his eleven thousand troops never caught the elusive bandit. The longer the Punitive Expedition stayed in Mexico, the harder it became to justify it as a use of force for retribution. In April, after a brief skirmish with Mexican civilians at Parral, the movements of the Punitive Expedition were restricted essentially to scouting parties. At the end of June, after a bloodier encounter with Carranzista soldiers at Carrizal, even scouting parties were prohibited. The Punitive Expedition remained encamped a hundred miles inside Mexico.

By the end of April, a month and a half after the Punitive Expedition crossed into Mexico, Wilson was no longer able to define the Punitive Expedition as chasing those who had attacked Columbus. Instead, he began to describe it as a means to protect the border by forcing Carranza to take care of his bandits. Secretary of War Newton Baker explained to General Hugh Scott, his chief of staff, that the expedition was their "means of compelling the *de facto* Government to take up and pursue to an end the chase of Villa and the dispersing of whatever bands remain organized." When Scott and General Funston, at that time the commander of the Southern Department bordering Mexico, met with Carranza's chief lieutenant, General Álvaro Obregón, in late April, their orders were to impress upon Obregón that the Punitive Expedition was "for the sole purpose of removing a menace to the common security and the friendly relations of the two Republics."[55]

Secretary of State Lansing also began invoking the cloak of protection to justify the Punitive Expedition's presence a hundred miles into Mexico. In a circular letter to U.S. legations in Central and South America dated 21 June, Lansing explained that "the most effective method of preventing raids of this nature . . . is to visit punishment or destruction on the raiders." When war threatened to break out between the United States and Mexico after the Carrizal fight, Lansing disclaimed any intention to intervene in Mexican affairs. Instead the United States was motivated solely by "the defense of American territory from further invasion by bands of armed Mexicans, protection of American citizens and property along the boundary from outrages committed by such bandits, and the prevention of future depredations." War with Mexico would be "without purpose on the part of the United States other than to end the conditions which menace our national peace and the safety of our citizens."[56]

Even as the Americans adamantly disclaimed any intent to intervene in Mexico, even as they wrapped the Punitive Expedition tightly in the cloak of protection, Wilson used Pershing's presence in Mexico to enter into discussions with Carranza. When the first chief agreed to negotiate the withdrawal of the expedition, Wilson used the Joint Mexican-American Commission to broach broader issues such as political and social reforms. The American representatives delayed any talk of withdrawing until they could help the Mexicans—with friendly advice and suggestions—end their revolution along democratic lines. Protection, like liberty, excused myriad crimes.

Similarly, Wilson finally decided on war with Germany to punish it for its illegal use of the submarine—a use of force for retribution. He also saw a U.S. declaration of war as the only way to ensure himself a seat at the eventual peace conference—a use of force for introduction. Making the world safe for democracy became a George Creel truism, a simplistic rallying cry to unite the American people. It actually covered a far more complex array of motives and goals. Saving the world for democracy required considerably more than the use of force for protection. It also entailed associating the United States with other nations united against Germany and introducing the United States to the peace conference.

Toward the end of World War I, the nations associated with the United States began pressuring Wilson to approve a Japanese intervention in Russia. They hoped that intervention would divert German forces eastward, perhaps even recreating the Russian front that had collapsed so quickly after the November 1917 Bolshevik Revolution. Wilson stood alone against the plan. His veto, though, left him isolated among his associates, who continued to pressure him. Since one of Wilson's premier goals for the war was the establishment of a League of Nations dependent on collective security among nations, the pressure proved unbearable. In the end, Wilson seized on the presence of some fifty thousand Czechoslovakian prisoners of war who were making their way home by way of Siberia to the United States and then to Europe. When open hostilities broke out between the Czechs and the Bolsheviks, Wilson grasped the opportunity to approve a joint U.S.-Japanese Siberian intervention to save the Czechs. A joint invasion with British forces in northern Russia was launched at about the same time to keep German forces from capturing significant amounts of leftover war supplies.

Wilson used the claim of protection to excuse both interventions. Though protection undeniably was a part of his motive, a more persuasive argument can be made for the use of force for association as the principal motive because of the extreme importance Wilson was then placing on collective action. The interventions helped prove the efficacy of the use of force for association. Association was the dominant motive, protection the recessive one.

More than the several other uses of force, protection ran as a common thread through all the interventions. It was the most readily accepted, the most commonly understood, the easiest to justify. Saving Mexicans, Haitians, Dominicans, Czechs, and even the world elevated the employment of force to a higher plane, one equal to the grand humanitarianism of the United States. Yet it should also be clear that there were times when protection dominated as a motive and other times when its part was recessive. When it dominated, Wilson seemed most intent on saving others from themselves. When protection was recessive, claiming it as a motive seemed the best way to excuse or, put generously, to justify an intervention.

In the Wilsonian way of war, there seemed to be much that needed protection.

3 FORCE
for Retribution

> . . . a government's resort to armed power to chastise another government or organized group operating within another country. It usually results from specific grievances over the attitude or behavior of the other government or organized group. In short, it is an international punishment.

In the Wilsonian way of war, justice was seldom swift, always sure, and dependably inconstant. When aggrieved, Wilson usually sought satisfaction through diplomacy before turning to arms. His patience disguised his tenacity. If negotiations ultimately failed, he unhesitatingly resolved his complaint with force. Curiously, once embarked on an intervention, Wilson never allowed the original grievance—whether insult, attack, or violation—to control the outcome. Retribution was sufficient to cause an intervention, but never to conclude one. Vengeance left Wilson strangely unsatiated.

On three separate occasions, Wilson redressed a grievance through force. With the occupation of Veracruz in April 1914, the United States punished the usurper government in Mexico for its insult to the American flag. Two years later, Pancho Villa, the former Mexican bandit turned revolutionist, led a ragged band of Mexican rebels in an attack on Columbus, New Mexico. Wilson decided immediately to respond with force. In April 1917, Wilson asked Congress for a declaration of war against Germany for its repeated infringements on American neutral rights, primarily the unlawful sinking of unarmed U.S. merchant ships by U-boats.

With each of these three instances of force, retribution provided the original motive and controlled the scope of the intervention. Retribution also legitimized each by providing an acceptable justification readily recognized by the international community. But Wilson never allowed vengeance alone to define the full course of a military intervention. Once American troops were engaged, Wilson changed the purpose of each intervention by adopting other, generally more ambitious policies, such as resolving the Mexican Revolution or restructuring the international system. In doing so, he did not expand the intervention by sending more troops or extending their field of operations, but shifted from one use of force to another. Each shift demarked a fascinating example of how Wilson used force and how he imposed on it a startling flexibility.

RETRIBUTION V. REPRISAL

International law provided a rationalized method for one nation to take vengeance on another through the processes of reprisal. By 1914 the purposes and procedures for conducting a reprisal had become well defined by precedent and well recognized by international jurists. They covered a multitude of sins and grievances, ranging from insults to the destruction of life and property. In the civilized, rule-infested world of international relations, reprisals were a perfectly acceptable way of taking an eye for an eye. Not surprisingly, of course, they were most often used by developed nations against underdeveloped countries. In those situations, reprisals could easily be controlled and contained; the risk of full-scale war, ever present among developed states, was hardly a consideration. By establishing rules for reprisals, the law provided a convenient vent for vengeance.

In 1914 Wilson used the law to excuse his actions, but he did not allow its myriad rules to interfere with his policies. Between the outer reaches of that excuse and the goals of those policies lay ample maneuvering room for Wilson's changing uses of force. The Wilson administration justified the occupation of Veracruz by calling it a legitimate act of reprisal, or by calling it by its euphemisms, such as a means "of enforcing redress for a specific indignity." American actions were directed specifically at Huerta and his subordinates and were not meant as an act of war against the Mexican people. Reprisal, of course, conveyed a specific legal meaning under international law. By invoking it, Wilson tried to legitimize the occupation even as he used the intervention to introduce himself to the revolutionary problems confronting Mexico.[1]

Five days after the Tampico insult, State Department counselor Robert Lansing pointed out that the president was well within his authority in "the enforcing of claims or demands by the display or use of force, or the making of reprisals." Although reprisals had the "characteristics of war in that they are appeals to force rather than to reason," they were "not deemed by governments to be actual warfare." Lansing offered several precedents, including the 1853 shelling of Greytown, Nicaragua, by a U.S. naval squadron. During that incident, Nicaraguan rebels seized the property of an American company in Greytown, destroying some of its buildings and arresting some of its employees. When the American minister arrived to investigate, the rebels tried to kidnap him, but succeeded only in wounding him, thereby literally adding injury to insult. In response, the USS *Cyane* arrived to obtain reparations. When the rebels offered none, the *Cyane* gave a twenty-four hour warning, during which it helped evacuate the city, then shelled Greytown into rubble.[2]

Wilson embraced Lansing's definition of reprisal. The president cited the Greytown incident in a press conference on 20 April, suggesting that problems then were similar to the problems he was having with Huerta. Later that day he consulted Congress about using "the armed forces of the United States in such ways and to such an extent as may be necessary to obtain from General Huerta and his adherents the fullest recognition of the rights and dignity of the United States." Wilson explained his policy as seeking a "full recognition of American dignity and a guarantee that it would not happen again." He repeatedly denied that the proposed reprisal was intended to eliminate Huerta. Rather, he believed himself fully justified "under international law" to seek redress for the insults without the consequences of war. Although Wilson did not specifically use the term *reprisal*, it is clear that it was his point of reference.[3]

Throughout the occupation, members of the administration defended it as a reprisal. Secretary of the Navy Daniels explained to Admiral Fletcher, commander of the occupying forces, that "there has been no declaration of war. Our purpose in seizure of port was to obtain specific redress for an affront." Secretary of State Bryan described American actions as "the employment of a means well recognized in international affairs to enforce a specific redress for specific indignities." Lindley Garrison, the secretary of war, outlined the powers of the military governor, General Funston, by expounding on the rules of reprisals. "The circumstances attending our occupation of Vera Cruz are peculiar," Garrison explained on 14 May. "The object of our Government is not conquest. Such control as we are exercising is incident to an act of reprisal performed." At the end of the occupation, the army's judge advocate general confirmed Garrison's understanding by specifying that the United States seized the port "by way of reprisals."[4]

From Wilson's point of view, claiming the intervention as a reprisal bestowed a shroud of international legitimacy on American actions. Under international law, reprisals were considered legitimate acts taken by one country against another. They were well established in precedent and practice. The term provided a simple, understandable justification that actually covered a complex array of motives and policies.

Despite the many invocations of international law to excuse the intervention, the occupation of Veracruz failed the contemporary tests of reprisal. The original intent of the occupation was to perform an international punishment, but this motive was shed shortly after the troops landed, when other policies and other motives took control. These later motives were reflected in other uses of force.

In 1914, reprisals were defined as violent acts employed by one nation in response to an international delinquency perpetrated by another nation. The purpose was to obtain reparations or redress. One source consulted by administration officials added the condition that the reprisal "must be in proportion to the wrong done and to the amount of compulsion necessary to get reparation." Reprisals ended when reparations were received or when obtaining redress proved hopeless. According to the leading international jurists of the time, reparations were defined by the tests of purpose, proportion, and duration.[5]

The occupation of Veracruz failed each test. Rather than point to a specific delinquent act on the part of Mexican authorities, the Wilson administration's main complaint concerned their attitude. Wilson told a meeting of congressmen on 15 April that "the studied and planned exhibitions of ill-will and contempt for the American Government on the part of Huerta" brought on the crisis. Huerta's attitude was "contemptuous and rebellious." The Tampico affair, in Wilson's view, merely sparked the controversy; by itself it meant little. "Really, it was a psychological moment," he later explained. "There was no great disaster like the sinking of the *Maine* and there was an adequate reason for our action in this culminating insult of a series of insults to our country and our flag." Secretary of the Navy Daniels, echoing Wilson, ascribed the cause to the "atmosphere of studied insult by Huerta."[6]

As soon as it became apparent that Huerta would not offer a salute to the American flag as an apology, Wilson determined on a reprisal. "Under the circumstances," Admiral Victor Blue, a senior aide to Daniels, recalled, "there was nothing for the United States to do but obtain reparations by the use of force." The impending arrival of the German-registered, munitions-laden SS *Ypiranga*, which was due to dock at Veracruz on the morning of 21 April, sped up the timing of the landing, but did not cause it. "Reprisal could have been made by seizing a custom house at any port held by the Huerta faction," Blue later explained. "Tampico and Vera Cruz were considered in this connection. Vera Cruz being the gate way to the capital of Mexico, through which the great bulk of commerce passes, and being the natural base of operations for an invading army in case of hostilities, was selected as the place where the custom house would be seized." The administration was already leaning toward seizing the customhouse at Veracruz before it learned of the *Ypiranga*. The army's extensive collection of Mexican war plans consistently specified Veracruz as the point of easiest entry. In fashioning the reprisal, Wilson's military experts fell back to the logic of their war plans. On issues of tactics, the president readily deferred to them.[7]

Wilson hoped to confine the scope of the reprisal to the seizure of the customhouse and related locations at Veracruz. Had he limited the occupation to those areas, the intervention possibly would have fallen within the proportional requirement for a reprisal. Daniels ordered Admiral Fletcher to take the customs facilities in the early morning of 21 April. He was to extend his control over the rest of the city only in the event of Mexican resistance or to restore order. Upon landing, Fletcher encountered unorganized opposition. He determined that the Mexican authorities, most of whom had fled, no longer controlled the city. Consequently, and in line with Daniels's orders, Fletcher expanded his operations by occupying the entire city.

As the marines and bluejackets fanned out across the city, the reprisal became increasingly disproportionate to the wrong done by the Mexicans. By almost any standard, an insult, even a series of insults reflecting an attitude of utter disrespect, hardly warranted the occupation of an entire city, particularly when it resulted in the death of at least two hundred Mexicans. The continuation of American control over Veracruz for seven months exacerbated the disproportionate nature of the punishment.[8]

Because Wilson directed the action taken at Veracruz specifically against Huerta and his supporters, the chance for obtaining satisfaction diminished considerably when Huerta fled the country in July. After that the United States had no reasonable hope that reparations would be offered. Nevertheless, American troops remained in possession of the port. Because Wilson's uses of force had changed, the troops remained for a reason different from punishing Huerta's insubordinate attitude. Only the excuse remained the same.[9]

Reparations were not forgotten, simply set aside. Other concerns, related to other uses of force, took the fore. This transformation became apparent during the mediation conference opened on 20 May 1914, arranged by Argentina, Brazil, and Chile. Three weeks later, on 12 June, Frederick Lehman, the junior American delegate, explained to the conferees that:

> We have not troubled you with Tampico insults, nor engrossed your attention with questions of salute. Our concern is of a more serious nature. We have interests of our own in the Mediation, but none that can be measured by indemnity, whether of land or money. We seek the larger and the better advantages that will come to us from the establishment of peace in Mexico, a peace established upon a just basis, making for the general welfare of the Mexican people.

Lehman was simply admitting that Wilson's use of force had changed from seeking reparations to settling the Mexican Revolution. As part of the protocol ending the conference, the United States pledged not to seek any compensation or "other international satisfaction." The promise effectively settled the question of reparations.[10]

Clearly Wilson and his advisers originally intended to punish the government of Victoriano Huerta for its contemptuous attitude and insulting behavior. In Wilson's mind, upholding American honor legitimized the intervention, even as, conveniently, the intervention itself allowed him to pursue other policies and other uses of force. By initiating the occupation as a use of force for retribution, Wilson left open the possibility of employing the occupation in the service of his other objectives. The opportunity quickly arose, which is why reprisals and satisfactions were so quickly, so easily forgotten.

RETRIBUTION, NEAT

Throughout the ten months that the Punitive Expedition remained encamped south of the border, the Wilson administration consistently denied any taint or intention of intervention in the internal affairs of Mexico. Wilson and his advisers defined it not as a reprisal—an action one government takes against another—but as a police action in hot pursuit of a band of outlaws. Like a shot of whiskey poured neat, the motive for the expedition seemed straightforward—at least in the beginning.

"To get Villa," Zachary Cobb, a State Department agent in Mexico, concluded the morning after the attack on Columbus, New Mexico, "we must send troops after him." Yet in perfect, unwitting summary of Wilson's evolving policies, Cobb explained that this meant "taking positive hold of and solving the Mexican problem in its entirety." As Pershing chased Villa across northern Mexico, Wilson determined to clean up the rubble of revolution. Out of that determination arose the changing uses of force.[11]

Early on the morning of 9 March 1916, Pancho Villa and his band of about five hundred soldiers attacked Columbus, New Mexico. Despite being taken wholly unaware, the U.S. Cavalry, under the command of Colonel Herbert J. Slocum, gave a good account of itself. Darting from their beds, the troopers fought the Villistas in the streets of Columbus. When Villa retreated southward, Major Frank Tompkins led a force of the Thirteenth Cavalry in hot pursuit. They fought a running battle with the Villistas, penetrating fifteen miles into Mexico before running out of ammunition. During the attack, eight American soldiers and eight civilians were killed, and seven soldiers and three civilians were wounded. Villa lost at least sixty-seven men, though some reports placed his losses as high as 190.[12]

The American response was immediate and unanimous. Although the State Department called on the de facto government of Venustiano Carranza to "pursue, capture, and exterminate this lawless element which is now proceeding westward from Columbus," others in the administration—soldiers and civilians—set up a howl to get Villa. General Funston, commander of the army's Southern Department along the border, immediately asked permission to send a force after Villa. "So long as [the] border is a shelter for them they will continue to harass our ranches and towns," Funston argued. On 10 March he pointed out that "unless Villa is relentlessly pursued and his forces scattered he will continue raids." The Carranza government, Funston believed, was "accomplishing nothing," which gave Villa full freedom to launch additional raids.[13]

Wilson's closest advisers supported chasing Villa. According to Secretary of the Navy Daniels, "there was no other course this Government could take than to pursue Villa and put an end to his forays." Wilson's personal secretary, Joseph Tumulty, urged on the president the importance of "getting Villa." General Pershing, once in Mexico, repeatedly suggested offering a cash reward for the illusive Villa. Secretary of the Interior Franklin K. Lane, whom Wilson would later ask to head up negotiations with the Carranza government over the expedition, originally believed that "to fail in getting Villa would ruin us in the eyes of all Latin-Americans. I do not say that they respect only force, but like children they pile insult upon insult if they are not stopped when the first insult is given."[14]

On 10 March the War Department telegraphed Funston to dispatch an armed force "with the sole object of capturing Villa." When General Scott, the chief of staff, pointed out that focusing American power against one outlaw was bad tactics, Newton D. Baker, the new secretary of war, broadened the language—though not the intent—of the original orders. As Baker advised the president, "a sufficient body of mobile troops will be sent in to locate and disperse or capture the band or bands that attacked Columbus." In addition, Baker authorized the army commands along the border to respond to similar raids with the "same tactics of defense and pursuit."[15]

Wilson insisted that the Punitive Expedition behave "with scrupulous regard to the sovereignty of Mexico." The administration repeated that refrain in its public and private announcements. At first, as Baker advised Wilson, the administration intended to withdraw the expedition "so soon as the forces of the de facto government can take control of the situation." Wilson wholeheartedly agreed. General Scott explained to one correspondent that Wilson "expects to confine the invasion of Mexico to Pershing's columns; have them go down there and make a sash of Villa's outfit and come back." Just before the Punitive Expedition crossed the border, Baker emphasized to Funston that

> the President desires that your attention be especially and earnestly called to his determination that the expedition into Mexico is limited to the purposes originally stated, namely the pursuit and dispersion of the band or bands that attacked Columbus and it is of the highest importance that no color of any other possibility or intention be given and therefore while the President desires the force to be adequate to disperse the bands in question and to protect communications, neither in size nor otherwise should the expedition afford the slightest ground of suspicion of any other larger object.

Wilson, Scott reiterated, wanted the expedition "for defensive purposes to break up that gang and come out without affecting the sovereignty of Mexico. It may be unable to get out, but none can foresee the effect."[16]

The United States, Scott advised American investors involved in Mexico, had no plans to enter in force. Villa was like "one of our dogs who has gone mad, and we have had to kill him to prevent further damage to everybody." On 16 March, just after Pershing led more than a thousand soldiers over the border, Baker issued explicit orders that "upon no account or pretext . . . shall this expedition . . . be given the appearance of being hostile to the integrity or dignity of the Republic of Mexico." As Secretary Lansing advised one of the State Department's many representatives in Mexico, "The intention of this Government . . . is to endeavor to take the bandit chief Villa." The Punitive Expedition was a pure act of punishment against the organized group that had attacked the United States. It was retribution, neat.[17]

The Wilson administration adamantly denied that the expedition represented an intervention in Mexico. As early as 13 March, Wilson insisted that "in no circumstances will [the Punitive Expedition] be suffered to trench in any degree upon the sovereignty of Mexico or develop into intervention of any kind in the internal affairs of our sister Republic." Both the president and his secretary of state feared that any claim or perception of American "intervention," a term they defined to their own purposes, would seriously offend other Latin American countries.[18]

"To intervene in the affairs of a neighboring independent state," Lansing argued, "means to interfere with its domestic affairs and the exercise of its sovereign rights by its people." What he meant was forceful, not diplomatic, interference. Both Wilson and Lansing expended considerable energy conceiving ways in which Mexico could end its turmoil through political, economic, and religious reforms. Later, during the Joint Mexican-American Commission negotiations over the Punitive Expedition, they urged these proposals on Mexico's representatives, even as they denied they were intervening in Mexico's internal affairs. Their definition of intervention belied their determination to reshape Mexico in the American image.[19]

Yet they were at least sensitive to the ugly connotations of the term *intervention*. Lansing strongly urged Wilson to "avoid the use of the word 'Intervention' and deny that any invasion of Mexico is for the sake of intervention." The word suggested a definite purpose to "clean up" the country. Neither the Mexican people nor their neighbors in the Western Hemisphere would easily accept any meddling. Rather, Lansing argued, the United States should simply claim that it intended only "to end the conditions which menace our national peace and the safety of our citizens." Within the obtuseness of that description hid several Wilsonian uses of force.[20]

"I agree to all this," Wilson responded. He wanted to be very careful to "do nothing which will put any doubt upon our purposes and our ability to keep faith with Latin America in all matters that touch independence and territorial integrity." As he wrote his friend Colonel Edward M. House, "INTERVENTION (that is the rearrangement and control of Mexico's domestic affairs by the U.S.) there shall not be either now or at any other time if I can prevent it." Wilson urged Lansing to send a note to the various governments of Latin America denying any American policy of intervention.[21]

The administration searched frantically for some way to legitimize the Punitive Expedition in the eyes of Latin Americans. Lansing claimed the legally sanctioned act of "hot pursuit," although the army's weeklong preparations allowed the trail—and the argument—to cool considerably. "It was beyond human endurance," he told Licenciado Elisso Arredondo, Carranza's representative in Washington, "to be attacked in the way the American troops had been attacked." Lansing assured Arredondo that "the case of 'hot pursuit' by a punitive expedition was a very different thing from the deliberate invasion by an expeditionary force with intent to occupy Mexican territory." During the ten months Pershing's forces remained in Mexico, this distinction became increasingly subtle.[22]

The de facto government of Venustiano Carranza inadvertently supplied the Punitive Expedition with its much-needed legitimacy. Fearing, with considerable justification, that Wilson would use the raid to impose himself on Mexico, Carranza proposed on 11 March that the two countries agree to allow each other to cross the border in pursuit of bandits, but only "if the raid effected at Columbus should unfortunately be repeated at any other point of the border." From Carranza's point of view, the request was merely a gesture of good faith, an assurance that his troops would handle any future problems.[23]

Lansing agreed to the proposal with alacrity, but twisted it to incorporate the Punitive Expedition. Although Carranza clearly had in mind only future incidents, Lansing calmly ignored the qualifier. After readily granting permission for Carranzistas to chase bandits into the United States, Lansing announced on 13 March that "the arrangement is now complete and in force and the reciprocal privileges thereunder may accordingly be exercised by either Government without further interchange of views." Down on the border, Pershing readied his command to cross into Mexico.[24]

Lansing's bluster was a bit of a bluff. As the time approached for Pershing to cross into Mexico, administration officials worried about the response of the Mexicans. "Officers of the Mexican Government do not seem to understand the attitude of the de facto government is to tolerate our troops crossing the border for the purpose of assisting in the capture of Villa," Acting Secretary of State Frank Polk advised John W. Belt, one of the American representatives in Mexico. Polk urged Belt to ascertain what instructions Carranza had sent his commanders on the border. Some information indicated that Carranza would not oppose the Punitive Expedition, but none among Wilson's advisers truly believed that.[25]

The military waited uneasily for the crossing. General Tasker Bliss, the assistant chief of staff who had previously commanded the Southern Department along the border, warned ominously that the United States should prepare itself for a full-scale intervention. "Whether the United States has to resort to general intervention or not, reasonable safety requires that we should make all the preparations for such a status," he advised Scott on 13 March, "If we do not make these preparations the Mexicans are the more likely to take such action as will eventually force intervention against our will." The members of the War College Division strenuously objected to the limitations on the Punitive Expedition. They preferred, instead, a simple, straightforward intervention. When Wilson declined, the War College refused to participate in planning Pershing's chase.[26]

After Pershing and his troops finally crossed the border, almost a week after Villa's raid, the Mexican government protested the invasion. Referring to the exchange of reciprocal privileges, Carranza stated that his note of 10 March "should and must not be understood as tolerating or permitting any expeditions into the national territory." When Arredondo delivered the protest to Polk, the acting secretary disingenuously explained that the Wilson administration considered the agreement fixed. Arredondo, Polk gratefully noted, "did not suggest the withdrawal of the troops, nor did he suggest the expedition be stopped." The fact that the Mexicans had sternly protested the invasion of their territory seemed to pass over Polk's head.[27]

Carranza continued to protest. The Wilson administration accepted the objections, vastly relieved that as long as Carranza kept talking and kept sending along diplomatic notes, Pershing could continue chasing Villa without hindrance. Polk even expressed regret that the original Mexican offer had been misunderstood, though he quickly added that the sole purpose of the Punitive Expedition was "to pursue and capture Villa, unless his prior capture should be effected by the forces of the de facto Government." The United States had no intention of withdrawing Pershing. The negotiations continued, as did Pershing's chase. And that was as much as Wilson sought during the spring of 1916.[28]

Unfortunately Pershing never quite caught up with Villa. A number of skirmishes left a few of the bandit's top lieutenants dead, but Villa himself escaped capture. As March gave way to April, then April to June, the original rationale for the Punitive Expedition changed to other uses of force. Unable to catch Villa, the Americans were unable to punish him. As General Scott realized, "It does not seem dignified for all the United States to be hunting for one man in a foreign country." Consequently, the Wilson administration began talking less about punishing Villa and more about protecting the border from future raids.[29]

On 13 April, a mob of outraged Mexicans, assisted by Carranzista soldiers, attacked a troop of American cavalry at Parral. During the fight, two cavalrymen were killed and several were wounded. Funston immediately called for reinforcements. Pershing begged permission to occupy the state of Chihuahua. Wilson demurred, preferring, in typical fashion, to negotiate first. Orders went to Pershing to restrict the movements of his command lest he further outrage the Mexicans. "Since we met armed opposition at Parral," Pershing complained to one correspondent a month later, "the diplomatic end of the government stepped in and called a halt, and so activities have since been limited to our immediate surroundings."[30]

When General Scott left on a tour of inspection along the border a few days after the Parral incident, Secretary Baker spelled out the changing nature of the Punitive Expedition. It was, Baker maintained, "different from either a war against or intervention in Mexico." Yet it was no longer focused on getting Villa. Scott was to explain to Funston "the theory of drawing in our outlying military parties and maintaining an establishment in Mexico as a means of compelling the de facto Government to take up and pursue to an end the chase of Villa and the dispersing of whatever bands remain organized." Although still intent on getting Villa, Baker no longer expected Pershing to do it. Instead Pershing's presence in Mexico would compel, passively, the Carranzistas to do the job. By mid-April retribution was no longer quite so neat.[31]

As Scott headed south, Lansing suggested inviting Carranza to send a representative to meet the chief of staff. Carranza dispatched his lieutenant, General Álvaro Obregón. During their talks, Scott was to assure Obregón that "the Government of the United States earnestly desires to avoid anything which has the appearance of intervention in the domestic affairs of the Republic of Mexico." The pursuit of Villa, no longer a simple act of retribution, was now defined quite differently. According to Baker, the Punitive Expedition was

> for the sole purpose of removing a menace to the common security and the friendly relations of the two Republics. So long as [Villa] remains at large and is able to mislead numbers of his fellow citizens into attacks like that at Columbus, the danger exists of American public opinion being irritated to the point of requiring general intervention. For, of course, depredations on American soil and the loss of lives of American citizens cannot be tolerated.

During the conference, Scott and Funston repeated Baker's explanation to Obregón. The Mexican general, however, had his own goal for the conference: He demanded the withdrawal of the Punitive Expedition. After a week of intense discussions, Scott finally obtained Obregón's agreement to an enhanced Mexican pursuit of Villa and similar raiders in exchange for the gradual withdrawal of Pershing's forces. Carranza, however, vetoed the arrangement by demanding the immediate withdrawal of all American troops.[32]

Although the Scott-Obregón conference failed to reach an agreement, it helped defuse the mounting tensions along the border. From Wilson's point of view, keeping Carranza talking diverted him from acting against the expedition. When Scott headed for home, Carranza resumed the exchange of diplomatic notes protesting the misunderstanding over his offer of reciprocal border crossings. The notes culminated in a particularly nasty missive from Mexico on 22 May. Its tone, Polk advised Wilson, was "decidedly unsatisfactory and, in some places, impertinent." Still, Carranza was expressing his hostility with words, not bullets, and that suited Wilson's purposes. In a further effort to calm the turbulence, the State Department took a month to answer Carranza's complaint.[33]

But Pershing was no longer actively chasing Villa. Restricted to the vicinity of Colonia Dublan, the most he was allowed was to send out occasional scouting parties. The longer his command remained in Mexico, the harder it was for the Wilson administration to claim "hot pursuit," or even to claim that it was there to punish Villa at all. Then on 21 June, one of the scouting parties clashed with Mexican soldiers at Carrizal. Most of the American soldiers were killed. Wilson responded, not with more force as his military demanded, but by again arranging for a conference with Carranza's representatives. Rather than go through mediators, as he had during the occupation of Veracruz, Wilson dealt directly with Carranza. During the conference, as will be explained in a subsequent chapter, the United States surrendered all claim that the Punitive Expedition was still in Mexico to punish Villa. Instead the U.S. negotiators offered American solutions to Mexico's revolution.

After Carrizal, the use of force for retribution no longer controlled the Punitive Expedition. Pershing's movements were strictly confined. Not even scouting parties were allowed. The opportunity to expand the expedition slipped past. "After Carrizal was the time, if ever there was a time," Pershing complained privately, "when red-blooded Americans felt that we should go in, but we did not advance." Punishing the Mexicans was of less importance than the chance presented by the Joint Mexican-American Commission to discuss Mexico's revolutionary problems. Wilson switched from the use of force for retribution to the use of force for introduction.[34]

RETRIBUTION AND WAR

On 2 April 1917, Woodrow Wilson went before a joint session of Congress to request a declaration of war against Germany. In his speech the president justified the war as an act of retribution, even as he outlined his vision of a world made safe for democracy. The pattern of the speech followed perfectly the twin policies Wilson had pursued during the two and a half years of American neutrality. From the outbreak of general war in Europe in August 1914 until April 1917, Wilson had held the belligerents strictly accountable for any violations of the rights of the neutral nations, particularly their rights to trade and ply the seas. At the same time, Wilson had repeatedly offered his services to mediate an end to the hostilities. He sought to uphold America's neutral rights and to ensure a seat for the United States at any peace conference. The failure of the former policy ensured the success of the latter.

Wilson took the United States to war because Germany chose to ignore the rights of neutral nations to freedom of the seas. "The extraordinary insults and aggressions of the Imperial German Government left us no self-respecting choice but to take up arms in defense of our rights as a free people and of our honor as a sovereign government," Wilson explained in June 1917. "The military masters of Germany denied us the right to be neutral."

Wilson could not, in the end, stand passive before German abrogations of international law and the rights of neutral nations.[35]

The previous January the Kaiser had announced that German U-boats would immediately begin sinking all ships, neutral or belligerent, trading with his enemies. "International law had its origin in the attempt to set up some law which would be respected and observed upon the seas, where no nation had right of dominion and where lay the free highways of the world," Wilson explained to Congress. Germany had violated the law:

> This minimum of right the German Government has swept aside under the plea of retaliation and necessity and because it had no weapons which it could use at sea except these which it is impossible to employ as it is employing them without throwing to the winds all scruples of humanity or of respect for the understandings that were supposed to underlie the intercourse of the world.

Germany's reliance on the submarine was no less than "warfare against mankind" and a "war against all nations." The sinking of American ships compelled the United States to go to war to punish Germany. The cause of the war was retribution.[36]

Although retribution underlay the decision for war, it had little to do with the way Wilson fought or with what he sought to achieve. After explaining to Congress the necessity of punishing Germany for its violations of neutral rights, Wilson described his objectives:

> We shall fight for the things which we have always carried nearest our hearts,— for democracy, for the right of those who submit to authority to have a voice in their own Governments, for the rights and liberties of small nations, for a universal dominion of right by such a concert of free peoples as shall bring peace and safety to all nations and make the world itself at last free.

Wilson spent the war defining the various points—which eventually totaled twice fourteen—that he identified as America's war aims. Although freedom of the seas and trade numbered among them, none had anything to do with punishing Germany or seeking retribution for its violations of international law. At most Wilson called for the destruction of German militarism, which he defined as the autocratic political system that allowed a few men to determine the fate of their peoples. But that was a common Wilsonian twist: retribution could cause a resort to force, but by itself was insufficient to end one.[37]

The history of Wilson's agonized efforts to defend America's neutral rights from encroachments by both Germany and England has been well told before and need not be extensively detailed here. England's interference resulted in the loss of property; Germany's in the loss of lives. In Wilson's view, the destruction of property was considerably less significant than the taking of life. He willingly protested British policies out of principle, but he just as willingly allowed the resolution to await the end of the war, when reparations could be demanded. But it was crucial that he protest British interference whenever it occurred. To have done less would have been to show an implicit favoritism toward the Entente powers. Neutrality demanded a balanced response.

Yet German transgressions were far graver. Resolving them could not be postponed until the war ended because they resulted in the loss of American lives. As Wilson explained when he accepted the Democratic renomination to the presidency in September 1916:

> Property rights can be vindicated by claims for damages when the war is over, and no modern nation can decline to arbitrate such claims; but the fundamental rights of humanity can not be. The loss of life is irreparable. Neither can direct violations of a nation's sovereignty await vindication in suits for damages. The nation that violates these essential rights must expect to be checked and called to account by direct challenge and resistance.

Germany's use of the submarine to sink commercial shipping and ocean liners attacked the "rights, commerce, and the citizens of the United States," Wilson argued. "The list is long and overwhelming," he wrote in May 1917. "No nation that respected itself or the rights of humanity could have borne those wrongs any longer."[38]

Sunken ships pointed the way to war. With each incident Wilson escalated his demand that Germany cease torpedoing ships without warning and without provision for the safety of the passengers and crew. With each demand Wilson stiffened the American position, leaving himself little flexibility to respond to the next crisis. When Germany announced in February 1915 that it would use submarines to police a war zone around the British Isles, Wilson protested that Germany would be held to a "strict accountability" for the unlawful sinking of American ships or the loss of American lives. A month later a German submarine sunk the British steamer *Falaba*. Among the dead was Leon C. Thrasher, an American citizen.

Thrasher's death initiated an intense debate among Wilson's advisers over the appropriate response. Secretary of State William Jennings Bryan favored a mild response; State Department counselor Robert Lansing recommended a harsh protest. Wilson waffled between the two. Then in quick succession, a German plane bombed the American freighter *Cushing*, the German government published a warning to Americans not to travel in the war zone, and a German submarine attacked the American tanker *Gulflight*. Each incident hardened the lines of debate within the Wilson administration. Still the president hesitated. "It may be that there is no way to meet a situation like this except by war," Wilson told his cabinet. "It is important that we should show how sincere is our belief that there are other ways to settle questions like this."[39]

Three days later, on 7 May 1915, a German U-boat torpedoed the British passenger liner *Lusitania*, killing eleven hundred civilians, including 120 Americans. The sinking of the *Lusitania* forced Wilson's choice. In three notes to the German government, Wilson explained the American objections to the use of submarines. "Principles of law and humanity" prohibited sinking ships without warning and without provision for the passengers and crew. Because U-boats could do neither, they could not be used. In the second note, Wilson called on Germany to respect the rights of humanity. The third note warned that the United States would regard additional sinkings as "deliberately unfriendly." Bryan, protesting the tone of the *Lusitania* notes, resigned as secretary of state. Lansing, who succeeded him, explained that "the essential issue between the Governments is one of principle and not of fact." Once Wilson defined that principle, he had no way to back down and no way to avoid further confrontations with Germany if it ignored his protests. He had drawn a line in the sand.[40]

Germany crossed that line in August 1915 by sinking the *Arabic*. Two Americans died. "Certainly the Germans are blood mad," Wilson exclaimed, yet he feared further escalating his protests to Germany. With Lansing and House pushing him to break off diplomatic relations, Wilson sought some avenue shy of that. After several days of debate, he had Lansing convey to the German government a demand for an apology, reparations for the American deaths, and a promise that such attacks would not be repeated. The Germans, unwilling to risk war with the United States, essentially gave their promise. Wilson had won a respite, though it cost him considerable flexibility in responding to future crises.[41]

The Germans remained true to the *Arabic* pledge for seven months. In the interim, Wilson stepped up his campaign to mediate an end to the war, but he made little progress in convincing the belligerents to take advantage of his services. Increasingly, Wilson feared he would be shut out of the peace talks. The prospect of that was intolerable.

Then on 24 March 1916, U-boat 29 sank, without warning, the French channel steamer *Sussex*, killing eighty people and injuring four Americans. Once again Lansing and House pressed the president to break relations or issue an ultimatum to Germany. Wilson delayed, caught between the need to stand firm and the fear that standing firm would mean war. In the end the position he had staked out the previous year left him no choice. Although he did not go as far as Lansing and House believed necessary, Wilson demanded that the German government disavow its use of submarines. If they did not, Wilson threatened to break off diplomatic relations. Germany agreed to obey the law, but only if the United States held England to the same standard. Wilson accepted the promise, but ignored the condition. Germany had no right to tell the United States how it should conduct its relations with other nations.

Once again Wilson won, but the victory hinged on Germany keeping its pledge. When, on the last day of January 1917, the Imperial Government announced that it would go back on its promise and that henceforth it would engage in unrestricted submarine warfare, Wilson immediately severed diplomatic relations. During February and March, German U-boats laid waste the shipping lanes to Europe. Four American ships were sunk, hundreds of lives were lost.

Wilson froze. "I was for a little while unable to believe that such things would in fact be done by any government that had hitherto subscribed to the humane practices of civilized nations," he later confessed. Throughout February and March, he secluded himself in the White House. Yet his own protests left him little choice but to go to war. By progressively threatening the Imperial Government from "strict accountability" to severing diplomatic relations, Wilson had cut off all avenues of retreat for his neutrality policy. Whether or not he could bring himself to believe it, the U-boats penned him in a corner. On 2 April 1917, Wilson asked Congress for a declaration of war to punish Germany for its continued, now unabated, reliance on submarines.[42]

Once war was declared, Wilson quickly set aside any demand for retribution. It was as though Germany was punished enough by the mere act of declaring war; actually waging it required a grander vision, a more potent passion. Wilson immediately looked to the larger purposes—the better world— of democracy, leagues of nations, and self-determination. As he had with Veracruz and the Punitive Expedition, he changed his use of force. Vengeance, for Wilson, was never sweet.

Retribution provided the rationale, or excuse, for three of Wilson's interventions. During each, retribution was a motive for force, not a goal; a cause, not an effect. Enacting the punishment consistently proved unsatisfying and inconclusive. Each intervention extended well beyond the time and circumstances that punishment alone, as a motive, required or could compel atonement. Each was ultimately resolved on grounds quite distinct from the original intent to chastise.

The origin of each could be traced directly to the desire for punishment, but by the time each was concluded, other policies, and other uses of force, had diverted them to other purposes, such as resolving the Mexican Revolution or restructuring international relations. For Wilson the recourse to force was punishment enough. He saw no further need to insist on apologies, reparations, or further satisfaction. Other issues, other opportunities, and other uses of force took precedence after American troops were engaged.

In the Wilsonian way of war, seeking justice was often the incentive, but never its own reward.

4 FORCE
for Solution

> . . . a government's resort to armed power to resolve a problem with another government or organized group operating in a foreign country. It usually results from the belief that the intervening government can dispose of a problem with a foreign government or group by imposing its solution with military action. In short, it is an international consummation of will.

In the Wilsonian way of war, force rarely solved problems. Wilson had no principled aversion to compelling others to accept his views. "If a man will not listen to you quietly in a seat, sit on his neck and make him listen," he said on 15 May 1916, the day the U.S. Navy occupied the Dominican Republic. He never hesitated to use force once the necessity for it seemed clear, but he was ever careful to avoid the excesses of armed power. Wilson simply questioned its long-term practicality when other forms of power were so readily available. In his mind, sitting on someone's neck was a far cry from breaking it.[1]

Wilson generally shied from acting the conquering hero. He remained unconvinced, despite repeated resorts to armed power, that forcing a solution was the best alternative. "To conquer with arms is to make only a temporary conquest," he avowed as late as November 1918. At the time U.S. forces had completed two interventions into Mexico and, in association with the Allied armies, had just defeated Germany. American troops continued to occupy Haiti and the Dominican Republic, and combined U.S., Japanese, and British forces had launched twin invasions of Russia. Temporary or not, under Wilson the resort to arms was certainly frequent.[2]

Despite the frequency with which Wilson turned to force, he believed that a permanent conquest required other types of power, particularly moral, diplomatic, and economic. "The world will always acclaim the fact that it is impossible to conquer it by arms," he argued in January 1919, "that the only thing that conquers it is the sort of service which can be rendered in trade, in intercourse, in friendship, and that there is no conquering power which can suppress the freedom of the human spirit." Wilson preferred to use force to open new opportunities he could exploit morally, diplomatically, or economically. Force, then, was but part of the process, not its culmination.[3]

Usually Wilson limited force to immediate, well-defined goals. Once his immediate objectives were achieved—Veracruz occupied, Villa chased from the border, or Germany sued for peace—other forms of power were brought to bear. Armed power (the actual use of force) was tightly constrained to the crisis of the moment. Beyond that, Wilson put no great reliance on force to achieve a lasting solution.

But on two occasions, Wilson shrugged off his usual caution. During the occupations of Haiti and the Dominican Republic, he relied on armed power to order the chaos plaguing both nations. With marines easily subduing all resistance and effectively controlling both countries, Wilson set out to reform the governments and peoples. The solution reflected American emphasis on liberal democratic government, free enterprise, and Western cultural prejudices. "What we wanted was clean little towns, with tidy thatch-roofed dwellings," proudly declared Major Smedley D. Butler, the marine who taught the Haitians how to police themselves. He, like Wilson, was bound "to make of Haiti a first-class black man's country." In neither country, Haiti or the Dominican Republic, did the solution hold.[4]

Once again actions taken during the occupation of Veracruz set the pattern. Although Wilson refused, to the chagrin of the U.S. military, to expand his use of force at Veracruz to solve the Mexican problem in its entirety, the occupation gave the Americans a chance to uplift those Mexicans within their reach. Despite a conscious decision to rely on Mexican laws and Mexican administrative methods, the soldiers who ran the military government brought with them an inflexible ethnocentrism. They infused their prejudices with an equally strong humanitarianism. The combination made a potent admixture for reform. During the seven-month occupation, Funston and his men determined to turn Veracruz into a first-class American city.

Their prejudices were pervasive. "It must be remembered that we are dealing with a people practically devoid of any sense of honor or fair dealing," General Funston advised the War Department three days after taking over Veracruz as the military governor. General Leonard Wood, who was stepping down as the army's chief of staff just as the occupation began, believed that Mexicans, indeed all Latin Americans, were ill-suited to self-government. The United States needed to train them to the discipline of law. "The Central American republics are not wanting in either constitution or laws, but they are often sadly wanting in that state of mind which makes either constitution or laws workable," he advised one correspondent on 28 May 1914.[5]

Soldiers serving in Veracruz concluded from the occupation that Mexicans and, extrapolating further, all Latin Americans, had neither the courage nor the finesse to fight by modern methods. In a rather curious memo prepared by Funston's staff in mid-August 1914, American ethnocentrism shone brightly. Based on the navy's experiences in taking Veracruz, the memo generalized "Methods to be Employed in the Capture and Occupation of Latin-American Cities." Although the conclusions were not entirely out of line—they offered useful suggestions for urban fighting against unorganized snipers—the premises reflected the base prejudices the Americans carried with them into Mexico. "In any warfare instituted against Latin Americans our troops will encounter a mode of defense rather foreign to modern teachings and more in accordance with medieval times," the memo began. "These people pursue a style of warfare which consists primarily in the attack and defense of cities." Latin Americans (not just Mexicans) preferred to fight from street to street, house to house, " 'sniping' from roof tops, cellars, etc." They fought as their forefathers had battled—individually and from hiding. "A native's patriotism is seldom sufficient to cause him to join his country's organized forces and engage in open battle," the report complained.[6]

Ironically the memo ignored the fact that Wilson had ordered the U.S. Navy to seize the Veracruz customhouse, not seek out Mexican armies. When the marines and bluejackets ran into unorganized street fighting, Admiral Fletcher decided to take the city. The United States, not unpatriotic Mexicans, had defined the intervention as an attack on the city of Veracruz. The lessons of the occupation, and there were several pertaining to the limits of force, had little to do with Latin American methods of warfare. Unfortunately, American ethnocentrism effectively blinded Funston and his men to all but the most biased conclusions.

Yet in dealing with a people they considered primitive and incapable of honor or self-government, Wilson and his soldiers determined to inculcate them with American principles. Secretary of War Garrison charged his troops with giving the Mexicans "an object lesson of national good will." He was particularly anxious that "our governmental activities at Vera Cruz to be dictated by principles of extreme liberality and to be such as to suggest to the inhabitants of the territory occupied that we entertain no thought of subjugation or conquest." The Americans came as teachers, not as conquerors.[7]

When Admiral Fletcher proclaimed the establishment of a military government over Veracruz, he invested it with those American "functions necessary for the establishment and maintenance of the fundamental rights of men." Consistent with those grandiose goals, the military government also adhered to the municipal administrative structure that had existed in Veracruz prior to the occupation. The military government was seen as temporary. Following Mexican administrative practices and using Mexican employees ensured that the ultimate return to Mexican control would go reasonably smoothly. Necessity compelled Funston and his men to use Mexican procedures; their ethnocentric humanitarianism pointed them to American reforms.[8]

Having come to maturity in their careers amid the wide-ranging reforms of the Progressive Era, the soldiers who administered Veracruz were appalled at what they found. Continuing Mexican practices only went so far. Without hesitation, Funston outlawed certain activities he found offensive, despite deeply imbedded Mexican traditions. Although Funston relied on the Mexican method of collecting taxes through the sale of revenue stamps for most every document and business transaction, he revoked all the gambling concessions, thus reducing city revenues by a whopping thirteen thousand pesos a month. Bullfighting "and various other matters of a similar nature" were also banned, which cut further into the city's income. Mexicans were expected to learn to enjoy wholesome American pastimes, not squander their money on gambling and barbaric sports.[9]

The Americans also cleaned Veracruz, applying standards of hygiene only recently introduced in the United States. A thousand men were hired to sweep, scrub, and wash the entire city, including private premises. "The streets, alleys, and patios were kept scrupulously clean," Funston reported, "and all suspicious unhealthy places disinfected." A thousand army garbage cans were distributed throughout the city. Each night the fireboat flushed the city with salt water. Ages-old trash at the city dump was burned, human waste was disposed of outside the city, and public health regulations were strictly enforced by fines and jail sentences. U.S. forces next went to war against the mosquitos and flies. "The most modern methods known to sanitary science were employed," Funston wrote. The Americans dug sixty-one miles of ditches to drain the nearby swamps and marshes where the mosquitos bred. Sixty-nine thousand gallons of crude oil were poured on the smaller ponds and puddles. Kitchens and messrooms were enclosed, garbage was kept covered, and forty-six thousand people were vaccinated.[10]

The city market, where all the city's beef, fish, and vegetables were sold daily, required special care. Major Paul A. Wolf, who ran the Department of Public Works, complained that "it was almost unbearable for a white person to remain in the vicinity of the market" because of the filth and flies. Screens were erected to enclose the stalls, the grounds were washed, and American standards of handling and preserving food were imposed on the grocers and butchers.[11]

As a result, Funston's command enjoyed no higher rate of illness than army posts in the United States. The death rate among Veracruz citizens dropped from 45.59 per thousand, the rate from January to May 1914, to 30.59 per thousand during June to October 1914. With considerable pride,

Funston considered the cleanup campaign the greatest accomplishment of the seven-month occupation. As soon as the Americans left, Veracruz reverted to its traditional habits.[12]

THE AMERICANIZATION OF HAITI

The cabinet crowned the secretary of the navy "Josephus the First, King of Haiti." Unfortunately, the new emperor perched uncomfortably upon his throne. "You know that the things we were forced to do in Haiti was a bitter pill for me," Daniels confessed to his assistant, Franklin D. Roosevelt, "for I have always hated any foreign policy that even hinted of imperialistic control." Taken by surprise when Admiral Caperton landed the marines in Port-au-Prince, neither Wilson nor Daniels quite knew what to do with their new subjects.[13]

Wilson felt most uncomfortable: The occupation was the first time that he would use force to solve a problem. It went against the grain. American actions were "high-handed," he confessed, though justified by "extraordinary circumstances." He could hardly blame those Haitians who resisted American help; they were "between the devil and the deep sea." His ambivalence confounded his policies. Rather than order Caperton to take over all of Haiti immediately, Wilson allowed events to sidle, stumbling hesitantly, if not quite inevitably, to full American control.[14]

In the end Wilson convinced himself that he was acting for "Haiti's salvation." The "dusky little republic," as he described it, was "depending entirely on our marines to keep the peace." Normally, he told his fiancée, Edith Boling Galt, he disdained the argument that the end justified the means, but "we should not stand on ceremony now unless we wish this country, as well as Haiti itself, to be seriously and perhaps fatally embarrassed." Wilson hoped simply "that it will be possible to bring some order out of the chaos." Matters in Haiti, he recognized, had "certainly come to a head." The immediate problem was determining which way the head was facing.[15]

Wilson, who was on vacation in New Jersey, and Daniels, who seemed consumed by guilt, originally deferred defining U.S. policy to Lansing, who was acting secretary of state after Bryan resigned. Lansing shared their uncertainty. "I confess that I dislike very much the idea which was involved in our action," he admitted, "but there was really no other practical way in which to handle the question." The intervention, he wrote Wilson on 13 August, "does not meet my sense of a nation's sovereign rights and is more or less an exercise of force and an invasion of Haytien independence."[16]

American policy was defined amid a befuddling sense that the United States was acting outside international law and custom. "We have no excuse of reprisal as we had at Vera Cruz," Lansing complained to Wilson on 3 August. "The situation in Haiti is distressing and very perplexing," he confided to the president. "I am not at all sure what we ought to do or what we can legally do." Almost a week after the landing, Lansing still had not come to any conclusion about what the United States should do there.[17]

Wilson shared his secretary's perplexity, particularly as they lacked the legal authority "to do what we apparently ought to do." Nonetheless, "the necessity for exercising control down there is immediate, urgent, imperative," he explained to Galt, adding that "our object, of course, is not to subordinate them, but to help them in the most practical and most feasible way possible." Almost a week after the landing, Wilson finally concluded that the United States had to keep sufficient forces in Haiti to control Port-au-Prince and the surrounding countryside. He also wanted the Haitian congress assured that it would be protected, "but that we will not recognize any action on its part which does not put men in charge of affairs whom we can trust to handle and put an end to revolution." Nor would the United States allow Haitian revenues to finance revolutions. "We consider it our duty to insist on constitutional government there," Wilson instructed Lansing, even if that meant taking charge of elections to ensure "that a real government is elected which we can support."[18]

Translating these Wilsonian generalities into practical action took time. Lansing delayed until 10 August before transmitting the gist of Wilson's intentions to the American legation in Haiti. Admiral Caperton waited impatiently for some direction from Washington. "It is very important that I be kept advised of the State Department's intentions relative to Haiti," he pleaded. In the meantime, he instituted a number of stopgap measures aimed at quelling Haitian resistance. He convinced the Haitian congress to postpone the presidential election. Rosalvo Bobo, the leading pretender for the presidency, was persuaded to disarm his army and risk his ambitions on a future election. On 6 August, Caperton banished all Haitian soldiers from the capital; two who resisted the order were killed. On the same day, the USS *Connecticut* landed marines at Cape Haitien.[19]

Still, the admiral later confessed, he received no definition of the administration's policy until 7 August, a full ten days after he had landed troops. Even then the policy was expressed in the vaguest terms. The United States, Caperton was ordered to proclaim to the Haitians, intended "to establish order and maintain Haitian independence." Unfortunately the American saviors privately believed that these were contradictory objectives. Achieving the former required sacrificing the latter.[20]

Supported by U.S. Marines, Caperton established himself as the American regent in Port-au-Prince. "Years of unrest, sudden political eruptions, frequently followed by murders of opponents, had ingrained in the Haitian character an expectation of disorder," he concluded. "We held that the United States must expect to remain in Haiti until the natives had been educated to respect a self-sustaining government, its laws and its decisions, as well as assist in their several functions." Through his subordinate, Captain Edward Beach, Caperton compelled the remnants of Haiti's leadership to accept an American-backed candidate for president, an American-dictated treaty, and an American-designed police force.[21]

Haitian congressmen, needing desperately a single voice to deal with the Americans, continued to press Caperton for permission to elect a president. Realizing that the election was imminent, Lansing finally translated Wilson's views into U.S. policy in Haiti. On 10 August he cabled the American legation in Port-au-Prince instructions to inform the Haitian congress that the United States would support it, "but that it cannot recognize action which does not establish in charge of Haitian affairs those whose abilities and dispositions give assurances of putting end to factional disorders." He also wanted the presidential candidates advised that the United States expected to retain "practical control of the customs," as well as such general financial control as it deemed necessary for an "efficient administration" of the beleaguered country. Finally, Lansing avowed, "the United States considers it its duty to support a constitutional government." He disavowed any political or territorial designs on Haiti, promising solely "to aid the people of Haiti in establishing a stable government and in maintaining domestic peace throughout the Republic." Later that same day Lansing assured Wilson that "we will be able to arrange matters very much as we please."[22]

Caperton, as though he was hiring an employee, interviewed the leading candidates for the Haitian presidency. Rosalvo Bobo flunked the test. Although intelligent and influential among the lower classes of Haitians, Bobo "is himself entirely without strength of character, is bigoted, has personal ambition and no patriotism." Sudre Dartiguenave, who wisely agreed to run only on the condition that the United States "sustained" his administration, struck Caperton and Beach as "a man of steadier mentality and greater ability than Bobo." Despite rumors that Dartiguenave was a "grafter," Caperton clearly favored him. He quietly passed his endorsement to the Haitian congress which, to no one's great surprise, elected Dartiguenave president on 12 August.[23]

The next day Lansing forwarded to Wilson a draft of a new treaty with Haiti. The terms granted the United States "extensive control" of Haitian finances and internal affairs. Although Lansing still felt a twinge of guilt over negotiating with Haiti while U.S. Marines policed its capital, it was not guilt enough to dissuade him from its necessity. "The only way possible, it seems

to me, of restoring to the Haytiens their political and personal rights and protecting them from the terrorism of unscrupulous military leaders is to obtain
control, for a time at least, of the prize which these chieftains seek, namely,
the public revenues of the Republic," he advised the president. Wilson
agreed. [24]

The terms of the treaty harked back to the proposals Wilson had been trying to impose on Haiti for a year, but with some significant amendments. The
new terms ensured that any government in Haiti would be little more than a
puppet regime of the United States. The treaty provided for U.S. control of
Haiti's customs revenues through the appointment of an American general
receiver and U.S. control of Haiti's finances through the appointment of an
American financial adviser. Revenues would be used first to defray the salaries
and expenses of the receiver and adviser. Second in priority was making the
scheduled payments on the public debt. Third was the expenses of a Haitian
constabulary. Only after these costs were covered could money be used to pay
the "current expenses" of the Haitian government. [25]

The treaty required the establishment of "an efficient constabulary composed of native Haitiens." This police force was intended for "the preservation of domestic peace, the security of individual rights and the full
observance of the provisions of this treaty." The constabulary would be "organized and officered by Americans" chosen by the American president,
though actually appointed by the Haitian president. Further, the treaty incorporated a promise from the Haitian government not to transfer title or
control of any of its territory to any foreign power nor to enter into any treaty
with any foreign power, save the United States, that impaired Haitian independence. The United States also took upon itself to develop Haiti's natural
resources and, shades of Veracruz, to improve the country's public health. As
if these terms were insufficient to complete Haiti's subjugation, the treaty
also entitled the United States "the right to intervene for the preservation
of Haitien independence and the maintenance of a Government adequate
for the protection of life property and individual liberty." All the bases
were covered. [26]

The Haitians balked. For a month President Dartiguenave and his new
cabinet slipped and slid through the negotiations, desperately running from
consummating the agreement. "Treaty negotiations are not progressing satisfactorily," Caperton complained on 21 August. Although Dartiguenave
seemed to favor the treaty, several among his cabinet and in the congress were
vociferous, their principal objections centering on American control of Haitian customs. Despite "friendly, explanatory, and patient" negotiations by
Caperton, the Haitians were recalcitrant. [27]

"But we must insist," Wilson well understood. "Control of the customs is
the essence of the whole matter." Lansing, anxious to begin the grand work

of rebuilding, proposed a modus vivendi implementing the treaty immediately while awaiting the approval of both congresses. As he envisioned the opportunities, putting Haitian finances in order would allow the government

> to pay promptly adequate salaries to its officials, to establish a good school system; to build roads and generally facilitate the transportation and marketing of the produce of the country; to extend and perfect the present telegraph lines and erect and maintain wireless stations; to undertake harbor improvements and municipal sanitation and by carrying a public works of this nature to furnish employment to the people and afford them opportunities to improve their industrial and intellectual condition.

A whole new world awaited the Haitians if only they would accept American help. [28]

But the Haitians remained blind to the opportunities. On 23 August, Dartiguenave and his cabinet threatened to resign if the United States continued to insist on customs control. "It is to be remembered," Caperton advised his superiors, "that there are practically no patriotic people in Haiti, in the sense of people being willing to unselfishly sacrifice their own personal interests for the good of the country." Although the discussions continued, Caperton prepared to establish a U.S. military government in the event the Haitians resigned. He understood that the United States was "bound not to abandon the Haitien situation until the affairs of the country are set at right and the predominate interests of the United States secured."[29]

In the meantime Wilson determined to expand the intervention across the rest of Haiti. On 19 August Daniels ordered Caperton to take the customhouses at Jacmel, Aux Cayes, Jérémie, Miragoane, Petit Goâve, Port-au-Prince, St. Marc, Gonaïves, Port-de-Paix, and Cape Haitien. Funds collected from these facilities would be applied to the establishment of the constabulary. As Caperton realized, the instructions meant that the "United States has now actually accomplished a military intervention in affairs of another nation." Seizing the customhouses by necessity meant taking the cities. To accomplish the task, he needed another regiment of marines, an artillery battalion, and three more gunboats or light cruisers.[30]

Caperton also wanted the reinforcements put to disbanding the cacos. "These lawless negroes," he later explained, "most of whom lived a carefree and irresponsible life in the mountains were professional bandits." Keeping them at bay "would do much towards the betterment of insular conditions in a political, as well as a moral way. . . . That could only be accomplished by force." Wilson and Daniels accepted Caperton's proposal. Thus even as the Americans pressed to legitimize their control over Haiti through the treaty, Caperton was consummating it through force. As the gunboats moved along the coast seizing the customhouses, the marines marched into the interior and the Wilson administration increased its pressure on Dartiguenave to sign the treaty. Within its terms lay not only American ambitions for Haiti's salvation but also the legitimacy for the intervention. Lansing, foreswearing Haitian territory and pledging his respect for its national sovereignty, threatened to set up a U.S. military government or install some other political faction that would sign. The United States, Lansing continued the refrain, sought no "treaty conditions other than for the welfare of the Haitian people." It was the purity of American humanitarianism that made Haitian obstinacy so frustrating.[31]

Dartiguenave and his cabinet, hanging desperately to the last threads of Haitian independence, promised to sign if the articles pertaining to customs control, the financial adviser, and the right of the United States to intervene were so modified as to render them essentially harmless. Caperton decided to proclaim martial law over Port-au-Prince. The proclamation, issued on 3 September, promised to protect "the fundamental rights of man." "I believe this move will strengthen the best elements in the present Haitian Government," Caperton assured Daniels, "and will serve to suppress the disloyal elements." The test of loyalty, of course, was acceptance of the treaty in its entirety.[32]

"Apparently the Haitian authorities are seeking to play fast and lose with us," Wilson wrote his fiancée, "I am wondering whether to blame them or not!" Caperton was not so sympathetic. While he continued the negotiations with the Haitian government, his gunboats seized the various customhouses along Haiti's extensive shoreline. Convinced that "our experience at Vera Cruz and sound military principles indicate that we cannot expect to seize a customs house and administer it unless we take military occupation of the town where it is located," Caperton soon had a dozen cities under military occupation.[33]

Still the treaty remained "the most important thing in Haiti." As Caperton privately confessed, he applied "military pressure at propitious moments in [the] negotiations," including the proclamation of martial law. "Successful negotiation of the treaty is the predominant part of our present mission," Caperton advised Daniels. "Any success that has been made so far toward the accomplishment of the treaty has been due to military pressure." By 8 September prospects for the treaty were favorable. Two cabinet members resigned, which earned Wilson's begrudging respect and cleared the path to signing the treaty.[34]

Because the Haitians were on the verge of signing, Caperton eased the military pressure. He delayed further offensive operations in Cape Haitien until Dartiguenave put his name to the treaty. On 14 September the Haitian government capitulated. It agreed to sign the treaty and to enter immediately into a modus vivendi implementing its terms pending ratification. The treaty was signed two days later.[35]

Once signed the treaty needed next to be ratified by both the U.S. and Haitian legislatures. No one in the Wilson administration expected trouble from either body. The U.S. Senate would naturally accept the burden of helping Haiti; the Haitian congress could hardly resist American control. In the meantime the modus vivendi would allow the good works to begin. Caperton resumed the take-over of Haiti's ports and the breakup of the cacos.

Because the congressional session expired on 17 September, President Dartiguenave called for a special session to convene three days later. Caperton applied to the Wilson administration to use its good offices to arrange for a $1.5 million loan to cover governmental expenses, including the back pay owed employees—particularly the congressmen. Dartiguenave assured the admiral that he expected no opposition to ratification. He intended to permit a full discussion in the congress to ensure that "acceptance may be made unanimous."[36]

The euphoria of finally having the treaty signed barely survived the re-convening of the congress. The senate immediately appointed a committee to study the terms and to raise objections. Within four days Caperton was complaining that the Haitians were "the most deceitful, unreliable, graft seekers on earth." The ministers in Dartiguenave's cabinet were "all against him," but they kept their opposition well hidden because the United States had so plainly indicated that "we are here for keeps and that we mean business." Caperton, though, also kept his impatience secreted from the Haitians. Although frustrated by the "outside influences and selfish motives" opposing ratification, he preferred to defer to Dartiguenave to lobby for a favorable vote. He drew the line, however, at any suggestion of reopening negotiations over the terms of the convention.[37]

In what he considered a generous display of forbearance, Caperton abstained from any "forcible measures" to compel ratification. Such blatant pressure was hardly necessary. His gunboats essentially controlled the coast; his marines were well on their way to conquering the interior. While the Haitian congress argued over accepting American control through the treaty, Caperton's forces were rapidly extending and solidifying it through force. While the senators talked, the Americans acted.[38]

Yet Caperton had a gentler side. He believed it best to rule benignly. Ratification ultimately depended on earning the good faith of the Haitians. That, he realized, would take time, but it would also ensure a wholehearted acceptance of American help. "To be sure," he later wrote, "we were powerful enough to accomplish by force anything we desired." But, he added, "a friendly attitude . . . would lay the foundation for future good relations between the two governments." Consequently, even as his marines and gunboats forcibly extended U.S. control, Caperton emphasized the humanitarian side of American rule. As he explained to his friend Admiral William S. Benson, the chief of naval operations:

> The work of our doctors in connection with the distribution of Red Cross funds, the prompt and efficient manner in which public works have been conducted, the adoption of sanitary measures, the abolition of petty graft formerly collected by local officials, the breaking up of marauding bands, all these have tended to create in the minds of the people, a belief that the Americans are unselfish in their purposes and have occupied the country for its own good.

The treaty, of course, held out the promise of even greater help.[39]

Although Caperton held back the stick, he readily proffered the carrot to the Haitian congressmen. On 18 October he authorized the expenditure of thirty-five thousand dollars from the customs receipts to pay the monthly salary of the legislators. The gesture underscored the irrelevance of the great debate. While the Haitians argued over agreeing to U.S. control of customs, Caperton showed he already had it. He lacked only the legitimacy a treaty would bestow. A Haitian choice had been mooted by events. What Caperton sought was not active acceptance but passive acquiescence.[40]

What he got was rejection. The senate committee reported against American control of the customs receiver, the financial adviser, the constabulary, and even the improvements in public works. The committee accepted American support of the Haitian government, but by stripping away the details of that support, it essentially negated all but the right of the United States to intervene if the government was threatened. Nor was that entirely assured, because the committee recommended that a new treaty be negotiated. Although Dartiguenave immediately assured Caperton that he had enough votes to ratify the treaty, the committee report rattled the admiral.[41]

The risks were high. As Caperton reported to Daniels, if ratification failed, the Haitian constitution required laying the treaty aside for a full year before it could be reconsidered. Even then it would be presented to the same senate. Caperton felt reasonably confident that the full senate would accept the convention, but he warned that "powerful influences are being exercised in that body against ratification." The general populace, he believed, favored the agreement, and "famine conditions and prostration of industries" demanded it.[42]

But doubts remained. Should the vote be negative, Dartiguenave proposed to dissolve the congress and immediately call elections for a "constituent assembly" to ratify the treaty and amend the constitution. Caperton endorsed the proposal, adding that the United States should uphold Dartiguenave. His government offered "the only hope for peace and prosperity in Haiti." The velvet glove was slipping from the iron hand.[43]

Wilson and Daniels thought it time to strip it completely off. On 10 November, the day before the scheduled senate vote, Daniels ordered Caperton to appear before Dartiguenave's cabinet. As though acting on his own authority, Daniels wanted Caperton to warn the ministers—and through them, the senate—that if the treaty failed, the United States still intended to "retain control in Haiti." In that event, U.S. forces would "forthwith proceed to the complete pacification of Haiti." The Dartiguenave government would be supported. Those who opposed could "only expect such treatment as their conduct merits." Daniels wanted Caperton to make the threat clear enough to thwart all opposition and secure ratification.[44]

Caperton succeeded admirably. His warning quickly spread throughout the senate. It had the desired effect. Late in the afternoon of 11 November, after another long day of debate, the senate ratified the treaty twenty-six to seven. The good work of the United States could now legitimately proceed.[45]

The newly signed treaty did not ensure full acceptance by the Haitian people. The cacos, in particular, fiercely resisted the take-over. They were, after all, fighting for their livelihoods. But they had rarely confronted an enemy that fought back—and they had never faced one so well trained, well equipped, and well fought. The skirmishes were so lopsided, the caco losses so heavy, that by 15 November, Daniels, the unwilling "Josephus the First," ordered Caperton to cease all offensive operations. Despite the admiral's vigorous protest, Daniels simply could not suffer the high loss of life.[46]

Daniels's discomfort typified the American position in Haiti. Emboldened by the purity of their own motives, they eagerly shouldered the white man's burden only to find that the mechanics of the task were unpleasant, the actions required of them were morally distasteful, and the very people they were trying to help were just plain unlikable. The marines who executed Wilson's policies in Haiti hardly tried to hide their displeasure. By American standards, the Haitians were immoral and dishonest, "a lovely bunch of cut throats and thugs," as General Littleton Waller described them to his sons in November 1915. One marine stepped ashore in Haiti to find that "it hurt. It stunk. Fairyland had turned into a pigsty. . . . Haitians of the working class have the ugliest feet in the world. In my bewilderment I somehow blamed them for the hornied things on which they stood. We were all annoyed." The marines overcame their distaste for the task by believing that they were rescuing the Haitians from their inherent inferiority. According to Major

Butler, the commander of the gendarmerie, the marines were "trustees of a huge estate . . . the Haitians were our wards."[47]

The marines went about the task of salvation with typical gusto. By April 1916 they had recruited, equipped, and trained almost two thousand Haitians, garrisoning the men throughout Haiti. They made the gendarmerie more than a police force. According to Butler they were "doing everything in their power to assist the native population in rebuilding their roads, their irrigation works, their bridges, to clean up their towns and generally better the condition of the people at large." He joshed that he had "been so busy trying to help my little black fellows get on their feet that I have hardly had time to eat." Sadly, despite the fervor with which he offered the Haitians his help, to Butler they were always just "cockroaches."[48]

And therein lay the problem. If Daniels's queasiness typified the approach, Butler's racism characterized it. The Americans were helping a people whom they believed were essentially beyond help—and their reliance on force proved unrelenting. In August 1916 Admiral Benson reported to Daniels that the Haitian people seemed "happy and prosperous," but "the necessity for putting absolute pressure" on the Dartiguenave government "to comply with the demands of the State Department seems absolutely necessary." A year later, in June 1917, Butler and his gendarmerie dissolved the Haitian congress when it refused to adopt a U.S.-written constitution.[49]

Yet despite the force, the Americans understood themselves to have embarked on a "great experiment." Major General John H. Russell, who commanded the marines during the early 1920s, described Haiti as a "laboratory of government." The Americans were the scientists experimenting to create a better country. "We stayed to help Haiti lift herself out of disease, poverty, ignorance, and political anarchy," Russell proudly remembered. Marshall Morgan of the State Department wrote in early 1919 that:

> The American Government is actively assisting in the restoration of the country. Public improvements of all sorts are being installed, roads are being built and steps to educate the illiterate are being taken. Instead of murder, anarchy, poverty and ignorance, peace, prosperity and happiness have been substituted.

Yet, what manner of creature were these American Frankensteins creating?[50]

The Haitians learned that a strong police force, well armed and loyal to the government, would put an end to the chronic revolutions. Who then needed public works, education, or general prosperity? It was dictatorship, not democracy, that the Americans bequeathed to Haiti when they released their control in 1933. It was the strength of the gendarmerie, not the improved roads and sanitation, not the schools or the improved finances, that had the lasting impact.

American control was as brutal as it purported to be charitable. In May 1920, Rear Admiral Thomas Snowden, the senior U.S. officer in Haiti, warned then-Colonel Russell not to allow his marines to use "inquisitorial" tactics of torture against Haitian prisoners. Snowden feared that the gendarmerie was being used "as a club." He ordered the "inquisition methods" stopped. "In trying to administer a foreign or dependent country it is absolutely necessary to be open, fair, and above-board," Snowden advised, adding, "We want to be just."[51]

Justice, though, proved elusive. The accusations of torture and indiscriminate killing continued to reach Washington. In 1920 Daniels ordered the judge advocate to establish a court of inquiry. The court's conclusions simply mirrored the approach the Americans had taken in conquering Haiti. It estimated that as many as 2,250 Haitians had been killed between July 1915 and October 1920. The judge advocate excused the killings because the marines were fighting "savage" Haitians "who operated free from all the restraints of civilized warfare." The ruthlessness of the cacos "forfeited any claim to treatment such as should be accorded to those who abide by the rules of land warfare." The marines would have been justified "to exterminate every last number of those bands," the court concluded. "That this was not done is clear enough proof that there was no indiscriminate killing of natives who had taken the field against us."[52]

But the marines' restraint was hard to discern. Over twenty-two hundred killed in five years was a staggering number for a self-proclaimed benign administration. The death rate illustrated the dangers of relying on force to solve international problems. The risk is always that force inures those who depend on it. Those who use force chance becoming habituated to violence, losing sight of the larger goals. Merely refraining from exterminating all who resist, however laudable, is hardly the best way to teach democracy and good government.

THE AMERICANIZATION OF THE DOMINICAN REPUBLIC

Wilsonian warriors were shy conquerors. Convinced of the purity of their motives, Wilson and his soldiers rarely hesitated to resort to force as an initial means to some greater end. But they never seemed comfortable using force to impose that solution. They wanted the conquered to embrace them as heroes, not disdain them as enemies. They were appalled to find that those they vanquished treated them with hostility.

In mid-May 1915, Admiral Caperton rushed his small fleet to the Dominican Republic. He landed troops at the capital, Santo Domingo, on 15 May and began again the long, stumbling process of imposing an

American solution. To Caperton's great chagrin, Dominican resistance ultimately pushed him into outright occupation. Within three days of the landing, Caperton was complaining that "we seem to have no friends here
whatever among the Dominicans." They were, he wrote Admiral Benson,
"very unfriendly. . . . Even the women and children almost turn up their
noses as we pass by and treat us with utter and silent contempt." His new
aide, Lieutenant Commander William D. Leahy, concurred that "the
Dominicans definitely did not like us." Because the Americans wanted only
to help, neither officer understood why the Dominicans were so "very bitter
towards Americans."[53]

With a bravado originally unmatched by action, Caperton courageously
promised that he would impose U.S. policies upon the Dominicans. He preferred to do this without force, he assured Benson, but "when force is
necessary we will not fail to act quickly and with our best efforts." Haiti would
be his model. "It looks to me as if we will have to take charge of matters
here and deal with them pretty much as we did in Haiti, if this is the policy
of the Government," Caperton concluded. "The country must be disarmed,
revolutions must be wiped off the calendar, and the people made to deal
honestly."[54]

As with Haiti the Americans faltered through the take-over of the Dominican Republic. Caperton received no fresh instructions until early June, half
a month after he originally landed U.S. forces in Santo Domingo. Daniels
instead referred him to the archives of the American legation, particularly
to a year-old cablegram from former Secretary of State Bryan insisting that
"no more revolutions will be permitted. . . . The people of Santo Domingo
will be given an opportunity to develop the resources of their country in
peace. Their revenues will no longer be absorbed by graft or wasted in
insurrections."[55]

U.S. Minister William Russell recognized immediately that the presence,
if not yet the use, of American military forces improved the prospects "for
ultimately obtaining permanent reforms." By the end of May, he was plead-
ing with the Department of State to recognize that it was time to take financial control of the Dominican Republic. The U.S. customs receiver should
collect all revenues, whether from customs or internal taxes, and establish
himself as the disbursing officer to the Dominicans, doling out monies only
on those projects and expenditures approved by the United States. Once financial control was firmly entrenched, the United States could insist on a
treaty embodying a Haitian-style constabulary, control of the country's communications and railways, and other reforms.[56]

Russell also argued that "a de facto Government headed by a man of our
selection and not hampered by a Congress would be ideal." Officials in the

department's Division of Latin American Affairs agreed. Obtaining the ideal proved difficult. Jiménez's resignation left a council of his ministers in charge of the government, and the Dominican congress, composed of a house of deputies and a senate, was still in session. Both bodies were anxious to elect a new president to deal with the American invaders. Russell described the legislature as "composed of the worst elements in the country." He and Caperton feared that any man elected by it would "bring nothing but disaster to the country."[57]

Consequently, American policy immediately after the landing was to block the election of a new president. The Wilson administration opposed the election because the congress was composed of the same rebellious members who had supported Desiderio Arias and impeached Jiménez. Russell feared that the senate would elect Arias, not just one of his supporters. In his view the "final elimination [of] Arias as a political or military factor must now be accomplished." Russell wanted the election delayed until Caperton could pacify the country and arrange, as he had in Haiti, for the selection of a U.S.-favored candidate.[58]

The Dominican congress refused to wait. On 18 May, three days after the landing, the House of Deputies endorsed Dr. Federico Henríquez y Carvajal of the Supreme Court. His name then went before the senate for its concurrence. Both Caperton and Russell demanded a delay in the vote, but the Dominican legislature refused even to reply. Admiral Caperton determined to "use force when necessary . . . to prevent election." Every day Caperton and Russell went among the Dominicans lobbying for a postponement. On 23 May the senate confirmed the choice of the house at the first reading. If the vote held through two more readings, Henriquez would be the next president of the Dominican Republic.[59]

Daniels ordered Caperton: "Within your power use all means to postpone election of president in Santo Domingo until after satisfactory conditions of peace have been restored." Thus bolstered, Caperton threatened "extreme measures." Already he had received "all sorts of promises from Congress not to elect a President." He was unsure, though, how long the Dominicans would keep their promises. "In my heart," he confided to Benson, "I believe that we will finally get what we want merely with the display of force." But he was doing more than exercising military power through the threat of force. Even as he wrote, American marines were stepping ashore at Puerto Plata and Montecristi.[60]

Russell lacked Caperton's confidence. He preferred a more blatant exercise of armed power at the capital, not just in the provinces. On 2 June he proposed as "one option" that American forces arrest enough senators to stop the election. At the least, he urged the Department of State, "We should at once proceed with the appointment of a financial controller" to take over the country's finances.[61] Russell's superiors vetoed any arrests. Reluctant, again, to resort to a naked exercise of force, Wilson and his advisers preferred to use economic, rather than armed, power. The choice reflected their natural hesitation to use brute power when more subtle, and less overbearing, options remained. Acting Secretary of State Polk considered arresting the senators "too high-handed and not necessary." With Wilson's full concurrence, he ordered Russell instead to "induce Congress to agree on a desirable candidate." As the inducement, Russell was to "impress on all factions that this government will not recognize any government in Santo Domingo not satisfactory to it and as this government intends to maintain financial control such recognition will be absolutely necessary."[62]

Wilson and his advisers unanimously agreed that the only way to salvage Santo Domingo was to take over its finances, create an American-trained constabulary, and teach the Dominicans peaceful ways to select their government. In early July, Secretary of State Lansing summed up American policy:

> I think that constant pressure should be exerted to bring about the necessary reforms to prevent the treasury being plundered by government officials. That and a constabulary system will insure peace in the republic. We should endeavor to secure a treaty or amendment of the present treaty so that it will be similar to our treaty with Haiti.
>
> The peace of the whole island depends upon similar financial control in the two Republics, otherwise revolutionary movements are fostered across the international boundary.

In effect, Wilson wanted to run the country until such time as the Dominicans could emerge from American tutelage as fully converted junior Americans. Because his motives were pure, Dominican opposition and willful independence surprised him. How could anyone refuse such selfless assistance?[63]

But like the Haitians before them, refuse the Dominicans did. Under intense American pressure, the Dominican congress delayed the vote for almost two months. At first, following Russell's suggestion and with Caperton's concurrence, the Council of Ministers arrested a handful of Arias senators. The arrests sent a shaft of fear through the congress. But the State Department remained uncomfortable with such blatant displays, and a day later, to Caperton's surprise, Russell arranged their release. The vote for Henríquez passed its second reading. At that point, those senators who sympathized with the American desire to help simply boycotted the senate proceedings, thus preventing a quorum and effectively blocking Henríquez's election.[64]

The stalemate continued through June and most of July. "These people still remain sullen and quiet," Caperton wrote Benson on 7 June. He added, "They are thoroughly imbued with the idea that this time the United States is in earnest." The admiral believed that the longer U.S. forces remained and prohibited further revolutions, the more the common folk would grow to "appreciate that we have come to help them and give them a chance to work their soil and make an honest living." Yet Dominican stubbornness in refusing American help grated. A week later Caperton bitterly complained that "these people are worse than the Haitiens, if such a thing be possible, and I am more convinced each day that the only way to handle them is by force and the big stick."[65]

The time had come to use force for solution. The deadlock in congress not only prohibited the Dominicans from expressing their preference, it also kept the United States from imposing, or even finding, its candidate. On 20 June Caperton ordered his marines to occupy Santiago, Moca, and La Vega. Proclaiming that "we were here to preserve law and order and protect life and property, and to support the present Dominican government," companies of marines moved out. They swept aside the sporadic resistance offered by the Dominicans and, in short order, firmly established U.S. control over the country.[66]

At the same time, the customs receiver expanded his control over Dominican finances. Clarence Baxter, the general receiver, believed it time to ignore the Dominicans's "tender susceptibilities as a sovereign people" and simply proceed, "under American compulsion if necessary," with the business of improving the country. Russell wholeheartedly agreed. "All factions," he reported on 6 June, "understand our policy and that troops will not be withdrawn until reforms demanded are in final form and successfully operating." On 16 June the Bureau of Insular Affairs ordered Baxter to take control of the finances. Since he already managed most of its revenues through customs collections, it was fairly easy to take over its expenditures. They simply steamrolled Dominican objections, "going right ahead regardless." Within ten days Baxter was "feeling rather optimistic." A month later he was prophesizing "a wave of prosperity will strike the country, and the revenues will rapidly increase." Powerless to stop the incursion, the Dominican minister of finance resigned in protest.[67]

While the American occupation expanded physically across the country and financially through control of the revenues and expenditures, Caperton tried to ease the natural fears of the people. On 26 June he issued a proclamation reminiscent of the promises he had made the Haitians a year earlier. By proclaiming the innocence of American motives, he tried to make the violence of their actions somehow more acceptable. The United States, he announced, was "supporting the constituted authorities" and "putting a stop to revolutions and consequent disorders." Caperton promised, "It is not the intention of the United States Government to acquire by conquest any territory in the Dominican Republic nor to attack its sovereignty, but our troops will remain here until all revolutionary movements have been stamped out and until such reforms as are deemed necessary to insure the future welfare of the country have been initiated and are in effective operation." According to the Haitian model, it was now time to find a Dominican agreeable to American control and manage his election to the presidency. Then the United States could consummate the remaining reforms it believed necessary for the republic's salvation.[68]

The Dominican congress rebelled. Using the only feasible retaliation it could muster, the senate and house of deputies elected Francisco Henríquez y Carvajal, Federico's brother, president on 25 June 1916. The election came with surprising swiftness, catching Caperton and Russell off guard. Russell considered the election a victory for Arias. Despite the new president's promise to seek U.S. help "to establish a government of order that will guarantee the peace and prosperity of the country," Russell thought it unlikely that Henríquez would easily consent to the reforms the United States considered essential.[69]

Henríquez lost from the start. U.S. Marines occupied most of the major cities in the Dominican Republic. U.S. customs receivers controlled the country's income, taking a staggering $200,000 a month out of circulation. The Wilson administration refused to recognize the new president, branding him instead an Arias puppet. "No good can come to the country from his administration," Russell concluded. That conclusion rang the death knell on the Henríquez administration. Its death throes, however, lasted a distressingly long time.[70]

Once again Wilson shied from forcing a solution. He preferred to exercise the less volatile forms of economic and diplomatic power. Each was sufficient to enervate the Dominican government; neither was enough to finish the task. In a normally scheduled rotation, Admiral Caperton left the island in mid-July, handing over his command to Rear Admiral Charles F. Pond, an incompetent who had difficulty staying awake through an afternoon. Pond interpreted his chief functions as to support Minister Russell's exertion of diplomatic power and to ensure that his command tread as softly as possible amid a population that "vehemently resent our presence among them." Unlike his predecessor, Pond did "not deem it advisable to mix at all in politics."[71]

From early August to the end of November, Russell threatened and cajoled Henríquez to accept U.S. control of the money, the establishment of an American-led constabulary, and the dissolution of the Dominican military.

In return the United States would recognize his government. Henríquez conceded U.S. management of the customs and promised to transform the army into a police force, but he did not believe he had the authority to put either promise in writing. Russell distrusted him. Lansing decreed that the provisional government would not be recognized "until such time as it shows itself to be favorable to our interpretation of Convention as to [financial] control, constabulary, and other reforms." He ordered that Arias be put under close surveillance and arrested if he tried to leave Santiago, and that acceptance of the reforms be in writing, preferably as a published decree.[72]

Negotiations continued, but with no real progress. Henríquez maintained that it was constitutionally impossible for him to give the promises in writing as the Americans demanded. Convinced that their control of the money would eventually compel the Dominicans to cave in, Lansing brushed aside Henríquez's constitutional qualms. If necessary, Jordan Stabler of the Division of Latin American Affairs advised the secretary, the United States had enough marines in the Dominican Republic "to prevent any disturbance and will, if necessary, place the country under martial law as we did in Haiti, with but very little effort and publicity."[73]

Economic power was failing the Americans, even as it was destroying the Dominicans. "Suspension of payments as a coercive measure," Baxter wrote, " . . . is not working out as expected by the diplomats." All it was accomplishing was to focus "the bitter animosity" of the Dominicans on the customs receivers. By the end of October, the general receiver had confiscated almost $600,000. "This will likely produce a monetary crisis throughout the country, for which we would not like to be held responsible," Russell finally warned, adding that "very many people are suffering who do not deserve to suffer."[74]

Russell returned to Washington for consultations. Forcing a solution was rapidly becoming the only realistic alternative to ending the stalemate with Henríquez. On 24 October Pond dispatched a small marine patrol to the outskirts of Santo Domingo to arrest a Dominican named Baptista. The Dominicans fought back, killing two of the marines and wounding a third. Two days later another squad of marines was attacked outside a gambling saloon. Fearing that the two attacks portended more violence, Admiral Benson recommended putting Santo Domingo, if not the whole country, under martial law. Russell agreed with the suggestion, which had the added advantage of offering economic relief to the bankrupt nation. Payments to the Henríquez administration would constitute recognition of his government, which no one wanted, but payments could be made once martial law was declared.[75]

On 31 October Jordon Stabler, Minister William Russell, chief of naval operations Admiral Benson, and navy captain Harry S. Knapp conferred about the deteriorating situation. "The landing of our forces," they agreed, "was for the purpose of upholding the then constituted government and of putting down revolutions." The time had come "to legalize our military action in keeping order and putting down any revolutionary activity." Such legality could only be obtained through a declaration of martial law. Captain Knapp, the conferees agreed, would replace Pond and declare himself military governor of Santo Domingo.[76]

Russell considered the solution "the only real remedy." On 12 November Knapp sailed the USS *Olympia* to Santo Domingo. Stabler urged Lansing to allow him to declare martial law when he arrived. The secretary agreed. "The situation in the Dominican Republic is approaching a crisis and we ought to determine immediately a course of action," he advised Wilson on 22 November, "as otherwise revolution and economic disaster are imminent." That course, he advised, should be a military government under Knapp.[77]

Upon his arrival in the Dominican Republic, Knapp found the situation largely unchanged. Henríquez remained adamant about the limit of his power to bow completely to the Americans. "They will never voluntarily consent to the measures of reform desired by our government," he cabled the Navy Department on 23 November, adding the next day that "there still exists a necessity for firm action."[78]

During this time Wilson had paid very little attention to the problems encountered in the republic. Other crises consumed him. Two months before the landing in Santo Domingo, the Punitive Expedition had crossed into Mexico. By November 1916 the expedition was encamped deep within Mexico. Negotiations over its withdrawal were dragging along. On 24 March, again but two months before the Dominican landing, a German U-boat sank without warning the French channel steamer *Sussex*, thus violating Germany's previous pledges to obey the rules of war. The Punitive Expedition kept the United States teetering on the brink of hostilities with Mexico; the sinking of the *Sussex* brought the country to the edge of war with Germany. Wilson ably sidestepped both crises, but his maneuvering left him little time or energy to attend to the difficulties in the Dominican Republic. And as Caperton, then Pond and Russell grappled with Dominican obstinacy, Wilson was running for reelection on the reassurance that "he kept us out of war." He deferred to Lansing and Daniels and their departmental subordinates to define U.S. policy toward the Dominican difficulties. They essentially followed the policies Wilson had spelled out a year earlier, but with little success. Now they were recommending force for solution.

"It is with the deepest reluctance that I approve and authorize the course here proposed," Wilson finally wrote Lansing on 26 November, "but I am convinced that it is the least of the evils in sight in this very perplexing situation." Although distracted by other, more pressing problems, Wilson none-theless intended to extend—and, if necessary, to impose—American help on the hapless Dominicans. He was indeed reluctant to use force for solution, but it was now the only way to achieve the reforms he considered essential for the Dominican Republic's salvation. On 29 November 1916 Captain Knapp proclaimed himself the military governor of the Dominican Republic. Amer-icanization could now begin in earnest.[79]

Knapp went eagerly to the task. He appointed naval officers to manage the several departments of government while Marines swept the country of Do-minican opposition. Afterward they began the work of training a native con-stabulary. Knapp also formed a commission of "distinguished Dominicans" to study the status of education in the country. Public works, particularly the construction of new roads and the maintenance of the old, also caught the new governor's attention.[80]

By mid-December 1916, Colonel Pendleton reported his confidence that "there will be no more signs of organized opposition." From this point, he assured Knapp, "our work . . . will be that of helping to teach these people to walk alone." A significant part of that effort was to establish the constab-ulary. Because the Dominicans suffered "the revolutionary habit," Knapp wanted to ensure that the police could never be used to support disgruntled leaders. Part of the plan, then, was to design the constabulary as small units dispersed throughout the country.[81]

"We are all working in harmony in the preparation of a broad and com-prehensive plan of government reconstruction and future development," Baxter assured his superiors at the Bureau of Insular Affairs. Knapp was "sur-prised at the ease with which the whole affair has thus far been consum-mated," but he was even more convinced that it would take a generation or more to complete the tutelage. Officials in the State Department agreed. In February 1918, F. Mayer of the Division of Latin American Affairs described the yearlong occupation as too short a period "to alter the fundamental conditions" in the country. The United States "would be derelict in its duties as Trustee for the Dominican people" if it turned the government back to them.[82]

The Americans were, if nothing else, consistent in their idealized hopes for the Dominican Republic. In June 1921 Rear Admiral Thomas Snowden, who succeeded Knapp, defined the goals prayed for the occupation: "The great object of the Military Government has been to pay off the public debt of the country; to advance the education of the country and especially to wipe out the large percentage of illiteracy in the country; and to draw the people away from every source of personalismo, that is, voting for the man, and to educate them toward higher ideals." They did not have a generation to realize the dream. During the presidential election campaign of 1920, Democratic vice-presidential candidate Franklin D. Roosevelt, who had been Daniels's assistant secretary, bragged that he had written Haiti's constitution—and that it was a pretty darned good one. The unfounded boast brought the issue of both occupations before the voters. Republican Warren G. Harding's election led to the early withdrawal of U.S. forces from the Hispanic Dominican Republic. The marines remained in black Haiti.[83]

In the grand humanitarian gesture, few compared to Wilson. Under his leadership, the United States embarked bravely on the bloody business of proselytization. The uses of force were incidental to the greater goal of spreading liberal democracy. With this as his objective, Wilson could forgive himself the violence. "What do you think is the most lasting impression that those boys down at Vera Cruz are going to leave?" he asked of his first intervention. His answer could have easily applied to most any of his several resorts to force:

> They have had to use some force—I pray God it may not be necessary for them to use any more—but do you think that the way they fought is going to be the most lasting impression? Have men not fought ever since the world began? Is there anything new in using force? The new things in the world are the things that are divorced from force. The things that show the moral compulsions of the human conscience, those are the things by which we have been building up civilization, not by force. And the lasting impression that those boys are going to leave is this, that they exercise self-control; that they are ready and diligent to make the place where they went fitter to live in than they found it; that they regarded other people's rights; that they did not strut and bluster, but went quietly, like self-respecting gentlemen, about their legitimate work.

Wilson readily excused the messier aspects of force as the burden of Americanization—the legitimate work of self-respecting gentlemen. Nonetheless, he sat uncomfortably with the consequences of domination. As humanitarian helpers, Wilsonian warriors were brave and strong; as conquerors, they were shy and hesitant. Only after events convinced them that to be the former required them to be the latter, did they swallow their distaste. Their hesitation was well considered. Force, though facile in subduing a nation, proved unwieldy in imposing a Wilsonian solution.[84]

In the Wilsonian way of war, force served better as an expedient to other forms of power, not as an end unto itself.

5 FORCE

for Introduction

> . . . a government's resort to armed power to compel or inaugurate negotiations with another government or organized group operating in a foreign country. It usually results from the belief that a military response will justify the intervening government's participation in negotiations. In short, it is an enforced invitation to discussion.

In the Wilsonian way of war, force was not the culmination of policy, but part of the continuum; it was rarely the ultimate. Force was a single aspect of a broader array of power. In Wilson's hands, the several types of international power were merged into a coherent policy mosaic. Wilson adeptly moved from diplomatic to armed power, economic to moral power, or whatever combination seemed best suited to the needs of the moment. The choice depended entirely on which appeared most likely to achieve his goals. Force in Wilson's hands was a tactical weapon drawn from a larger arsenal. It was nothing more than one kind of power among several, an arrow, however distinctive, in a full quiver.

Wilson was not the first national leader to incorporate force into foreign policy. From time immemorial nations have depended on armed power to achieve national objectives. It was used to subdue an opponent, taking over for other types of power once those had failed or were frustrated. Typically, though, armed power was held in reserve as the last resort, then unleashed in its full fury. The temptation had always been to rely on unrestrained force to solve international problems. War was far better known by its excesses than its limits.

Carl von Clausewitz, the master war theoretician, first recognized war as "the continuation of policy by other means." Clausewitz stressed, however, that it was the "peculiar nature of its means"—its violence—that distinguished war from other exertions of policy. War required "that the trend and designs of policy shall not be inconsistent with these means." In other words, even as war expressed policy, policy, for its part, would be modified according

77

to the unique nature of warfare. As a "pulsation of violence," war compelled policy to adapt to it even though war itself was nothing more than a political instrument.[1]

According to Clausewitz, the central aim of war was the defeat of the enemy. War was "an act of force to compel our enemy to do our will." Three broad objectives governed all wars: the destruction of the enemy's forces; the occupation of the enemy's country; and the subjugation of the enemy's will. Though individual wars varied in the degree to which they obtained each objective, all wars were fought "to render the enemy powerless." To the extent that political considerations modified these goals, then "the art of war will shrivel into prudence," moving from "real wars" to "half-hearted" wars.[2]

Still, Clausewitz believed that "in essence war and peace admit of no gradations." At its highest level, the "art of war turns into policy—but a policy conducted by fighting battles rather than by sending diplomatic notes." Essentially, political considerations determined the extent of war: "As policy becomes more ambitious and vigorous, so will war, and this may reach the point where war attains its absolute form." Conversely, policy could just as easily transform the "terrible two-handed sword" into the "lightest rapier—sometimes even a harmless foil fit only for thrusts and feints and parries." But the latter extreme foiled war's peculiar nature.[3]

Within the controlling political context, warfare retained an operational purity aimed always, if by varying degrees, at the defeat of the enemy. Although politics determined the direction of the war, the conduct of the war held true to immutable, universal principles derived from the science of warfare. "Political considerations," Clausewitz asserted, "do not determine the posting of guards or the employment of patrols." Politicians interfered with the conduct of the war at their hazard: "Only if statesmen look to certain military moves and actions to produce effects that are foreign to their nature do political decisions influence operations for the worse." As an instrument of policy, war could only be used to achieve what it had been designed to gain—"to compel our enemy to do our will." One simply could not use a sword as a plowshare.[4]

Wilson embraced, perhaps too tightly, the Clausewitzian dictum that war was an instrument of policy. Yet he refused to be bound by the uniqueness of the tool. On several occasions Wilson applied military moves to create new situations that he could then exploit with other forms of power. He was far less interested in war's ability to defeat an enemy—or even its ability to compel an enemy to his will. Rather, Wilson saw in force a particularly effective method of transformation. Armed power introduced him to new opportunities by creating new situations. With that introduction, Wilson could begin afresh using the other types of power at his command.

Wilson shied from using force to solve problems, to defeat the enemy. He much preferred to apply armed power in essentially the same way as he did other types of power. He quickly learned to use force opportunistically, controlling it with almost surgical precision, then following through with an innovative regimen of different types of power—diplomatic, economic, and moral. Rather than overwhelm or subdue an opponent, under Wilson force offered a way to inject the United States into an issue. Wilson used it to grab an opponent's attention, to give the United States standing to negotiate, or to kick stalled relations forward. Armed power never became his end play. It was neither the last resort of his policies nor his ultimate weapon.

From the beginning Wilson recognized that force was but one aspect of policy, its utility equal to the other instruments at his command. He denied the peculiar nature of war that undergirded Clausewitz's theory. For Wilson, war was not merely policy expressed by other means—though it was that, too—it was simply one means among several. All offered distinct benefits, but none was so peculiar as to stand entirely alone. Wilson not only defined gradations between peace and war, he depended on them in the conduct of his foreign policy. In the Wilsonian way of war, the limits on force defined the essence of force.

In large part, Wilson's predilection to deny the "peculiar nature of force," even as he used it repeatedly, derived from the distinctive Wilsonian knack of applying force against peoples whom he adamantly denied were his enemies. Wilson frequently relied on force for purposes other than compelling an enemy to do his will. Under Wilson, the United States twice invaded Mexico in the name of friendship and neighborliness. He sought not to compel Mexico to accept his policies, but to create new opportunities for his frustrated efforts to promote democracy. The twin interventions in Russia followed the same logic, turning warfare into a humanitarian gesture of international assistance. When Wilson tried the same tactics in Haiti and the Dominican Republic he found it necessary to pursue Clausewitzian logic. That was far from his original intent. Wilson perceived both occupations as unavoidable results of the need to tutor the Haitians and the Dominicans in the mysteries of democracy. He wanted to help his friends, not subdue his enemies.

Because Wilson so assiduously coordinated his uses of force with the other types of power at his command, the operational details of posting guards and dispatching patrols were important to him. He generally deferred to the military to develop the tactics to take Veracruz, chase Villa, impose peace on Haiti and the Dominican Republic, fight World War I, or launch the twin invasions into northern Russia and Siberia. But he had no qualms about interfering with the military's meticulous designs. Thus to the military's chagrin, he pulled in the sentries posted outside Veracruz, he suspended the patrols dispatched by General Pershing during the Punitive Expedition, and he ordered Admiral Caperton to go gently with the offensive operations in Haiti and the Dominican Republic.

Wilson boldly declared World War I a war for amateurs. "Nobody ever before conducted a war like this and, therefore, nobody can pretend to be a professional in a war like this," he told the astonished officers of the Atlantic fleet on 11 August 1917. "The experienced soldier—experienced in previous wars—is a back number so far as his experience is concerned," he added. Similarly, Wilson overruled the eminently practical objections of his military advisers and ordered them to invade northern Russia and Siberia. Throughout each resort to force, the military consistently decried the wars that were not quite wars, the limitations imposed on force, and the anti-Clausewitzian approach taken to armed power. [5]

Force inspired no awe in Wilson. "There is nothing noble or admirable in war itself," he declaimed in November 1914. Wilson measured force strictly by its purposes. "There is something very noble and admirable occasionally in the causes for which war is undertaken," he explained. "A war of aggression is not a war in which it is a proud thing to die," he said on the occasion of the return of the American dead from Veracruz, "but a war of service is a thing in which it is a proud thing to die." To enable that service, Wilson frequently found it necessary to apply armed power. [6]

FORCE AND MEDIATION: VERACRUZ

Wilson consistently abjured any suggestion that the occupation of Veracruz was an intervention in the internal affairs of Mexico. He admitted that "things have taken an ugly turn in Mexico" and confessed that his heart ached "to think of what we have been forced to do." But the president adamantly denied that what he had done was intervene. In early August 1914, after his troops had been ensconced in Veracruz for four months, Wilson explained to Secretary of War Garrison:

> We shall have no right at any time to intervene in Mexico to determine the way in which the Mexicans are to settle their own affairs. I feel sufficiently assured that the property and lives of foreigners will not suffer in the process of the settlement. The rest is political and Mexican. Many things may happen of which we do not approve, and which could not happen in the United States, but I say very solemnly that is no affair of ours . . . There are in my judgment no conceivable circumstances which would make it right for us to direct by force or by threat of force the internal processes of what is a profound revolution, a revolution as profound as that which occurred in France.

Months later, as Funston's forces were evacuating the city, Wilson bragged to the press that the purpose of the occupation had been "to finish Huerta, and that was accomplished." Yet his cockiness was misleading. From the initial landing to Huerta's resignation the following July, Wilson made no effort to force Huerta to leave or to compel the Mexican factions to accept an American solution to the revolution. Indeed, Wilson repeatedly rejected all suggestions that he expand the occupation or otherwise exact an end to the turmoil. As soon as Admiral Fletcher gained control of Veracruz, the United States fought no more.[7]

Instead, Wilson used the occupation to resuscitate his moribund policies. By April 1914, Wilson had exerted just about every form of power available to him, save armed. Through diplomacy he had managed to isolate Huerta from the international community, effectively cutting him off from any European support. Economically, he had allowed the Constitutionalists to obtain weapons and supplies, and he had warned foreign investors to take care in their dealings with the Mexican dictator. Morally, Wilson had repeatedly denounced Huerta's illegal usurpation of power. And through military power, the presence of U.S. troops along the border and U.S. ships in Mexican ports reminded Huerta of the power of his northern neighbor.

Yet each of these exercises had stalled. Huerta retained his power; the revolution ground along with disconcerting, though destructive, slowness. Wilson remained intent not merely on forcing Huerta from power but also in using "every influence . . . to secure Mexico a better Government" and to protect foreign economic interests. By the summer of 1913, though, his efforts had devolved into a self-described "watchful waiting."[8]

By April 1914 Wilson desperately needed a fresh start. His principal emissary in Mexico, John Lind, had long recommended intervention. "Mexicans respect power and nothing else," Lind had advised in October 1913. "Hence a demonstration of power justly, efficiently and generously exercised is the most effective argument we can make." Wilson was briefly tempted to intervene that fall when Huerta reneged on a promise to hold elections, but ultimately he could not bring himself to do it. Lind kept up the campaign. On 1 April 1914, he argued that "the dictates of humanity seem to compel" intervention. Again Wilson demurred. Force for solution seemed to him no solution at all.[9]

Then Huerta made a mistake. On 9 April Huertista soldiers arrested a handful of American sailors. Compounding the insult, Huerta refused to apologize with a twenty-one-gun salute. After an intense period of negotiation, Wilson ordered the occupation of Veracruz by way of reprisal. In his mind, force for retribution was far more justifiable than force for solution.

The landing of the marines and bluejackets created an entirely new situation. The first step was to limit the use of force. The Wilson administration moved immediately to downplay the seriousness of the incident, thus reducing the risk that it would have to expand the occupation into a full-fledged intervention. Secretary of State Bryan advised Venustiano Carranza, the Constitutionalist first chief, that the United States carefully distinguished between Huerta and the Mexican people. The occupation was directed strictly against the former for his refusal "to make proper reparation for the arrest of the American sailors." Bryan applauded the Constitutionalist attitude of "standing aloof from the controversy." Throughout the occupation Wilson and his advisors claimed it as a reprisal seeking a specific redress. The Mexican people had no cause to interpret U.S. actions as war. [10]

Escalation would not come from the United States. "I still in my stubborn optimism do not believe that the present trouble is going to assume very great proportions," Wilson advised one correspondent. He left it to Huerta to make the next hostile move, though he "sincerely pray[ed] God it may not have to go to the length of definite war." As Secretary of the Navy Daniels advised one associate, "We entertain hopes that it will not be necessary for us to go further than we have already gone." He added, "I believe everything is going to come out all right."[11]

Wilson could not leave it to chance. He used the occupation to jumpstart his stalled policies, to quit waiting and act. If before he had only friendship to excuse his interference in Mexico's affairs, the presence of U.S. forces in Mexico and the grievance that brought them there provided Wilson with negotiable issues. He no longer had to stand on the sidelines a hamstrung observer, but could now claim a part in resolving the problems besetting Mexico. Where before he had neither cause nor standing to justify his meddling, he now had an interest—7,150 soldiers and marines—to protect and an insult to assuage. He lacked only a forum. [12]

Wilson quickly maneuvered to bring about negotiations. Sometime between 23 and 24 April, Bryan intimated to the French Ambassador to the United States the "desirability of mediation" by Argentina, Brazil, and Chile. The ambassador contacted the Argentine minister, Romulo S. Naón, who claimed "the greatest love" for Bryan. Naón suggested mediation to his government, which approved the idea and invited Brazil and Chile to join. The three governments extended their offer of a conference on 25 April. In a brilliant diplomatic maneuver, Wilson transformed his use of force for retribution into a use of force for introduction. Armed power had provided him his venue. The next difficulty was to control the topics of the conference. [13]

The original invitation was too limited for Wilson's purposes. The so-called ABC powers offered their "good offices for the peaceful and friendly settlement of the conflict between the United States and Mexico," by which they meant the specific controversies—the insult and demand for a salute—leading directly to the occupation. But that simply was not enough. Having forcibly introduced himself into diplomatic discussions pertaining to Mexico's turmoil, Wilson had no intention of restricting himself to insults and their amends.[14]

In accepting the offer of mediation, Bryan hoped that the "several elements of the Mexican people," and not just the Huerta faction, would be allowed to "discuss terms of satisfactory and, therefore, permanent settlement." Privately Wilson explained to the mediators what he meant by "permanent." The elimination of Huerta was essential, followed by the establishment of a provisional government "acceptable to all parties." This temporary administration would be pledged to the "establishment of a permanent government constituted in strict accordance with the Constitution of Mexico and committed to the prosecution of such reforms as will reasonably assure the ultimate removal of the present causes of discontent." According to Wilson, "the essence of any hopeful settlement would of necessity be a concert of the contending elements of the republic and that such a concert can be obtained only upon the basis of such reforms as will satisfy the just claims of the people of Mexico to life, liberty and independent self-support." As State Department counsellor Robert Lansing opined, the United States viewed the mediation as "an attempt to restore peace between Mexican factions and to obtain guarantees from them which will insure the reestablishment of constitutional government in Mexico." The "real quarrel of the United States" was not with the individual factions in Mexico, but with the "intolerable conditions" that the fighting caused. In this sense, the mediation was actually between the various groups of the Mexican people, not between the United States and any single political element. Lansing perceived the role of the United States as that of interested and friendly witness. "The principal that I am going on," Wilson affirmed, "is that we ought studiously to seek to leave the settlement in their hands and that our only part is to see that they get a chance to make it."[15]

But in truth Wilson considered himself something more than friend. Just as important, the mediation was "by no means to be laughed at." He confessed a "passionate desire to see something come out of this struggle which will redound to the permanent benefit or at least partial emancipation of the great body of the Mexican people." Mexico's economic lopsidedness, which concentrated most of the land and wealth in the hands of a few, was the cause of the revolution. "A landless people," Wilson wrote, "will always furnish the inflammable material for a revolution." As he explained at a Fourth of July rally in Philadelphia:

Eighty-five percent of the Mexican people have never been allowed to have any genuine participation in their own government or to exercise any substantial rights with regard to the very land they live upon. All the rights that men most desire have been exercised by the other fifteen per cent.

This problem was further compounded by the disruption of the revolution and the consequent loss of individual rights and property. "But back of it all," Wilson was convinced, "is the struggle of a people to come into its own."[16]

Success for Wilson's policies no longer depended on the further uses of force, but on diplomatic power and, specifically, on the participation of the two most important factions in Mexico, the Huertistas and the Constitutionalists. At Wilson's urging, the mediators also invited the Constitutionalists, but conditioned the invitation on their agreeing to a general armistice. The mediators notified the State Department on 29 April that both Huerta and Carranza had accepted the invitation. "This enables the mediators to deal with the entire Mexican Situation," Bryan exulted. The announcement, however, was premature. Carranza accepted mediation only in principle, and only to discuss the dispute between the United States and Huerta. Because he opposed expanding the scope of the mediation, he saw no value in agreeing to an armistice between his forces and the Huertistas.[17]

The ABC representatives, though, believed just as strongly that mediation was "practically impossible" as long as hostilities continued. Negotiations in that case would only serve to weaken Huerta while strengthening the Constitutionalists. They worried that Carranza would win before the mediation could be concluded. He might try to delay the progress of the discussions until his victorious armies muted the purpose of the conference. An armistice, they decreed, was an essential precondition for admittance to their mediation.[18]

For Wilson, it was just as necessary that the Constitutionalists attend, even if it meant accepting Carranza's terms. "Our object," Wilson proclaimed, "is the pacification of Mexico by reforms and changes instituted by her own leaders and accepted by her own people." Constitutionalist attendance was not simply desirable, it was "all but essential to the success of the Conference." Mexico could not be pacified without their cooperation.[19]

Wilson simply shrugged off Carranza's objections to the expanded scope of the discussions. Carranza, he insisted, must be admitted, "for if he participates he will be under the stronger compulsion before all the world to accept the results." The mediators seemed to be operating under the mistaken assumption that the Constitutionalists were the ones "who must be made to yield" in any Mexican settlement. Obviously, it was Huerta who should give way. If the Constitutionalists were not brought in, Wilson threatened, the

United States would be obliged to appoint itself as their representative, "to constitute ourselves judges of what would be just to them and reasonable to expect them to accept." Since he had no way of knowing the exact demands of the Constitutionalists, Wilson pointed out, he might ask more for them than they would themselves demand.[20]

The mediators remained unswayed. They refused to relent on their demand for an armistice. Carranza proved equally adamant. Wilson then anointed himself the Constitutionalist advocate in the mediation.[21]

Even as this argument played out, the mediation continued. The mediators were Minister D. de Gama of Brazil, Romulo S. Naón of Argentina, and Eds. Suárez Jujica of Chile. Despite the Wilson administration's desire to hold the conference in Washington, where Wilson and Bryan could more readily keep track of the discussions, the mediators chose Niagara Falls, Canada, as the site. Wilson appointed associate Supreme Court justice Joseph Lamar and former solicitor general Frederick Lehman to represent the United States as the "Special Commissioners of the President of the United States Near the Mediators." The cumbersome title was suggested by Lansing to avoid any hint that the United States recognized or accepted the Huerta regime.[22]

Huerta sent Emilio Rabasa, Luis Elquero, Augustin Garza Galendo, and Augustin Rodríquez. According to the State Department's information, Rabasa was an "extreme Scientifico," who opposed the Catholic church's influence, but who was among the principal conspirators against President Madero. Elquero was an aristocrat and a devout Catholic, but never particularly active in politics. Galendo, though also inactive politically, did hold "pronounced liberal views." All the department could learn about Rodríquez was that he, too, was "a most devout Catholic."[23]

Unconcerned now with insults and apologies, Wilson expected much from the mediation. According to one news report, he told his commissioners that "the settlement of the entire Mexican problem in some definite form must come before our forces are recalled from Vera Cruz." As defined by his State Department experts, this meant addressing a full range of issues, such as land ownership, taxation, wages, and peonage, as well as political conditions, official corruption, social conditions, racial prejudices, and individual interests. "Whether the Mexican people are capable of conducting a republican system in accordance with provisions of the Constitution remains to be proved," one department position paper concluded.[24]

And that was precisely what Wilson intended to see. "We shall merely try to secure an orderly reorganization of the Government of Mexico and a choice of president by the Mexicans themselves," Bryan modestly set as his goal for the conference. The mediators, too, saw their chance to reshape

Mexico. Through the use of force, Wilson had created seemingly unlimited opportunities to reform Mexico along democratic, American-style lines. Only the Mexican people—and the triumphs of the Constitutionalists— stood in his way.[25]

The mediation opened on 20 May 1914. Bryan immediately cabled the American commissioners calling for Huerta's retirement and "the establish- ment of a provisional government made up of men favorable to agrarian re- form." While the provisional government arranged elections, it would also decree carving up the large landed estates into more equitable divisions among the populace. All the candidates in the election would have to pledge themselves to support the decree.[26]

The mediators, too, caught the spirit. They proposed that Huerta resign in favor of his minister for foreign affairs, who would become the provisional president responsible for holding the elections and, most important, for im- plementing initial reforms "leading to permanent results." Upon Huerta's re- tirement, hostilities in Mexico would immediately cease and the United States would embargo the importation of arms and weapons of war. Wilson and Bryan were "pleased and encouraged" by the progressive attitude of the mediators, although they had some qualms about their plan. They pointed out that the Constitutionalists, as the "now victorious party," would have to be represented in the provisional government. The issue of agrarian reform needed more discussion, which both sides took up with enthusiasm.[27]

For the next several days, the mediation covered in detail the transition from Huerta to a provisional government and the changes it would imple- ment. In the meantime the Constitutionalists grew stronger, their advance on Mexico City unstoppable. Worried by Carranza's inevitable success, the me- diators and the Mexican representatives began urging the imposition of a neutral provisional government and an arbitrary end to the revolution. They expected the United States to enforce the plan, if necessary with force.[28]

The suggestion appalled Wilson and Bryan. On 24 May Bryan advised the commissioners of the president's views:

> It is clear to us that the representatives from Mexico are keenly aware that Gen- eral Huerta no longer has the force or standing to insist on anything; and they of course cannot expect us to supply him with the force or influence he lacks. We get the impression that the Mexican representatives are chiefly anxious that we should by some means intervene to prevent the complete success of the rev- olution now in progress. We on our part cannot afford in right or conscience to do that.

Instead, the United States "can deal only with the facts in Mexico as they now stand." Wilson refused outright to "use the armed force of the United States" to try to change the situation. The mediation should recognize that

Huerta's elimination and the Constitutionalists' victory were now inevitable. Trying to stop the revolution would be "impractical and futile" and would "very soon force active intervention upon us and delay and confuse all we have hoped for." Wilson urged the mediators to "set the stage for a settlement and demand guarantees that a settlement will be effected."[29]

The revolution outpaced the mediation. The mediators' plan of a neutral provisional government—one without Constitutionalist representation— became increasingly unrealistic. "Events have moved very fast and far since mediation was agreed upon," Wilson wrote on 26 May. The United States was trying hard to understand the changing situation and devise a plan for peace, with no further use of force. Any "programme which involved intervention and coercion would involve the interests and pride of the Mexican people much more deeply than an accommodation with the constitutionalists," Wilson believed. "Even the occupation of Vera Cruz seemed for a little while to bring the danger of war with a whole people."[30]

The discussions now focused on the provisional government. Neither Wilson nor, certainly, the mediators wanted a direct transfer of authority from Huerta to Carranza. Both preferred to slow the revolution with a coalition government pledged to hold elections and effect the necessary reforms. Where they differed, however, was on the composition of the coalition. Wilson wanted a Constitutionalist majority, the mediators insisted on a neutral balance. Throughout the closing days of May and into June, they discussed in detail individuals and percentages, reforms and revisions. While they talked, Carranza's troops plowed forward.[31]

Wilson's aversion to further fighting robbed the United States of its strongest power to determine the results of the revolution. "A provisional arrangement established by force, especially if established by the force of the United States, would inevitably be temporary at best and the prelude to other revolutions," Wilson believed. Because he looked to a Constitutionalist victory, his policies were based on influencing that party to implement reforms. Carranza, however, had no intention of allowing anyone to decide the outcome of the revolution.[32]

In mid-June Carranza sent representatives close enough to the scene of the conference for the American commissioners to meet with them. Carranza's agents objected strongly to everything that the commissioners thought they had done for them. "They say that Mexican conditions raise no international questions and that they are entitled to fight out their own fight in their own way," Lamar and Lehman reported. The Constitutionalists wanted "no outside interference," a disillusioning blow for the Americans. "From the beginning," Lamar and Lehman complained, "we have persistently endeavored to secure from the Mediators a plan that would be accepted by Carranza while the Mediators and the Mexican Representatives have just as persistently opposed it. We are suddenly informed that Carranza would not accept it if we secured it." Repudiated in trying to help, the commissioners brazenly suggested ignoring Carranza and proceeding with the mediation and the selection of a provisional government. [33]

But the mediation was now deadlocked. Neither the mediators nor Huerta's representatives would agree to the American criteria for the provisional government. On 20 June they shelved the discussions. A few days later, they signed a protocol essentially ending the mediation. The Constitutionalists were invited to negotiate privately with the Huertistas. "We have done what they [the Constitutionalists] wanted," Bryan confessed. As Wilson understood, the United States now took the "part of patience, toleration and perserverance." Carranza, under the excuse that he had to consult his subordinates, and daily nearing his triumph, delayed sending a representative. Finally he refused to talk with anyone. His generals, he said, disapproved. [34]

In mid-July Huerta resigned and fled the country, barely outdistancing the rapidly advancing Constitutionalists. Wilson crowed, crediting his policies with ensuring Carranza's victory. Carranza clearly did not accept that theory. To Wilson's increasing disappointment, in the months ahead Carranza showed he had no intention of allowing Wilson to introduce himself further into the outcome of the revolution.

Despite Wilson's ultimate failure to reshape the Mexican Revolution in the American image, what was most intriguing about the occupation of Veracruz was his innovative use of force to introduce himself to mediation. His efforts, first to convene the mediation and then to expand the topics, showed an impressive ability to combine force with the several other forms of power available to him. That the mediation was eventually frustrated was a failure of diplomatic, not armed, power. Nor was it a fluke of fate. Two years later, with the Punitive Expedition deep in Mexico, Wilson again used force to introduce himself, not to mediation but to straight negotiations with Carranza's de facto government. Wilson preferred not to bludgeon his opponents, but to use force like a schoolmaster's cane to gain his student's attention or to discipline them toward the path of happiness and success.

FORCE AND NEGOTIATION

Barred by Carranza from guiding the revolution, Wilson was again reduced to helplessly watching and waiting as the Constitutionalists gained their victory then promptly began warring among themselves. United against Madero's murderer, Carranza and Villa split soon after they defeated Huerta. The first chief established himself in Mexico City; Villa took again to rebellion. Wilson, though more comfortable with Villa's seemingly sympathetic malleability, kept himself out of the fray, only occasionally exercising what little diplomatic power remained to him south of the border.

It proved a frustrating period. Wilson considered Carranza "an honest but a very narrow and rather dull person." Despite Wilson's repeated efforts to help, Carranza consistently turned him down. Compounding this, the first chief had also openly opposed the occupation of Veracruz. Villa, on the other hand, had accepted it, thus convincing Wilson that the former bandit was by far the easiest Mexican leader with whom to deal. [35]

Villa, though, was losing. By the spring of 1915, it was clear to Wilson, if not yet to Villa, that Carranza had established himself as the strongest power south of the border. In a series of maneuvers Wilson tried again to end the fratricide. Threatening an American intervention, he demanded that the leaders of the various factions set aside their differences. When they ignored this use of military power, Wilson turned again to diplomacy by promising Carranza recognition if he would convene a peace conference among his opponents. That, too, the first chief ignored.

Lansing suggested imposing a new government on Mexico composed of individuals, if such could be found, who had remained independent of the several factions. Tempted, Wilson decided to work with other nations to effect Lansing's proposal. He convened a Pan-American meeting to devise a common approach to the Mexican Revolution. By the time it met in August, however, Carranza had clearly shown his dominance. On 13 September Wilson determined to recognize the first chief. A month later the United States announced its de facto recognition of Carranza. [36]

Villa turned his considerable wrath on the United States. Over the next several months, his band brutally murdered several American civilians in Mexico. The vendetta led him to Columbus, New Mexico, and the subsequent chase by the Punitive Expedition. Once again Wilson found himself with U.S. military forces inside Mexico, and again he looked for ways to use those forces to effect his larger purpose of reshaping the Mexican Revolution.

Wilson's first chance came late in April. After a troop of U.S. cavalry was attacked by Mexican civilians and soldiers at Parral on 13 April, Wilson ordered Pershing's forces to concentrate at Colonia Dublan. Tensions, though, remained high. Army chief of staff General Scott traveled to the border in late April to study the situation first hand. Responding to Lansing's hints, Carranza proposed that Scott and Funston meet with General Álvaro Obregón. Wilson greeted the suggestion with immense relief. To his mind, talking was always better than fighting. Scott, though doubtful that anything productive could come from a meeting, settled in El Paso to await Obregón. [37]

The Wilson administration expected to use the impending conference to explain its purposes to the Carranza government and thereby alleviate the tensions between them. Scott's orders were to explain that the United States had no thought of intervening in Mexico. Quite the contrary, the purpose of the expedition was to assist Carranza in neutralizing or removing bandits along the border. The United States, after all, had been attacked; it had legitimate cause to take retribution. The Punitive Expedition would not be withdrawn until the Wilson administration was sure that the bandits were punished and that such attacks would not be repeated. Beyond that, Wilson stood ready to counsel and guide the revolution.[38]

The Scott-Obregón conference began on 29 April. Obregón had but one objective, which he repeated with monotonous obstinacy: the Punitive Expedition must be withdrawn from Mexican territory. Scott and Funston, with equal monotony, reviewed the injuries to Americans and American interests and the failure of the Mexican government to police its side. Their argument was buttressed by two more raids on the United States at Glenn Springs and Boquillas. After wrestling with Obregón all day on 2 May, Scott emerged with an agreement, although he admitted it was "not altogether satisfactory." In exchange for Scott's assurance of the "gradual withdrawal" of Pershing's forces, Obregón promised that Mexico would vigorously pursue any raiders who attacked American territory. The extrication of the Punitive Expedition was tied directly to Carranza's performance in protecting the border.[39]

Wilson approved the agreement immediately; Carranza took his time to refuse. The wait left Scott and Funston "sick with apprehension." Finally on 8 May, Scott, Funston, and Obregón met again for the latter's announcement that the first chief would not accept the proposal. Carranza demanded that the Americans set a firm date for the withdrawal of the expedition. He would not allow Mexico's ability to protect the border to become the hinge for Pershing's withdrawal.[40]

Both Scott and Funston cried foul, accusing Carranza's counterproposal of being "redolent with bad faith." Fearing a surprise attack, the two generals pled for 150,000 reinforcements. Wilson mobilized the national guard units along the border into federal service, but reminded his soldiers that they were not to attack first. Scott and Funston met again with Obregón from 9 to 11 May, which allowed the sense of crisis to pass, but achieved no better results. For the moment, as Scott understood, that was enough.[41]

Though the crisis stilled, Wilson's policies were equally becalmed. Scott returned to Washington, Obregón to Mexico City. Pershing remained encamped at Colonia Dublan, occasionally sending patrols out to scout, but no longer pursuing Villa with any vigor. Wilson, preoccupied with the sinking of the *Sussex* by a German U-boat, which threatened his efforts to introduce himself to any peace negotiations to end the Great War, allowed his policies toward Mexico to drift through May.

Wilson's second chance came at the end of June, some three months after Pershing crossed into Mexico. On 21 June one of Pershing's scouting patrols, composed of two troops of the Tenth Cavalry, clashed with Mexican soldiers outside the dusty village of Carrizal. Nine Americans were killed, twelve were wounded, and twenty-four were taken prisoner. Mexican casualties were probably the same or higher. From Mexico City, James L. Rodgers, the State Department's "special agent," cabled that news of Carrizal was "generally interpreted as [the] announcement beginning hostilities." Lansing immediately assumed that the fight relieved him of troubling further with Mexico. He would make his scheduled vacation in early July, he wrote the day after the fight, because the problems with Mexico now "will be military rather than diplomatic."[42]

Officials in the Wilson administration immediately assumed that the U.S. forces had been attacked by the Mexican soldiers without provocation. The assumption led to a chorus of demands from inside Mexico and without demanding war. Lansing peremptorily insisted to Carranza on the release of the prisoners and immediate restitution for the dead and wounded. He dismissed any suggestion of mediation because the "American demand, of which the justness is beyond controversy, is not a proper subject for mediation."[43]

Even Wilson slumped, though he kept his resolve not to intervene—as he defined intervention. "We are apparently getting into deep waters to the south of us," he wrote Louis Wiley of the *New York Times* on 22 June, "but we must be the more careful in entering them to do nothing which will put any doubt upon our purpose and our ability to keep faith with Latin-America in all matters that touch independence and territorial integrity." He and Lansing discussed the difference between intervention and war. The former they abjured, the latter they believed was now imposed upon them. Baker urged Wilson to send a message to his soldiers calling them to "honorable and fair fighting." He wanted the Mexicans to think of them as "foes who came to help rather than to hurt."[44]

As the accounts of the surviving troops reached Washington, however, it began to look as though the Americans had in fact provoked the attack. Most agreed that Captain Charles T. Boyd, who commanded the American troops, had instigated the fight—and had died leading the charge. The fine sense of outrage gave way to a sheepish embarrassment. Lansing began to think less of war and once again of diplomacy. On 3 July—four days before his scheduled vacation—he proposed to Wilson that they try again with diplomatic power. Lansing wanted to suggest to Carranza the establishment of a joint commission of four to six members to discuss the range of problems between them.

"If the Carrizal incident was a clear case of Mexican aggression," he advised the president, "I doubt if I would be favorable to this policy, but it appears to me that Captain Boyd was possibly to blame."[45]

Typically, Lansing's idea went beyond the simple issue of the Punitive Expedition. As he described it to the president, the joint commission should take up such issues as Carrizal, the general lawlessness in Mexico, the treatment of their respective citizens, cooperation between the two governments, the right of hot pursuit, the use of railroads (which the Mexican government had denied Pershing's forces), cooperation on border protection, and the withdrawal of the Punitive Expedition. Lansing also believed it important that the suggestion for a conference come from Carranza. While they waited, Lansing wrote, "I would not abate for an hour the military preparation which we are making."[46]

Wilson agreed immediately. Lansing suggested privately to Arredondo, the Mexican representative in the United States, that Wilson would be receptive to the establishment of a joint commission. Carranza, who wanted war no more than Wilson did, responded positively. Quiet negotiations began over the scope and purpose of the commission. These negotiations showed quite clearly that Wilson intended to use the Punitive Expedition, as he had before with Veracruz, to introduce himself to negotiations over the full range of problems wracking Mexico.[47]

From Mexico City, Rodgers reported that Carranza was now ready to discuss Mexico's problems in depth. On 7 July he advised the department that the de facto government, convinced it would lose any war with the United States, saw in the joint commission a chance to "open [the] whole question [of] Mexican future and enable acceptance [of] aid financial and otherwise from United States without loss [of] face." Carranza and his advisers now realized, Rodgers assured Lansing, "that [the] United States is [the] only nation which can save them." Reassured by the Mexican response, Wilson and Lansing dared to hope for "a very sensible and peaceful settlement of our difficulties with Mexico." Thus buoyed, Lansing took his vacation, leaving Frank Polk to work out the details with Arredondo.[48]

Carranza played a fascinating game. He coyly tantalized Wilson with private hints of the great things the commission could discuss. Officially, however, he repeatedly and stubbornly insisted that only Pershing's withdrawal and the protection of the border were suitable topics. His people, he implied, would allow no other course. Although Rodgers continued to report that Carranza would "open [the] whole Mexican question" to negotiation, the actual Mexican proposal, handed to Polk on 12 July, proved disappointing. Carranza suggested appointing three commissioners on each side to discuss the withdrawal of the Punitive Expedition and to draft a protocol for reciprocal border crossings. The commission would also be charged with "tracing to their source the invasions that have taken place . . . so as to be able to find the responsibilities."[49]

Polk thought the agenda "rather too limited." As he described it to Wilson, "There does not seem to be any provision in this communication for an investigation along the broad lines you and the Secretary have in mind." Rather than make a counterproposal, Polk wanted to suggest informally that Carranza "broaden the powers of the Commission."[50]

On 13 July Rodgers reported that Carranza's "expectation is to discuss whole Mexican question." Yet Arredondo's official response, handed to Polk six days later, restricted the commission to the Punitive Expedition and the border, with a promise to take up other matters once these issues were happily resolved. When Polk continued to insist that the topics be broadened, Carranza signalled through Rodgers that he privately agreed, but could not publicly avow it. As Rodgers explained on 21 July:

> General Carranza as well as others advising him on subject are thoroughly in accord with the President in desire to have scope [of] proposed conference broadened but General Carranza resists idea of having it appear in beginning that conference is for any other purposes than settling questions of retirement of troops from Mexico and effecting border protocol agreement.

To underline his point Carranza released to the public his agenda for the commission.[51]

Although the publication of the Mexican agenda embarrassed the Wilson administration, the first chief's seeming dilemma made sense to Lansing. He advised Polk that they accept Carranza's agenda publicly, while privately agreeing to broaden the topics once the commission met. In a note dated 28 July, Polk tried Lansing's tactic. He instructed Rodgers to inform the Carranza government that Wilson accepted Carranza's suggestion to appoint three commissioners to discuss the pressing issues before them, namely, the Punitive Expedition and the border. Polk also wanted it explained, lest Carranza misunderstand the American position, that the United States

> had hoped that, as a result of the deliberations and findings of this Commission, a settlement of all the perplexing questions outstanding between the two Governments might have been arrived at. He feels that the questions arising out of the border difficulties can be settled by direct negotiations; that a commission for the settlement of these questions alone would be unnecessary.
>
> There are, as the Carranza Government must be well aware of, other and very important questions which have been raised by or have grown out of, the

disturbed conditions which have so long prevailed in Mexico. It is not intention or desire of this Government to interfere with the internal administration
of Mexico, but American lives have been lost and American property injured
and destroyed, and this Government feels that it is its duty to spare no effort to
prevent a repetition of those occurrences.

At this point, negotiations stalled briefly with neither side able to concede.[52]

For two anxious days Polk heard nothing. Then on 25 July Rodgers reported that Carranza was willing to broaden the topics, but that he could not
make the promise in writing or through Arredondo. Polk drafted the official
U.S. reply to Carranza's note of 12 July, pointing out that the United States
firmly believed "that the powers of the proposed Commission should be en-
larged." The United States was willing to discuss withdrawing the Punitive
Expedition and protecting the border. But, Polk added in a new, vaguely
worded formula he hoped Carranza would be able to accept, Wilson also
wanted to "consider such other pending questions, the amicable and friendly
solution of which would tend to improve the relations of the two countries."
These latter discussions, Polk promised, would not be binding on either
government.[53]

Once again Carranza hinted privately at better things while officially denying them. Polk, his patience with the negotiations exhausted, despaired.
On 3 August he wrote Lansing:

> Personally, I have a feeling that nothing is going to come of this conference.
> Carranza is acting with even more stupidity than usual, if that is possible, and
> I think when the Commission meets his Commissioners will decline to discuss
> anything until the evacuation of Mexican territory by American troops is dis-
> posed of.
>   Arredondo seems very suspicious of any suggestion to widen the scope of the
> Commission and has told people in confidence that he sees nothing for them
> to consider beyond the border difficulties. This also seems to be opinion of
> many in Mexico City.

In a plaintive conclusion, Polk wrote: "They certainly are a discouraging people to try to help."[54]

Wilson could not afford Polk's despair. His policies were now entirely dependent on getting Carranza's representatives to the negotiating table. Consequently, he grasped at the first chief's private hints and ignored his official
disclaimers. On 4 August Carranza applauded the American acceptance of
his invitation to establish a joint commission. He specifically pointed out
that the topics of discussion were the withdrawal of the Punitive Expedition
and the formulation of a protocol for reciprocal border crossings. Privately

Arredondo assured Polk that Carranza meant that these topics would be discussed first. Once they were settled, other issues could be raised. "Thank you," Wilson wrote Polk, adding, "I think the matter is now in as satisfactory a position as we can get it into."[55]

Thus, exactly as he had two years earlier, Wilson gambled that once he got Carranza negotiating, he would be able to expand the discussions to cover the whole range of Mexico's problems. At Wilson's behest, Lansing invited Richard Olney to serve as a commissioner. "The scope of the work of the Commission," he wrote Olney, "has been left more or less indefinite in order that there may be a very free and informal discussion of the various questions which have arisen between the two countries in addition to the troubles along the border." Lansing explained that the chief difficulty facing Mexico was financial. "If the de facto Government could be financed," he believed, "there would be little reason why it would not succeed in the pacification of the country." Wilson fully agreed that economic problems "undoubtedly lie at the bottom of the whole Mexican domestic settlement." Both men fully expected the negotiations to cover in-depth ways to help the Mexican government straighten out its finances.[56]

After some difficulty in finding "high calibre" men to serve on the commission, Wilson chose Secretary of the Interior Franklin K. Lane, Judge John R. Mott, and George Gray. They were supported by a range of assistants and experts, including General Tasker Bliss as the military specialist on border problems. The Mexican delegates were Foreign Secretary Luis Cabrera and two engineers, Ignacio Bonilles and Alberto J. Pani. After an introductory luncheon in New York City on 4 September, complete with optimistic speeches by Lansing, Lane, Arredondo, and Cabrera, the Joint Mexican-American Commission settled down to business in New London, Connecticut, on 5 September.[57]

Unfortunately, of course, each side arrived with an entirely different agenda. Both Arredondo and Cabrera opened the conference with very general platitudes about the importance of the negotiations and the need to restore Mexican-American friendship. Neither remarked on widening the topics of discussion; neither referred to any specific issues. Lansing, though, interpreted the comments as indicating "very clearly the desire of the Mexican Government to adjust not only the boundary difficulty but all other controversies which have arisen between the United States and Mexico." Lansing was particularly anxious that the commission take up the financial problems besetting Carranza's government. These, in Lansing's view, were the root problem for all of Mexico's other difficulties. "I have real hope that the American-Mexican Commission will satisfactorily adjust our differences," he wrote his father-in-law.[58]

Although Secretary Lane had earlier complained that Carranza "won't let us help him," he clearly saw the joint commission as the chance to do precisely that. In his opening remarks, he admitted that they were there primarily to discuss border problems, but he did not let that hold him back for long. "We have started it without much noise, but very agreeably," he wrote Wilson on 6 September. After studying the correspondence leading to the commission, Gray reluctantly concluded that they were bound to discuss the withdrawal of the Punitive Expedition and the border problems before moving to other issues. Indeed, for the first two meetings, Lane patiently allowed Cabrera to demand the withdrawal of Pershing's forces.[59]

As soon as they could, the American commissioners introduced new topics for discussion. Rather than pull the Punitive Expedition out, Lane suggested ways it could cooperate in catching Villa. From there he went boldly on to other issues. As he assured Lansing within four days of the start of the conference, "The principle of our negotiations has been and is—what is the wise thing to do now so as to help Mexico most without any sacrifice of American dignity, and so as to secure as speedily as possible such a re-establishment of conditions in Mexico as would permit the re-entry of Americans to their properties in that country." By 11 September, a week after the conference began, the Americans had the Mexican commissioners defending Carranza's recently promulgated "confiscatory taxes" on mines owned by Americans. The intent, Lane advised Lansing, "was to further our plan to secure from Mexican Commissioners a complete picture of internal conditions in Mexico"—a topic well beyond Carranza's agenda.[60]

For a time the strategy seemed to work. "As far as I can judge," Lansing wrote Lane on 15 September, "your efforts to broaden the scope of the subjects to be considered by the Commission are meeting with marked success." The progress was so satisfactory that Lansing succumbed to an uncommon optimism. He believed, he commended Lane, "that a practical and satisfactory solution will be found to the whole vexed question of Mexico." Other officials within the State Department looked forward to even wider ranging discussions over Mexico's problems, including Carranza's recently published mining and oil decrees, taxes, confiscations, and forfeitures. Meanwhile, General Tasker Bliss, the assistant chief of staff and former army commander along the border, studiously prepared a plan of border control for the approval of the commission.[61]

Their initial successes completely deluded the American commissioners. When the Mexican representatives reminded them that their instructions required that they first address the withdrawal of the Punitive Expedition and a plan for border protection before they move to other topics, the American commissioners first tried to reject the contention, then responded angrily. Lane urged the Mexicans to consider those problems "which lie back of the border raids and upon the solution of which the reestablishment of internal order depends." Both Lane and Gray agreed that if they resolved the Punitive Expedition and the border issue first, then the "Mexicans are likely to get the belly ache or some other complaint and break up our conference."[62]

And that was the heart of the stalemate. By using the Punitive Expedition to introduce the United States to negotiations with Carranza, Wilson could not risk withdrawing it for fear that Carranza would quit talking. Wilson would then lose his chance to lead Mexico in the democratic direction. Consequently, Lane, Gray, and Mott determined that they would have "to be very helpful, aggressively helpful."[63]

Their aggression made Mexico's rejection of American help all the more frustrating. On 22 September the American commissioners submitted an agenda for the negotiations. They proposed discussing the protection of life and property of foreigners in Mexico, the establishment of a claims commission, and the promotion of religious tolerance. The Mexican commissioners responded with an agenda of their own—the withdrawal of the Punitive Expedition and the establishment of a joint military commission to determine the optimum distribution of troops to protect the border. It was not the answer the Americans sought.[64]

Astoundingly, Lane and his fellow commissioners concluded that Carranza had firmly bound their Mexican counterparts with "strict secret instructions" to obtain the withdrawal of the Punitive Expedition and an arrangement for border protection before moving to any other subject. Bliss believed that Carranza was following the same strategy that he had taken during the Scott-Obregón conference in late April. The Mexican commissioners "are being perfectly polite about every subject advanced for discussion or consideration but declining really to consider anything except the immediate withdrawal of General Pershing's troops."[65]

"I despair often," Lane wrote his brother. "The hardest part of all," he advised one correspondent, "is to convince a proud and obstinate people that they really need my help." Yet Lane privately believed that the Mexican position went beyond obstinacy. They were, he complained to Lansing, ingrates incapable of saying thank you: "Nothing that is fine springs spontaneously from their nature." The Mexicans, he wrote, "eternally cry 'give, give,' but there is no evidence whatever of a thought that they have either a duty to the world, responsibilities to us, or that we have done anything for them that was kindly or generous or big." Nonetheless, Lane remained committed to helping Mexico secure a stable government; to reestablishing its industry and agriculture; and to implementing a program of primary, industrial, and agricultural education. He understood, too, that they were enduring "not merely a political revolution, nor an economic revolution. It is a social revolution also."[66]

"Our purpose now," Lane reassured his brother cabinet officer, "is to take up these internal questions which make Mexico so bad a neighbor, one by one and demand that manifest injustices shall be undone." For that reason, the troops in Mexico and the militia on the border played an important role in his negotiating strategy. His task now was

> a slow insistent process of education, the education of three men here and a fourth in Mexico City, partly by reason and partly through fear. The troops in Mexico are not "doing nothing." The militia on the border have in a very real sense already intervened, and there is a power not yet invoked that it may be necessary to invoke, to make the well-intentioned Mexican do the thing that will bring through his cause.

Although Carranza kept insisting that the Joint Commission effect the withdrawal of the Punitive Expedition, Lane's determination to achieve a "satisfactory solution of the entire group of international questions" depended on the expedition's remaining south of the border as a forceful inducement on the Mexicans.[67]

The talks continued throughout the fall of 1916 and into 1917. The Mexican commissioners occasionally allowed their American counterparts to bring up the issues of most importance to Wilson. Still they were but brief detours of little consequence. Lane grew increasingly frustrated and bitter. The Americans had approached the negotiations "in the spirit of helpful cooperation," whereas the Mexican attitude had been "negative and permeated with distrust." When the commissioners actually discussed the withdrawal of the Punitive Expedition, the Mexican commissioners would not allow any conditions to be placed on their government. Pershing would have to come out, period.[68]

"I don't see what good result from the military point of view it is possible for the commission to obtain," General Bliss wrote on 23 October. "They have now talked for a long time and thus far have decided nothing." But the talking continued. The Mexicans, according to the Americans, were "negative and destructive." "But oh!" Lane exclaimed, "the misery of dealing with people who are eternally suspicious and have no sense of good faith!" Even after the commissioners finally drew up a plan of withdrawal and border protection, which essentially incorporated Bliss's premise that each side do its best to prevent "its own bad men from inflicting injury on the other side,"

Carranza rejected the settlement. "You certainly have had the greatest discouragements and rebuffs to overcome," Wilson condoled Lane, "and I value the service which you and your colleagues have performed all the more."[69]

The commission adjured sine die on 15 January 1917. No agreement had been reached; Pershing remained in Mexico. Yet the negotiations were not without some good effect. Once again Wilson showed that he preferred talking to fighting, even if he had to fight to talk. The conference also allowed the United States to express its views on many of Mexico's most pressing problems. If the Mexicans seemed to ignore the suggestions, they had nonetheless heard them. And most important, the talks had defused the Carrizal crisis by allowing Carranza to show his supporters that he was pushing to get the Americans out of Mexico while giving Wilson the chance to broach the issues he believed most important to Mexico's future.[70]

Once again Wilson had used force to introduce himself to negotiations. That the talks reached no firm resolution was, as with Veracruz, a failure of diplomatic, not armed, power. In both instances Wilson had gone beyond the Clausewitzian dictum that war was policy by other means. Rather than accept Clausewitz's definition that war was a substantially different means from other expressions of policy, Wilson showed that force was in fact but an integral means—among many—of implementing policy. Defeating the enemy was irrelevant, perhaps even counterproductive, to the real goal of converting a land and its peoples to the American style of democracy and liberty. With that the objective, force fit comfortably within the larger continuum that combined all aspects of power. It was an impressive innovation.

WAR FOR PEACE

When the guns of August kindled Europe, Wilson stood to the side. He intended with this stance to be more than an uninvolved observer watching Europe consumed. From the first days of the war, he posed himself "ready with calmness of thought and steadiness of purpose to help the rest of the world." Remaining apart, unscorched by "the fires of hate and desolation," enabled the United States to "keep law alive while the rest of the world burns." The posture differed from the traditional American policy of noninvolvement. "We are not trying to keep out of trouble," he explained, "we are trying to preserve the foundations upon which peace can be rebuilt." Through neutrality, Wilson took custody of the very soul of civilization.[71]

From August 1914 to April 1917, Wilson's restrained neutrality assumed American leadership in the reconstruction of the world. Because he looked beyond the war, Wilson's purpose was "to serve mankind by reserving our strength and our resources for the anxious and difficult days of restoration and

healing which must follow, when peace will have to build its house anew."
Until then Wilson sought "the right opportunity to influence, if I may, the
course of events toward peace." Only after the belligerent powers made it
clear that such an assumption was baseless did Wilson turn again to the use
of force for introduction.[72]

Peace, not war, inspired Wilson. "It would be a calamity to the world at
large if we should be drawn actively into the conflict and so deprived of all
disinterested influence over the settlement," he believed. As he worked to
bring the combatants to the peace table, Wilson devoted himself to designing
a new postwar world based on international cooperation and law. He intended to offer the world a new order once the opposing sides were ready to
talk. Only after it became clear to him that the price of implementing his
vision was fighting did Wilson reconcile himself to war for peace. "Neutrality," he finally realized on 2 April 1917, "is no longer feasible or desirable
where the peace of the world is involved and the freedom of its peoples."[73]

Wilson's slow, painful evolution from frustrated mediator to warrior for
peace has been well told; it need only be highlighted here. Even as Wilson
sought to defend the ancient principles of international law from the new
technologies of war, he searched for a way to insinuate himself into crafting
the peace. It took both policies to fail before Wilson could bring himself to
enter the United States into the war. Once a belligerent Wilson fought only
so long as it took to bring Germany to the peace table. He sought neither
unconditional surrender nor the complete defeat of the enemy. Even though
embroiled in a total war, he used just enough force to compel the other side
to talk peace.

Originally Wilson contented himself exercising diplomatic and moral
power. He made no concerted effort to exert America's growing economic
power, particularly over the Entente nations. Instead, through the private
channels established by his confidant, Colonel Edward M. House, Wilson
monitored an almost continuous correspondence with British and German
officials. House focused his efforts on how and when to bring the belligerents
to the peace conference. Through Lansing and the State Department,
Wilson defended neutral rights under international law, thus preserving
America's preeminence as the impartial neutral. Publicly, Wilson reminded
the country of the need to stay above the fray—and he described for the combatants a postwar world of peace.

Immediately after the outbreak of the war, Wilson offered to mediate.
Over the next two and a half years, working principally through House,
Wilson signaled repeated reminders to the combatants that the United States
was "the mediating nation of the world." This role required complete impartiality in thought and action. Only by proving the purity of its neutrality

could the United States gain the confidence of each side and thus arrange the ultimate peace. That was why it was so necessary for the United States to prove itself too proud to fight.[74]

House traveled to Europe in January 1915 to confer with both sides. Wilson instructed him specifically that "our single object is to be serviceable, if we may, in bringing about the preliminary willingness to parley which must be the first step towards discussing and determining the conditions of peace." He urged House to offer the combatants a "channel of confidential communication." House played a sly game of enticement. As he explored several avenues to peace, he emphasized to each side what they most wanted to hear. With British officials, he spoke of democracy and free trade; with the Germans, he talked of freedom of the seas. The sinking of the *Lusitania*, unfortunately, brought an early halt to the discussions. Shortly thereafter, House returned home.[75]

From New York, the honorary colonel continued a lively correspondence with officials on both sides. During the summer of 1915—or perhaps as a result of what he learned from his visits to Europe—House came to understand the war as a grand challenge pitting democracy against military autocracy. By mid-June House was advising Wilson that entering the war might not be such a calamity. "The war would be more speedily ended and we would be in a strong position to aid the other great democracies in turning the world into the right paths," he advised Wilson. "It is something that we may have to face with fortitude being consoled by the thought that no matter what sacrifices we make, the end will justify them."[76]

During the summer of 1915, Wilson was not quite ready to embrace a forceful solution. Although still shying from belligerency, he tried to stand tough against German violations of international law. While responding to the sinking of the *Lusitania* and, three months later, the torpedoing of the *Arabic*, Wilson also began to plot the shape of the world after the war. Slowly Wilson embraced the concept of a league of nations. Capitalist internationalism, democracy, freedom of the seas, the Open Door, and arms control would be the hallmarks of the new system. And the United States would finally shed its ages-old isolationism and assume its rightful place as world leader. It was an ambitious program for a neutral nation to propose.

During the winter of 1915–16, House again visited Europe. Although denying any interest in "local settlements,—territorial questions, indemnities and the like," Wilson urged his friend to make clear to the combatants that the United States was vitally interested in "the future peace of the world." To achieve a lasting postwar era, Wilson now thought it essential to obtain "(a) military and naval disarmament and (b) a league of nations to secure each nation against aggression and maintain the absolute freedom of the seas."

And, Wilson instructed House, it was time for mediation talks to begin. If but one side indicated its willingness to talk, Wilson promised "to use our utmost moral force to oblige the other to parley."[77]

House, whose personal sympathies lay with the Entente powers, twisted these instructions to aid the British. In a private memorandum of agreement with Edward Grey, the British foreign minister, House promised on 22 February 1916 that the United States would enter the war against Germany if the Kaiser refused an American offer to mediate. The timing of the offer would depend on a signal from the Entente powers that they were ready. House advised Wilson: "The Allies will agree to the conference and if Germany does not, I have promised for you that we would throw our weight in order to bring her to terms." Wilson accepted the House-Grey memorandum, but only after toning down the promise by specifying simply that the United States would "probably" enter the war.[78]

Thus by early 1916, House had privately allied himself with the Entente powers. Lansing, too, clearly sympathized with the British, French, and Russians. Wilson leaned that way, but he was not yet prepared to express his sympathies either openly or with action. He continued to protest belligerent—German and British—encroachments on neutral rights in an increasingly vain effort to maintain U.S. impartiality.

The sinking of the *Sussex* in April brought the issue of neutral rights to a head. Its ambiguous resolution gave Wilson just enough space to maneuver away from war. During the summer and fall, other issues—the Punitive Expedition, his reelection, and the occupation of the Dominican Republic—kept Wilson from devoting his full attention to the problems of the war.

But by November 1916, safely, if barely, reelected, with the Joint Mexican-American Commission earnestly debating the scope of its agenda and with Captain Knapp enthroned as military governor of the Dominican Republic, Wilson was again ready—eager—to address the end of the war. Over the strenuous opposition of his closest advisers, Wilson prepared a note to the belligerents calling on each to define its war aims. Germany bluntly refused to share its goals with a neutral. The Entente nations, after considerable delay, finally answered, but their rather lengthy list of objectives required major concessions from Germany. Wilson understood from the responses that both sides were still far from ready to accept his mediation.[79]

Increasingly desperate to arrange an end to the war, Wilson called for a "peace without victory" on 22 January 1917. He promised American cooperation in any fair settlement, which he believed should include some type of a congress of nations. The United States stood ready to assume its rightful place of active leadership in world affairs. It now depended on the willingness of the belligerents to accept its mediation. But neither side was interested. By

30 January Wilson realized that his policy of keeping the United States an impartial neutral ever ready to negotiate an end to the war had failed. The world would not accept him as its referee.

On 31 January Germany announced the resumption of unrestricted submarine warfare. Appalled by the complete collapse of both his neutrality policies, Wilson isolated himself within the White House during February and March. By April he had accepted the need for war as retribution against Germany, but also—and just as importantly—as the only way left to introduce himself to shaping the peace. In his request to Congress for a declaration of war, Wilson first explained the outlawry of Germany, then described his vision of the future. "But the right is more precious than peace," Wilson proclaimed, "and we shall fight for the things which we have always carried nearest our hearts,—for democracy, for the right of those who submit to authority to have a voice in their own Governments, for the rights and liberties of small nations, for a universal dominion of right by such a concert of free peoples as shall bring peace and safety to all nations and make the world itself at last free." During the war Wilson continued to enunciate, if not so clearly to define, the purposes for which the United States warred. The 1917 Bolshevik Revolution compelled him to expound the liberal-democratic, capitalist alternative to communism. Wilson proposed making the world safe for democracy through the power of cooperation. He summarized his war aims in fourteen points on 8 January 1918, then added another fourteen or so points over the course of the year. By the fall of 1918, the world well knew, even if it did not entirely understand or accept, Wilson's goals.[80]

Germany's utter defeat was not among them. Wilson sought simply its acceptance of peace negotiations. As soon as the German government signaled its readiness to talk, Wilson moved quickly to arrange an armistice. It came just as the United States was finally geared to total war. Thus Wilson ended the fighting in November 1918 at just the time the United States was in a position to steamroll over the German armies and compel Germany's unconditional surrender.

But that was not the Wilsonian way of war. Once assured that Germany acknowledged the "military supremacy of the Allies" and accepted a peace based on the Fourteen Points and related principles, Wilson was satisfied. When his associates balked at the leniency of his peace terms, Wilson threatened to sign a separate peace. The threat forced the Entente powers to accept most of the terms, save the British who refused to concede freedom of the seas and the French who insisted that Germany pay for its damages to civilians.[81]

The Armistice allowed the Allied and associated forces to occupy the German Rhineland. The American component of these forces remained until 1923, far beyond the time Wilson had intended them to stay. By then many of his dreams had crumbled. Collective action forced him to change many of his plans; senatorial obstinacy compelled him to drop most of the remaining ones.

In the end, force introduced him to the war's resolution, but Wilson had no stomach for using it to compel the outcome. As soon as Germany indicated that it was prepared to talk, he promptly quit fighting. Wilson consistently showed his belief that force was a useful tool to initiate diplomatic negotiations. He almost as consistently refused to carry through with force to resolve the issues before him.

Similarly, after considerable hesitation, Wilson embarked on a joint British-Japanese-American intervention in Siberia and a twin intervention in northern Russia. His primary motive for both interventions was to prove the efficacy of collective international action. Pressed relentlessly by his associates in the war, Wilson finally agreed to send U.S. troops to Russia because he no longer felt comfortable in turning his colleagues down. For his excuse he relied on the presence of a substantial number of Czechoslovakian former prisoners of war who needed saving from Bolshevik hostility. He had no higher ambition than that.

But once there, Wilson could not resist tampering. He sent William C. Bullitt to Russia to try to arrange a conference on Prinkipo Island with the Bolsheviks and other factions. The Bullitt mission ultimately failed. Nonetheless, months after the war ended, when the Czechs could have obtained clear passage home and the Allied and associated forces could have been withdrawn to leave Russia to its own fate, Wilson agreed to a plan for the protection of the Trans-Siberian Railroad. The plan involved establishing a six-mile zone along the rail route. Within that zone, Japanese and U.S. forces would maintain the peace and keep the rails running.

In July 1919 Wilson explained the continued presence of American troops in Siberia to the Senate:

> The purpose of the continuance of American troops in Siberia, is that we, with the concurrence of the great Allied powers, may keep open a necessary artery of trade and extend to the vast population of Siberia the economic aid essential to it in peacetime but indispensable under the conditions which have followed the prolonged and exhausting participation by Russia in the war against the Central Powers.

But with troops on the ground, Wilson could not withstand the seductive opportunity to guide the course of the Russian Revolution, just as he had offered his guidance to the Mexicans. As in Mexico he searched for some leader who best represented the liberal, democratic impulses he held so dear. At first Admiral Alexander Kolchak, leader of the White Army, promised the best hope. During the summer of 1919, Wilson dispatched U.S. ambassador to Japan Roland Morris to Siberia to feel out Kolchak's democratic tendencies. Morris was to promise Kolchak American aid if he would agree to a platform incorporating various democratic reforms.[82]

While he awaited Morris's report, Wilson tried to tie aid to Kolchak to extracting a promise of liberal, democratic reforms. Although convinced that bolshevism would fail of its own weight, Wilson primarily feared the resurgence of "Imperial Russia." Desperate for help, Kolchak issued a proclamation promising an array of reforms, including elections to a constituent assembly and land for Russia's starving peasants. Wilson described it as "a very good proclamation," but by then it was too late; Kolchak had no chance of defeating the Bolsheviks. In August Morris confirmed that Kolchak teetered on defeat. Although U.S. troops remained in Siberia another year, Wilson was left with no one to introduce him to Russia's salvation.[83]

What is most revealing about Wilson's clumsy handling of the Russian problem is not that he failed so miserably to direct the Russian Revolution, but that he tried at all. In times of turmoil, Wilson could not help but extend the guiding hand of American principles and programs. Force offered him the easiest way to introduce himself to the problem, but once the troops were on the ground, Wilson quickly lost interest in using them to consummate his policies.

In the Wilsonian way of war, talking was far preferable to fighting, even if all too frequently it was necessary to fight to talk.

6 FORCE

for Association

> . . . a government's resort to armed power to
> ally itself with specific governments or groups
> or in response to demands from its allies. It
> usually results from the belief that a military
> response will cement or maintain collective
> international action. The associates may be
> motivated by different uses of force. In short,
> it is an international act of cooperation.

In the Wilsonian way of war, friends
were indispensable. Wilson did not shirk from fighting alone, nor was he reluctant to act independently. Once engaged, regardless of his associates, he
never shied from assuming his natural place of leadership. Like a knight er-
rant, he simply needed to fight for someone. Wilson preferred to raise his
banner in the service of some grand endeavor, saving those who could not
save themselves or leading to democracy those who had somehow lost their
way. He was ever seeking the right crusade.

Having lately achieved its majority as a great power, Wilson intended the
United States to act with commensurate greatness. He was determined to ab-
solve his interventions of any hint of self-aggrandizement. Under his command, the uses of force became altruistic gestures. Repeatedly Wilson
denied, by word and deed, any territorial or selfish ambitions. His interventions were never simply to promote the self-interests of the United States
or its citizens. He sought neither trade advantage nor economic benefit, neither territorial expansion nor material gain. The Wilsonian way of war
seemed always fought for something or someone else—democracy or freedom or friendship.

Goodness was its own reward. As early as December 1902, Wilson prayed
for his country "that vision may come with power." As the United States
emerged on the world scene, he urged his countrymen to "ponder our duties
like men of conscience and temper our ambitions like men who seek to serve,
not to subdue the world; let us lift our thoughts to the level of the great tasks
that await us, and bring a great age in with the coming of our day of strength."
Although he understood the benefits of trade and financial growth, economic
advantages were not his principal motivations. Building empires—of trade or

territory—was never his ambition. Free trade and liberal capitalism fit snugly into an overall conception of democracy as "not so much a form of government as a set of principles."[1]

With these principles Wilson sought to proselytize the world. He never hesitated to resort to force as part of the process of conversion. "Liberty is a spiritual conception," he believed, "and when men take up arms to set other men free, there is something sacred and holy in the warfare." In Wilson's mind the divine purpose of America was to serve the world; its most effective power was its essential morality. It could not, then, remain neutral while others struggled or fought for freedom.[2]

Like the missionaries of old, Wilson plundered for more than simple earthly treasures. Once embarked on his peculiarly American crusades, Wilson sought not only souls to save, but disciples to maintain the salvation. He screened the various internal groups—Mexican Constitutionalists, Haitian and Dominican politicians—to find some political faction strong enough to carry the cross of liberty. He then tried to imbue the select with the true fervor of those who, though once damned, were now saved. Wilson wanted not merely to transform but to transubstantiate.

By supporting these native, budding democrats, Wilson hoped to ensure the flowering of democracy once American forces withdrew. He intended not simply to impose his politics on others but took the much more delicate and complicated approach of carefully, lovingly nurturing the newly sprouting seeds of democracy abroad. Those seeds needed to take root within their own soil to survive. Tending those internal groups meant using force for association.

In Mexico Wilson saw himself fighting for the "eighty-five percent" of the people long excluded from self-government. He chose the Constitutionalists under Carranza as most representative of the disfranchised. Whether he was punishing Huerta or chasing Villa, Wilson used the opportunity to associate himself with the Constitutionalists. In 1914 he put the United States forth as Carranza's representative before the ABC mediation. Throughout the Niagara Falls conference, the American delegates demanded those conditions which they—in good, misguided faith—believed would be most beneficial to the Constitutionalists. That Carranza eventually spurned their help came as a shock, although it was not enough to convince the Americans to see their crusade as simple meddling. Whether Carranza wanted assistance, Wilson stubbornly intended to give it to him.

Two years later, in 1916, Pancho Villa's raid on Columbus, New Mexico, provided Wilson with new opportunities to guide the Constitutionalists toward democracy. Claiming the approval of Carranza, Wilson launched the Punitive Expedition to rid Mexico of its worst band of outlaws. Doing so would spare the newly recognized de facto government from its greatest threat, thus allowing it to focus its energies on transforming Mexico. After Carranzista and American troops clashed outside Carrizal, Wilson used the resultant conference to propound an ambitious program of social, economic, and political reforms. Whether Carranza wanted it, he had become Wilson's principal apostle in the conversion of Mexico.

In Haiti, Wilson moved quickly to establish a new Haitian government so that he could fight for it. Admiral Caperton expended considerable effort searching for the right candidate for the presidency. Once he identified Sudre Dartiguenave as most amenable to the American program, Caperton arranged his election to ensure that the United States would have some internal political element with which to associate. After Dartiguenave's installation, the United States absolved its actions under the claim of supporting legitimate government in Haiti. Through their affiliation with Dartiguenave, American forces spread the gospel of democracy.

Wilson tried the same tactic, with considerably less success, in the Dominican Republic. Once again Admiral Caperton searched for some native leader qualified to carry the American banner of democracy and liberty. When the Dominicans proved too recalcitrant for their own salvation, the U.S. Navy installed one of its own as the republic's savior. Captain Knapp's primary mission was to resurrect democracy in the Dominican Republic. By that point, it mattered little what the Dominicans wanted.

Through the use of force for association, Wilson tried to refine the rude application of American power by allying it with native elements within each country. He was merely assisting these internal groups as they staggered along the path of democracy. By associating with Carranza, Dartiguenave, and someone—if only they could find him—in the Dominican Republic, Wilson hoped to blunt the sharper edges of the American interventions by showing he had no selfish ends to serve. The United States helped its friends, even if it had to search high and low to find them.

In 1917 Wilson warred against Germany in a grand association of democracies. In the Fourteen Points, he outlined a set of typically vague promises, including open diplomacy, freedom of the seas, freedom of trade, disarmament, and self-determination—all guaranteed by the nations of the world in league together. Subsequent promises expanded and refined the original points by specifying that justice would guide the final settlement, the discredited balance-of-power system would be discarded, territorial settlements would be accomplished for the good of the people affected, national aspirations would be taken into account, and honor and law would henceforth guide international relations. With these promises and more, Wilson determined to save the world for democracy.[3]

So enraptured did Wilson become in drafting everyone to the great cause, that he tolerated, if not actually encouraged, the suppression of dissent at home. Pacifists, conscientious objectors, and opponents of the war were tried, convicted, and harshly sentenced on the slightest complaints. While U.S. troops fought for the grand ideals of freedom and liberty, U.S. Marshals arrested enemy aliens at home, imprisoning them in army camps without benefit of due process or court hearings. Liberal tolerance was an early casualty of war.[4]

In 1918, cooperating again with the British, French, and Japanese, Wilson sent troops into northern Russia and Siberia. As always, he sought to help his friends and enlighten the dark. But both interventions went beyond the typical Wilsonian goal of fostering liberty and democracy. They were the first tests of Wilson's most cherished wartime goal: the principle of international collective action. The experience taught him that acting cooperatively was not without cost. The highest expense was having to take unpleasant actions simply because one's associates were intent on doing it.

After the war Wilson tried desperately to establish the peace on the basis of collective security. Through the League of Nations, the countries of the world associated themselves to ensure an end to all war. Security would come from the power of collective action. Change would come through rational agreement, not through force or compulsion. Renegade nations risked the wrath of a united world. The league was the culmination of the Wilsonian vision, shared now by the majority of other nations, yet ultimately spurned by the U.S. Senate. Democracy had its own frustrations.

ASSOCIATION FOR WAR

Wilson interpreted the war as an association of the world's democracies (rather loosely defined) in pitched battle against military autocracy. The March 1917 revolution in Russia, which toppled the Romanov dynasty and replaced it with an embryonically representative government, confirmed the interpretation. As Wilson explained a month after the United States declared war, its purpose "is not aggression, is not punishment; it is not inspired by resentment nor fed by ambition, but it is loyalty to an ideal, and that ideal is freeing the world from an impossible international philosophy, a philosophy in which, if it should prevail, no freedom is left or is safe." Seven months later, in December 1917, he stated the case with stark simplicity: "We are fighting for Freedom, not to obtain it for a favored few or for a group of nations. It must embrace mankind; it is for all."[5]

Yet Wilson knew quite well that the associated nations did not necessarily accept his view of the war. In the spring of 1917, he learned—at least in broad outline—of the various secret treaties allying Britain, France, Italy, Russia, and Japan. These agreements spelled out the spoils of war for each nation once Germany and Austria-Hungary were defeated. Wilson wanted no part, nor did he want to be bound by the promises. "Our people and Congress will not fight for any selfish aim on the part of any belligerent," he insisted. To avoid any wartime promises, Wilson strictly maintained that the United States was "associated" with the Entente powers, not allied with them. It was a subtle, yet crucial, distinction.[6]

Among the associated democracies, the United States adamantly insisted on retaining its independence even as it strove to cooperate in the defeat of Germany. Secretary of War Baker clearly spelled this out in his orders to General Pershing, who was dispatched to Europe as commander of the American Expeditionary Force in May 1917. "In military operations against the Imperial German Government," Baker ordered, "you are directed to cooperate with the forces of the other countries employed against the enemy; but in so doing the underlying idea must be kept in view that the forces of the United States are a separate and distinct component of the combined forces, the identity of which must be preserved." Despite considerable pressures throughout the war, Pershing successfully resisted amalgamating American soldiers into British and French units. The United States would cooperate, but only as an equal, not as piecemeal reinforcements to the decimated armies of Britain and France.[7]

American independence did not imply any hesitation about cooperating militarily with the associated nations—far from it. Wilson intended to avoid any postwar commitments while carving out a distinct role for the U.S. Army and Navy. In the fall of 1917, he sent Colonel House and General Bliss to Europe to explore ways that the United States could expand its cooperation. Both advisers strongly urged the establishment of a council of war to coordinate military operations. Wilson thought it a splendid suggestion, so he urged House to insist on "a unified conduct of the war." Still the president strictly drew the line at military cooperation. "It is not practicable for us to be represented *in the same way* as the other governments on the civil side," he reminded himself to tell House, "but we will on the military."[8]

The associated nations agreed to the establishment of a Supreme War Council on 27 November 1917. The council consisted of the prime minister of each associate, save the United States, as well as military representatives from each, including the United States. Its purpose was to set the general direction of the war effort and to determine the best allocation of resources. Wilson immediately appointed Bliss the American military representative. Bliss campaigned strenuously to go beyond the Supreme War Council to establish a unified command over all the armies. Such a structure was finally established with Marshal Ferdinand Foch of France selected as supreme commander of the Allied armies in April 1918, a month after Germany launched its last, great offensive.[9]

Admiral William S. Sims was sent to England under orders to establish "hearty cooperation" with Britain, France, and Italy. At Wilson's insistence, the several navies began convoying men and war material from the United States, in the process further cementing a cooperative war effort. Through the "Northern Barrage," British and Americans worked together to mine the North Sea. As with the Allied and associated armies, the navies established their own Allied Naval Council to develop strategies and determine the best use of resources. Effecting cooperation sometimes proved impossible, as with Sims's frustrated efforts to launch a naval campaign in the Mediterranean. Still, the Allied and associated navies were planning together, even if that meant some suggestions were never approved.[10]

The Bolshevik Revolution in November 1917 underscored the need for cooperation—Germany seemed now free to turn its full force to the western front—while emphasizing the liberal war aims so eloquently defined by Wilson. Communism threatened everyone because it proposed an altogether new system of government, indeed, of living. Following the revolution and the propaganda unleashed by the new Russian regime, Wilson increased his efforts to publicize his vision of the postwar world. "The Democratic form of government is worth spending the lives of millions of men and billions of treasure to preserve," he affirmed. Three months after the revolution, in January 1918, he listed his Fourteen Points. Throughout that year he used every opportunity to proclaim the liberal, democratic alternative to military autocracy on the right and bolshevism on the left.[11]

Despite Wilson's emphasis on a cooperative war effort, he never had any intention of allowing the association to bind too tightly America's freedom of action. His insistence on an association, however cooperative, rather than an old-fashioned alliance underscored his determination to stay well clear of entangling conditions. He wanted nothing to interfere with or drag on the certain emergence of the United States as world leader. In the great association of democracies arrayed against Germany, Wilson assumed that the United States was first among equals.

Because he wanted no wartime agreements to hamstring his postwar agenda, Wilson studiously refused to enter into any political discussions with his associates. As House advised in late April 1917, "The best policy now is to avoid a discussion of peace settlements." House worried that "if the Allies begin to discuss terms among themselves, they will soon hate one another worse than they do Germany." The United States should insist that "the only thing to be considered at present is how to beat Germany in the quickest way." There would be time enough to design the peace after the war. Wilson wholeheartedly agreed.[12]

While serving on the Supreme War Council, Bliss was fully authorized to address purely military questions, but he was reprimanded on the few occasions that he allowed himself to be drawn into what Wilson defined as political topics. Unfortunately for Bliss, the president's definition of what was appropriate and inappropriate was excessively restrictive. Bliss soon learned simply to abstain if the talks turned too political. Only Colonel House—and then only rarely—was allowed to broach postwar issues with the associated nations.[13]

In September 1917 Wilson authorized House to supervise an inquiry into possible terms and conditions of peace. Working with an impressive collection of scholars and others, House oversaw the preparation of dozens of position papers and specialized reports, each addressing particular aspects of the peace settlement and the postwar world. Eventually Wilson took to the peace conference this quickly assembled, though for that no less important, library of peace issues, as well as many of the experts recruited by House. Sadly, it is not clear that the president ever made much use of the inquiry's resources.

By cooperating with the Entente nations, Wilson hoped eventually to coopt them into embracing—how loosely or tightly was as yet unclear—the American vision of the postwar world order. Beginning in April 1917, Wilson rather arbitrarily defined the grand war aims of the Allied and associate armies. He simply ignored the secret treaties and the rumors of the deals and territorial prizes the Allies had agreed to among themselves. It was the Wilsonian conception of collective security, freedom of the seas, liberal democratic capitalism, and self-determination that quickly became the rallying calls of the war. As historian Betty Miller Unterberger has suggested, the Wilsonian clarion had a potent appeal to the disparate peoples of the world.[14]

Although he shunned private talks with his associates, Wilson felt no hesitation about publicly defining the war. With a fundamental egotism, he independently specified the war's goals and purpose. Without any reference to the Entente powers, Wilson peremptorily declared that the war was "to make the world safe for democracy." He arbitrarily dismissed the "discredited" balance-of-power system and insisted on replacing it with collective security. Without consulting his colleagues, he drew up his Fourteen Points, many of which contained specific terms of territorial and political settlements. Whether or not his associates might have agreed with his proposals, he never really gave them the opportunity to endorse, much less refine, his postwar vision. In the Wilsonian way of war, Wilson alone defined the objectives.

His associates seemed to have no other choice but to follow Wilson's lead. With military autocracy crumbling to their right and rabid communism erupting to their left, the leaders of Britain, France, and Italy (less so Japan) fell in behind the Wilsonian alternative. Wilson well understood the unique role now afforded the United States. "This seems to me to be a war in which the American people are privileged to play a singular and noble part because they have no selfish ends to serve and are fighting for the principles and ideals which have always lain at the very foundation of our nation's life," he wrote in September 1918. "We are trying to extend to the world the gift of liberty and conscience and disinterested service of mankind." Earlier he had pressed the same gift on Mexico, Haiti, and the Dominican Republic.[15]

And Wilson imposed his vision on the Entente powers in the same conceited way he had pushed it on his neighbors in the Western Hemisphere. Although he interpreted the war as democracy pitted against autocracy, he clearly believed that America was democracy's purest representative, freedom's best standard bearer. His associates did not quite measure up. Because they lacked some essential quality of goodness, Wilson let it clearly be known that he was not too concerned with attending to their postwar programs. In April 1917 the Great War became Wilson's war.

As long as the United States continued flooding Europe with men, material, and money, Wilson's vainglorious approach seemed a small enough price for the Entente powers to pay. They would suffer him his ideals, and sometimes even applaud them, as long as American troops and supplies kept debarking in France. They would go along with the cooperative ventures, too, even proposing many of their own, and agree in principle to the idea of collective security. But they did not abandon their own agenda for the peace. Their peoples had suffered too much, had paid too high a price already, for them to forswear easily the spoils of war. Wilson's conceited promise to "make the world safe for democracy" was not so abrasive as long as the war lasted: the Entente powers were also fighting to save their world. But once saved, then what?

ASSOCIATION FOR INTERVENTION

Cooperation, Wilson learned during the war, burdened both sides to any joint venture. From before the war, the American military insisted on devoting its full measure of effort to defeating Germany on the western front. The officers of the War Department opposed divvying up U.S. troops among the British and French. They objected just as strenuously to diverting those soldiers to any sideshow of the Great War. "The War College Division is of the opinion that there must be no yielding to a popular demand to send small expeditions composed of one or two divisions of our regular army," Bliss advised in March 1917. Even at that the War College estimated it would take two years to put an army in France.[16]

But their new associates had run out of men and money—and had little time left. A month after the declaration of war, a British-French mission to the United States revealed the desperate condition of the Allied armies. The information, shocking as it was, confirmed the military in its initial recommendation that nothing deflect the U.S. contribution. "As the foreign gentlemen spoke more and more freely, it became evident that what they want and need is men, whether trained or not," Bliss advised Secretary of War Baker. Immediately Wilson sent General Pershing and an initial American Expeditionary Force of about twelve thousand soldiers. Within fourteen months, Pershing's command grew to one million men. It was an astounding achievement for a nation so completely unprepared for war as the United States had been in April 1917.[17]

Exhausted by three years of fighting against the German military machine, Britain and France made no serious effort to redirect American participation from the western front. So desperate was their condition that Secretary of War Baker concluded publicly that "the human race is a waif left to die unless we, as trustees, accept the task of rescuing it." Over the summer and into the fall of 1917, the associated nations arrayed against Germany seemed content for Pershing and his troops to take up stations on the southern flank of the western front—the area stretching from the Argonne Forest to the Vesges Mountains. After a relatively brief training period, Pershing started deploying his troops. Meanwhile America's enormous, slumbering industrial might began to awaken.[18]

Then in November 1917, the Bolshevik Revolution knocked the already staggering Russian armies out of the war. Voting with their feet, to use Lenin's phrase, the Russian soldiers fled in droves. The new regime quickly sued for peace. The Treaty of Brest-Litovsk, signed on 3 March 1918, merely formalized what had already become quite apparent: all was quiet on the eastern front.

Russia's desertion completely unnerved the remaining allies. "We can no longer count upon the Russians to keep the Teutons in the field on the eastern front," Lansing noted in December 1917 "This means that the German armies in the west and the Austrians in Italy will be largely increased. The situation is dark for the Allies who are now putting forth all their strength." For Lansing, Russia's withdrawal from the war boiled down to one essential question: "Can we get there in time to save the situation?" The Allies felt even more urgently pressed for that answer.[19]

Having had such difficulty fighting Germany on two fronts, officials in Britain, France, and Italy could not imagine how they could stand alone against the Central Powers, regardless of the exponentially growing contribution of the United States. In their desperation they struck upon a wild, practically absurd plan to recreate the eastern front by landing British, Japanese, and American forces in Siberia. Later they proposed a twin intervention in northern Russia to protect large quantities of war supplies sent to buttress the Russian armies before the Bolshevik Revolution.

Both proposals were ill defined, ill conceived, and poorly planned. At no point did either intervention ever have a concisely defined objective or a precisely explicated purpose. How an intervention would recreate the eastern front, or even compel Germany to retain its massive armies in the east, was never adequately explained. It was taken almost as a matter of pure faith that landing forces on one side of Russia would make Germany keep its troops thousands of miles away on the other side.

During the first half of 1918, Wilson alone blocked any intervention in Russia. He saw no benefit to either of the schemes, particularly as they detracted men, ships, and supplies from the true arena of the war. But his opposition stood in stark contradiction to his emphasis on wartime cooperation. Only after he came to understand each intervention as the price of international cooperation was Wilson able to rationalize sending troops into Russia. Ultimately the twin interventions were the last of Wilson's uses of force, but they were the first implementations of his vision of collective security.[20]

Wilson resisted as long as he could. Increasingly, though, he grew uncomfortable with the divergence between his plans for postwar collective security and his wartime refusal to cooperate in Russia. Baker remembered that Wilson agreed with the American military's opposition to both interventions, but the eagerness of the associate nations to embark on the Russian adventures convinced him to go along. "Baker," the secretary recalled Wilson saying, "I wholly agree with all you say from a military point of view, but we are fighting this war with allies and I have felt obliged to refuse to do so many things they have asked me to do that I really felt obliged to fall in with their wishes here." The pressures of cooperation finally convinced him to join Japanese and British forces in Siberia and British forces in northern Russia.[21]

When he announced the joint interventions in mid-July 1918, Wilson defined his policy as endeavoring "to cooperate in every practicable way with the Allied Governments, and to cooperate ungrudgingly. . . . [The United States] has sought to study every proposed policy or action in which its cooperation has been asked in this spirit." Although he had several qualms about each intervention, specifically any taint of political intervention in Russia's internal affairs, Wilson accepted the "modest and experimental plans" put forth by his associates to limit each one. Beyond that, he announced, he would not go.[22]

The Entente powers pressed their plan on Wilson both individually and, most difficultly for him, collectively. The pressures began shortly after the Bolshevik Revolution toppled the remnants of democracy in Russia. On 23 December the military representatives to the Supreme War Council, with Bliss wisely abstaining, approved Joint Note Number 5 to their respective governments. The note urged the Allies and their associate to support any group in Eastern Europe that evinced the slightest disposition to continue the war against Germany. To ensure the effectiveness of that support, the Supreme War Council's military members voted to establish direct communications "with our friends in Russia either by way of Vladivostok and the Siberian Railway or by operations in Turkey."[23]

Although always sympathetic to helping friends, in this instance Wilson was not sure just who his friends were. The United States had lent its strongest moral support, enlivened by some practical assistance, to the democratic government of Alexander Kerensky. But Kerensky's defeat by the Bolsheviks left a void. The situation for the Americans was much too confusing, the factions contending for power too undefined, for Wilson to feel much confidence in calling any friend. Lansing described it accurately enough as "an unanswered and unanswerable riddle." Until some solution to the enigma emerged, Wilson preferred to stand to the side.[24]

His associates pressed him to take a stand. On 19 February 1918, the military representatives to the Supreme War Council specifically nominated Japan to take the Allied mandate in a Siberian intervention. In Joint Note Number 16, they resolved that the "occupation of the Siberian Railway from Vladivostock to Harbin together with both terminals presents military advantages that outweigh any probable political disadvantages." The specific pluses and minuses were not detailed in the joint note.[25]

Arthur Balfour, the British foreign secretary, argued that a Siberian intervention would help Russia confront Germany. "Since Russia cannot help herself she must be helped by her friends," Balfour argued to Wilson. Jules Jusserand, the French ambassador to the United States, believed the chief advantage would be "keeping open for us all and the shutting to the enemy of the transiberian route, for us henceforth the only means of access to Eastern and Southern Russia." Japanese officials informed the American ambassador in Tokyo that an intervention by them would "arrest the sinister activities of Germany in Siberia." None of the proposals got much more detailed than that.[26]

Wilson was not enthused with the idea of taking action in Siberia when the only forces available to do anything were Japanese. His relations with Japan had never been comfortable. Discrimination against Japanese immigrants to the United States angered Tokyo, whereas Japan's ambitions in

China, which culminated in the outrageous Twenty-One Demands of 1915, disturbed Wilson. It was not until the fall of 1917 that the two countries were able to reach some understanding. Through the Lansing-Ishii Agreement, the United States acknowledged Japan's special interests in return for a Japanese promise to respect China's political and territorial independence and America's Open Door. The agreement simply resolved the immediate crisis, and had little effect on the underlying problems plaguing U.S.-Japanese relations.

Giving Japan the Allied and associate proxy in Siberia played to Wilson's distrust. In January 1918 Secretary of the Navy Daniels dispatched the USS *Brooklyn*, flagship of the commander in chief of the Asiatic fleet, to Vladivostok to observe events, particularly any action by the Japanese. The deployment was not intended as preparatory to intervention. Rather, Wilson was signaling his intention to keep Japan under close scrutiny. The British, showing again that they truly did not understand the American president, argued that as Japan was about to intervene anyway, it would be better that it act under the mandate of the Allies, which would put some restrictions on its ambitions, rather than let it go in unilaterally. The argument merely bolstered Wilson in his decision to oppose any landing—collectively by the associated powers or independently by Japan.[27]

Equally as important, Wilson objected to intervening in Siberia because it would seriously detract from the more important efforts on the western front. Not only would it drain away much-needed manpower from the decimated armies, but it also would divert the shipping of desperately needed supplies. Wilson and his subordinates argued repeatedly that the war had to be won in France.

Finally, Wilson opposed the intervention because, at the least, it would be interpreted by the Russian people as political interference in their internal affairs. At the most, of course, Wilson feared—with considerable justification—that it easily could become meddling in the Russian Revolution. As he had before with each intervention, Wilson adamantly denied any ambition to interfere in the internal politics of the distraught nation. This time the difference seemed to be that his actions would actually match his words.

Thus by the spring of 1918, Wilson understood that he alone stood opposed to a Japanese landing in Siberia. He also believed that his stance had effectively blocked the plan. In March the situation was further complicated when about two hundred British marines landed in Murmansk to protect a large stockpile of war supplies sent to Russia when it had been an ally. They were guarding the stocks, not from Germans but from the Russians. Although even the Allies agreed that they had insufficient resources to support an intervention in northern Russia, the issue, once on the table, refused to clear away. From March on, the Allies talked of two separate operations: one spearheaded by Japan in Siberia (Vladivostok) and another led by Britain in northern Russia (Murmansk and Archangel). Wilson opposed both.[28]

Although that opposition, for the moment at least, effectively stymied each intervention, it also left Wilson exactly where he did not want to be: isolated from his associates. His plans for the future peace of the world depended essentially on what his associates were here proposing; that is, collective action to resolve an international problem. Wilson may not have agreed on the solution, nor even on the importance of the issue, but he could not so easily deny that his associates understood it as an international problem and, more important, that their solution was to respond collectively. Ironically, Wilson risked the United States thwarting joint action at precisely the time he was putting forth collective security as the best—even last— hope for world peace. As Lansing complained, it was the "biggest problem and most complicated" he had ever faced.[29]

As the Russian spring thawed to summer, the situation grew more complex. Hoping somehow to escape the onus of singlehandedly blocking his associates, Wilson indicated that he would neither oppose nor request a landing by Japan. On 5 April, after three Japanese nationals were murdered in Vladivostok, five hundred Japanese soldiers deployed ashore, joined by fifty British troops. On learning of the landing, the military representatives to the Supreme War Council again resolved themselves in support of a Siberian intervention headed by Japan. Joint Note Number 20 argued that an intervention would prevent Germany from obtaining food and raw materials from the area, stop any German incursions there, and force Germany to keep its troops on the eastern front. It seemed a lot to ask of a single intervention.[30]

But soon more would be asked. In late April a ragtag army of eight thousand Czechoslovakian prisoners of war began moving across Russia toward Siberia. Anxious to see their homeland an independent nation, the Czechs planned to join the fighting against Germany on the western front by heading east to the United States, then east again to Europe. Although the Bolsheviks were eager to rid themselves of this troublesome collection of well-trained, well-armed, hostile Czechs, the animosity each felt toward the other eventually erupted into open fighting. Wilson's associates immediately added rescuing the Czechs to their reasons for intervening in Siberia.[31]

But in saving the Czechs from the Bolsheviks, the Allied powers also saw a way to draft the Czech legion into the interventions in Siberia and northern Russia. This would solve the manpower problem, ease the shipping problem, and all the while put an Allied presence in Russia. In Joint Note Number 25, dated 27 April, the military representatives to the Supreme War Council recommended that "all Czech troops, which have not yet passed East of Omsk on the Trans-Siberian Railway, should be . . . employed in defending Archangel and Murmansk and in guarding and protecting the Murman railway." Those portions of the Czech legion that had passed east of Omsk could be used "to co-operate with the Allies in Siberia."[32]

Although Wilson remained opposed to a Siberian intervention, he was beginning to cave in to the pressures for action in northern Russia. Secretary of State Lansing explained to Lord Reading, his British counterpart, in mid-May that the United States distinguished between the two Russian proposals. Wilson, Lansing wrote, believed "that the problem had really become two problems in that intervention in [Archangel and Murmansk] in no way involved the racial difficulty which had to be considered in regard to Siberia." The United States "could understand the military advantage of the former but had been unable, thus far, to find any advantage in sending troops into Siberia." Wilson hoped to end the talk of intervening in Siberia by supporting action in northern Russia.[33]

Because the northern Russia proposal seemed the least noxious of the proposed interventions, Wilson agreed to the use of the Czechs, supplemented by British and U.S. forces, in Archangel and Murmansk. Bliss advised his counterparts on the Supreme War Council on 1 June that Wilson concurred with Joint Note Number 25, at least as it pertained to northern Russia. Bliss cautioned that his president was finally "in sympathy with any practical military efforts which can be made at and from Murmansk or Archangel, but such efforts should proceed, if at all, upon the sure sympathy of the Russian people and should not have as their ultimate objects any restoration of the ancient regime or any other interference with the political liberty of the Russian people."[34]

Only practical problems—lack of shipping, war material, and troops—prohibited an immediate intervention. During June vague reports of German troops massing outside Petrograd, swarming over Finland, and marching toward northern Russia enhanced Allied fears. In Joint Note Number 31, the military representatives to the Supreme War Council concluded that the willingness of that portion of the Czech legion diverted to Archangel and Murmansk to defend the two ports "will be conditional on the moral and material support of a few Allied units on the spot to cooperate with them against the Germans." Although hesitant to divert from the gigantic effort needed to carry men and material to France, Wilson was much more sympathetic to the intervention in northern Russia than he was to the Siberian adventure.[35]

Unfortunately for Wilson, the Allies drew a distinction between the two interventions. In their minds, however, supporting the operation in northern Russia had no effect on the issue of action in Siberia. Each was equally important. No one but Wilson was satisfied to land troops only in Archangel and Murmansk. Thus during June 1918, the pressure on Wilson grew and, increasingly, he saw himself alone among his associates, the sole stumbling block to their plans. State Department official Breckinridge Long observed on 31 May that:

> from all sides there are now coming pleas for intervention in Siberia. Paris cables a meeting will be held there tomorrow between Lloyd George, Clemenceau, and Italian Premier on subject; Reinsch [U.S. ambassador to China] advises it from Peking; various cables from other ports, Russian and Siberia, urge it; and a general sentiment of personnel all over the Northern Hemisphere seem setting toward Allied intervention.

The whole world, save Wilson, seemed intent on landing troops at Vladivostok.[36]

Wilson's associates went out of their way to point out his isolation. At the sixth session of the Supreme War Council, convened at Versailles during the first three days of June, the prime ministers of Britain, France, and Italy agreed that Wilson had effectively vetoed the scheme; hence, only Wilson could get it going. The French foreign minister, Stephen Pichon, reported that the consensus among the foreign ministers was that "all the Allies with the exception of the United States thought Japanese intervention in Siberia desirable." Furthermore the foreign ministers concurred that "of course no final steps should be taken without the approval of the President of the United States because the Allied Governments would not wish to take any action in opposition to him." In order to set Wilson's mind at ease, Pichon suggested that the Allies query Japan as to its intentions in Siberia, particularly eliciting from Tokyo a promise to respect Russia's territorial and political integrity. Once reassured on these questions, Pichon felt sure Wilson would give his blessings to the intervention.[37]

The Japanese response further segregated Wilson from his associates. The Japanese government affirmed its refusal to intervene in Siberia unless it was assured not only of Wilson's approval but also of the "active support of the United States Government." It readily promised its respect for Russia's territorial and political integrity, which gave Wilson "genuine delight," but on the whole, the answer simply refocused all the pressures for intervention on the White House. By July the champion of collective security was single-handedly frustrating the unanimous desire of his associates for collective action in Siberia.[38]

On June 29 that portion of the Czech legion which had managed to reach Vladivostok overwhelmed their Bolshevik hosts, with whom they had been squabbling for weeks, and took over the city. The cry went up among the

Allies to save the Czechs. Pointing out that General Foch, the recently appointed supreme commander of the Allied and associated armies, believed
such an intervention was essential to the defeat of Germany (though how it
would contribute to that was never quite explained), Wilson's associates again
pleaded with him to cooperate before it was too late. "The Allies," Betty
Miller Unterberger has concluded, "were never so unanimous as they now
appeared to be on the necessity for intervention." Their unanimity left Wilson farther out in the cold. [39]

The Czechs, though, gave him a way in. He had never been comfortable
with the rationale behind the Siberian intervention—the reestablishment of
the eastern front—because it struck him as uncommonly absurd. America's
associates, Wilson told his cabinet, "propose such impractical things to be
done immediately that he often wondered whether he was crazy or whether
they were." But now the Czechs needed help. As Lansing pointed out, that
introduced "a sentimental element into the question of our duty." Wilson
seized the chance to use force for the protection of the Czech legion. He
could now claim that he was not intervening in Russia's internal affairs nor
making some futile effort to recreate the uncreatable. "Furnishing protection
and assistance to the Czecho-Slovaks, who are so loyal to our cause, is a very
different thing from sending an army into Siberia to restore order and to save
the Russians from themselves," Lansing explained. "There is a moral obli-
gation to save these men from our common enemies, if we are able to do so."
At a White House conference on 6 July, Wilson ordered the use of American
forces in Siberia. He specifically rejected the goal of reestablishing the eastern front because it was "physically impossible." The purpose of the intervention was to cooperate with Japan and Britain in rescuing the Czechs. As
he had so often before in his military interventions, Wilson again called on
the use of force for protection to excuse his actions. [40]

And as had happened so often before, the excuse of protection covered a
multitude of sins. Increasingly the twin interventions were used by the
British, and especially the Japanese, to meddle politically in Russia's internal
affairs. Wilson found cooperating with them no great comfort, although not
cooperating risked their untrammelled interference in Russia. The Japanese
clearly hoped to use the Siberian adventure to their own advantage. Not only
did it promote their ambitions for certain Russian territories but it also advanced their interests toward China. The United States contributed about
seven thousand men to the joint force; the Japanese deployed around seventy
thousand men, and they insisted on assuming the joint command.

When Wilson expressed his uneasiness over the rapidly growing size of the
Siberian intervention, officials in Britain and France first defended it, then
pressed for even more reinforcements. General Tom Molesworth Bridges of

the British Military Mission to the United States defined both interventions as the best way "to help Russia onto her feet again." Bridges, admitting to Baker that "we probably trust the Japanese more than you," even suggested the possibility of using "unlimited numbers of Japanese in the field without disturbing Russia." Typically for these interventions, he gave no hint as to how that could be accomplished.[41]

Wilson continued to feel somewhat isolated from his associates, despite their joint effort. As he explained to Lansing on 23 August:

> The other governments are going much further than we and much faster,—are indeed, acting upon a plan which is altogether foreign from ours and inconsistent with it.
>
> Please make it plain to the French Ambassador that we do not think cooperation in *political* action necessary or desirable in eastern Siberia because we contemplate no political action of any kind there, but only the action of friends who stand at hand and wait to see how they can help. The more plain and emphatic this is made the less danger will there be of subsequent misunderstandings and irritations.

For as long as the interventions lasted—and they lasted long past the time Wilson thought them necessary—he tried to temper the activities of his associates and keep them in line with what he understood to be the original intent. But the presence of Allied and associated forces in revolutionary Russia was too tempting. More and more, particularly after the November armistice with Germany, the interventions took on an anti-Bolshevik character. Once again Wilson succumbed to the enticing prospect of redirecting a revolution along democratic paths.[42]

Unfortunately, using force for introduction in Russia proved of no avail. Unlike Mexico, the situation in Russia was too amorphous, the contending factions too shifting, too weak, and yet too independent to brook much interference from the Allied and associated powers. Wilson never found a Carranza for Russia; he could never accept Lenin as a substitute. Thus he never had an internal element with which to associate American support. Without that he remained very much the outsider pressing to get in but never given standing to exert his influence. The contrasting ambitions of Japan merely complicated an already impossible situation.

Yet despite the conflicting goals and frustrating demands of working with other nations, Wilson showed with World War I and the twin Russian interventions that international cooperation could work. Their joint effort had defeated Germany and Austria-Hungary; limited interventions were launched into Russia. After illustrating the principle in practice, Wilson traveled to

Europe in December 1918 well prepared to redefine the international system according to the fundamental precept of collective security. With the League of Nations, Wilson proposed a formal way to express the use of force for association.

ASSOCIATION FOR PEACE

On the eleventh hour of the eleventh day of the eighteenth year of the twentieth century, Woodrow Wilson reached the pinnacle of international power. Although late to war on Germany, he had successfully imposed on the world his own definition of that war. In the process he transformed it from a nineteenth-century imbalance of power into a twentieth-century ideological crusade. He gave the disparate peoples of the world hope that they would be able to determine for themselves their individual destinies, unmolested by empires and aggressors. Self-determination, Wilson promised, would be protected by a new system of international relations secured by a revolutionary concept of collective action. The peoples of the world cheered him and loved him and awaited his every pronouncement, his every promise. They believed that he was pledging himself to their particular causes.

American military power was at its peak, the men under arms now fully equipped, trained, and experienced. The American economy, politics, and society were fully committed on a war footing. Clearly the United States had won the war, saving not only British but also French and Italian chestnuts. With scant reference to his associates, Wilson negotiated the terms of the armistice with the new German government. Having made the cease-fire his, he expected to make the peace his as well.

Victory found the Allied powers exhausted, depleted, and embittered. They were deeply indebted to the United States for men, material, money, and victory. Wilson was invigorated and triumphant. Fortified by the full stretch of American power, he was armed, as well, with an ideological vision to apply it. He knew what he wanted and had the wherewithal to obtain it. On 11 November 1918, he was the most powerful man in the world. No other contender stood close.

Within the year, he would lose most of his power; within three, it would all be gone. At Paris his associates would distort his vision of the peace, and he would be blamed for the contortions. At Washington the Senate would reject his peace treaty, and he would be blamed for its recalcitrance. And his body would fail him, leaving him a crippled invalid barely able to continue the functions of his office. In January 1921 he would retire, a prophet scorned in his own land. It was a tragedy of Greek proportions; a Shakespearian tale of ideals defeated, power collapsed, dreams unattained.

Wilson journeyed to Paris in December 1918 in the full blush of his power. He arrived determined to write a peace that implemented his Fourteen Points. Among those points he placed particular emphasis on collective security expressed through a league of nations. With the league he expected not only to protect the international system but also to provide peaceful means to reform and fine tune it. Wilson was prepared to accept less of the peace than he would have preferred, precisely because he saw the League of Nations as the best hope for mankind. By deferring to the league the problems that proved unsolvable at the Paris Peace Conference, he burdened it not only with his dreams of peace but also with his many unfulfilled promises to the peoples of the world. The burden would prove too much.

During the Paris Peace Conference, Wilson concentrated most of his energy on hammering out the details of the league. He showed himself an adroit negotiator, twisting and turning amid the contradictory demands of his associates, yet all the while moving the negotiations steadily forward. He compromised on specific terms while preserving the fundamental premise of collective security. His associates could have their reprisals against Germany, their huge war indemnity, their occupation of the Rhineland, and a dozen other minor concessions if that was what it took to gain their acceptance of the league. Wilson saw himself as preparing a great charter for the future of the world. Obtaining it superseded everything else.

He agreed readily enough to French demands for a military alliance with the United States and Great Britain against a possible resurgent Germany despite the precedential break with America's traditional policy of no entangling alliances. Wilson rationalized the departure by explaining it as a function of collective security. "I have promised to propose to the Senate a treaty in which we shall agree, subject to the approval of the Council of the League of Nations, to come immediately to the assistance of France in case of unprovoked attack by Germany," he explained to Tumulty, "thus merely hastening the action to which in any case we should be bound by the covenant of the League of Nations." In exchange the French accepted the league.[43]

The use of force for association was the fundamental premise upon which Wilson erected the Covenant of the League of Nations. The league proposed a comprehensive system of international relations based on a commitment to collective security. International boundaries were guaranteed against all military aggression. Those peoples yet too politically or socially undeveloped to stand on their own were protected under a mandate system whereby one of the developed powers, working with the approval of the league, guided them to development. An executive council consisting of the major powers—Great Britain, France, Italy, and the United States—ensured the supremacy of the war's victors. And finally, the peace of the world was ensured by the active cooperation of the member states to maintain it, by force if necessary. As Wilson proclaimed on 28 April 1919, the league promised "to maintain justice in international relations and peace between the nations of the world." The maintenance of the system depended entirely on the associated power of the world.[44]

Wilson traveled to Paris in December 1918 with a grand sense of himself as a pragmatic negotiator prepared to push for as much as he could get. Braced by a set of ideals, Wilson had the confidence of righteousness, the might of fidelity to the cause. He philosophically accepted that he would not get everything because he fully expected the League of Nations, once underway, to achieve the rest. The league was it. Once he had that, then he had all he needed.

And it was that attitude of gambling everything on the league that explains the great inconsistencies between Wilson's compromising pragmatism in Paris and his ideological inflexibility in Washington. At Paris he bowed to French, British, and Italian insistence on a huge war indemnity from Germany. He acquiesced to France's demand for a military alliance and to Japan's territorial ambitions in Shantung. He accepted occupation of the Rhineland, distorted national boundaries around the world, continued the intervention in Siberia, and compromised on a dozen other minor concessions all to gain international support for the league.

Once gained, Wilson gambled that the league would resolve all disgruntlements. As he told the conferees on Valentine's Day 1919:

> There are many complicated questions connected with the present settlements which perhaps can not be successfully worked out to an ultimate issue by the decisions we shall arrive at here. I can easily conceive that many of these settlements will need subsequent reconsideration, that many of the decisions we make shall need subsequent alteration to some degree; for, if I may judge by my own study of some of these questions, they are not susceptible of confident judgments at present.

But the league promised to resolve these issues and others that from time to time would arise. It was in Wilson's mind—if not quite anyone else's—"the keystone of the whole program which expressed our purpose and ideals in this war and which the associated nations have accepted as the basis of the settlement." He quite consciously gambled that the league would iron out the difficulties that the peace conference could not.[45]

Unfortunately the gamble depended on the purity of the league and the peace treaty as Wilson delivered it to the United States Senate on 10 July. "The light streams upon the path ahead," he warned the senators assembled, "and nowhere else." The Senate, though, had its own illumination, its own ideas for the postwar world. Wilson, having given in so often at Paris, refused to listen to any proposals in Washington. "My clear conviction is that the adoption of the Treaty by the Senate with reservations would put the United States as clearly out of the concert of nations as a rejection," he maintained. "We ought either to go in or to stay out." His stubborn rejection of any changes exacerbated the problems by infuriating the opposition. The Senate rejected the treaty; the United States stayed out of the League of Nations.[46]

In rejecting the peace treaty, the United States signaled the world that it was on its own. Wilson's immediate successors—Republicans all—retreated, not into isolationism but into independence. They spurned Wilson's ideal of acting in association with the nations of the world. As several scholars have suggested, the United States was hardly isolated from international affairs during the 1920s. It remained quite active in world trade, it was a major proponent of limiting international armament, and it continued to guide events in the Western Hemisphere. Although the military government was dismantled in the Dominican Republic in 1922, U.S. Marines continued to control Haiti for another decade. During the 1920s the United States would keep an intent eye on affairs in Mexico and Cuba and would send troops to Nicaragua.

The difference was that the Republican administrations of the 1920s preserved their independence of action. They shrugged off Wilson's sense of international community and his commitment to collective security. They preached a self-reliance in action, a selfish determination to move unfettered by allies or associates. That, more than anything else, was the true rejection of Wilsonian internationalism.

In the Wilsonian way of war, success bred its own failure.

7 The Abuses of FORCE

Infatuated, Paris kidnapped Helen. Infuriated, Agamemnon demanded her release, then mobilized the Achean tribes into a Greek army. When negotiations broke down before Paris's virile passions, the Greeks attacked the fortified city of Troy, intending to rescue Helen and punish Paris. With Troy surrounded but unconquered, the war settled into a ten-year siege, broken by frequent skirmishes and contests at one-to-one combat. Finally, by equine subterfuge, the Greeks sacked Troy and saved Helen.

The Trojan War, though infinitely complicated by the toying interference of the gods, involved specific, identifiable stages. The conflict followed a steady, albeit lengthy, progression from committing the grievance to demanding satisfaction, then raising the armies, dispatching the fleet, besieging Troy, constructing a hollow horse, destroying the enemy, and making the odyssey home. Most instances of force before or since have followed a similar pattern: grievance, dispute, clash, resolution.

Each stage of conflict can be as straightforward as Penelope's diurnal weaving, as ingenious as her nocturnal unraveling. The grievance can be of the heart—the kidnapping of Helen—or it can be about peoples, land, money, or ideals. The dispute can be a simple demand—the release of Helen—or it can be intricate applications of diplomatic, economic, moral, or military power. The clash can contain simple contests of arms—Achilles's duel with Hector—or it can array shifting uses of force. The resolution can be the destruction of the enemy—the sack of Troy—or it can be a negotiated settlement, stalemate, or defeat. Each stage presents a delicate intersecting of alternatives—choices and actions interlacing like the strands of Penelope's never-finished shroud.

Unraveling that cloth into its component threads allows a much fuller understanding of armed power. Reducing force to its elementary parts and then examining how they intersect with policy provides a way to understand the base elements of any instance of force. As Penelope's weaving transformed individual fibers into a garment, so the resort to armed power may contain several uses of force interlaced with policy to compose action. With policy the weft, the separate uses of force become the warp that, interweaved, constitute armed power. By discerning the motives behind force, it is possible to define the uses of force by the policies that control them.

National leaders have long recognized that force offers numerous advantages. Its uses are relatively straightforward; its controls are reasonably manageable; its outcome is generally self-evident. Power expressed through force is easier to measure than most any other international contest. Economic power is difficult to assess and requires considerable time to take effect. Moral power helps spotlight another nation's transgressions, but by itself can only effect the conscience of the world. Military power can be effective but ultimately risks war by the very presence of military force. With armed power nations' simply pit their guns, soldiers, and accoutrements against other nations' guns, soldiers, and accoutrements. The outcome hangs in the balance. The greatest unknowns are the will to employ force, the ingenuity of its application, and the risk of losing control.

When Cain slew Abel, man found in force a primal resolution to myriad problems, from soothing jealousies to stealing riches to protecting home, hearth, and dream. From time immemorial, national leaders have embraced force as a convenient, comparatively simple alternative to the subtleties of negotiations, the intricacies of diplomacy, or the headaches of foreign policy. But therein lies the rub. Using force is a temptation of irresistible dimension, even though succumbing to it imperils as much as it can secure. In turning to it with such alacrity simply because it seems so easy, without first assigning it clear motive or precise purpose, the uses of force chance sliding into the abuses of force. It is those abuses that ultimately risk all.

The abuses of force are the misapplications of armed power, either because the means do not match the objective or because there is no clearly defined objective to begin with. The ease with which force can be applied frequently results in national leaders resorting to force simply because they see no other alternative or their other choices seem too difficult, too costly, or too complicated. Armed power is used to its minimum effect the more obscurely its intent is defined, the more vaguely its objectives are delineated.

War too often seems the result of impatience or frustration, impetuous and unnecessary. In April 1812 the United States boldly declared war against Great Britain in retribution for a long list of grievances against American trade and American sailors. But the declaration contained no clear purpose or intent other than to prove the new nation's standing as a fullfledged, independent member of the international community. This lack of clear purpose was illustrated throughout the war in the clumsy way the United States fought. Lacking a precise objective, the U.S. military hustled willy-nilly from Canada to the Chesapeake to New Orleans. The war ended as it began, ill-defined and clouded by emotion. In any war what is needed most is a clear, well-defined understanding of the uses of force.

The uses of force are the motives and policies guiding a military contest at any of its several stages, from the initial deployment of troops to their ultimate withdrawal. The uses are defined by the goals sought (though not necessarily achieved) and by the ways in which armed power is applied to gain those objectives. The clashes can range from limited interventions to all-out war, from one nation fighting its own rebellious citizens to global conflagrations. Regardless of the size or scope of the battle, the uses of force are defined by policy. As motives change, so, too, do the uses of force. As conditions change, so, too, can the uses of force. Armed power is used to its optimum effect the more clearly its intent is defined, the more precisely its objectives are delineated.

In the Wilsonian way of war, international power incorporated an impressive selection from the several uses of force. Wilson moved with ease among the uses of force for protection, retribution, solution, introduction, and association. By recognizing force as an integral part of policy, Wilson harnessed its power directly to his purposes. He adeptly bolstered his policies with force, switching from one to the other to suit the needs of the moment. Not all of his uses of force accomplished what he had hoped of them, but the precision with which he used force allowed him each time to control it directly to his purposes. In using force Wilson may have sat astride an angry tiger, but he always managed to keep it well in harness, the bit tight against the fangs. Never did force get away from him; never did any intervention become something more than he intended or accepted. For a man of peace, it was an impressive integration of force to policy, a sly juggling that accounted for the changing, dramatic nature of force unfolding.

As Wilson found, force works best as but one weapon in a nation's arsenal, not when it is treated as something unique or *sui generis*. Rather than accept it as something distinct from the other forms of power, Wilson incorporated it into his foreign policy. He was not afraid to use force, nor was he afraid not to use it or to bring its use to an abrupt end. The frequency and determination with which he turned to force attests his recognition of it as one of many tactics at his disposal, but one arrow jammed into a very full quiver. By accepting force as one type of power among many, Wilson used it powerfully.

The focus of this study has been on the Wilsonian way of war because, far more than any other American president, Wilson resorted to force more often and for more diverse purposes. Studying his uses of force helped develop a vocabulary to describe force as a function of policy. Through that vocabulary instances of force can be dissected into their several elements and can be compared across time or space. Motives can be isolated and policies identified. Yet despite Wilson's repeated and multiple uses of force, he did not have recourse to all types of force conceivable. Other presidents at other times have resorted to other uses of force. Although each deserves more study than can be given here, they can at least be identified and tentatively defined.

Force can be used for *revolution* to change the status quo, gain independence from some other power, or reshape the prevailing political system. It is rebellion. The American declaration of independence from Britain exemplified this type of force, as did the failed attempt by the Southern states to secede. Nations or political entities within a nation claim their independence through armed power. A use of force for revolution is the violent effort to transfer power from the ruling group to a subservient or subject group.

At other times, force has been used for *aggression*, that is, to steal another nation's land or resources. It is limited only by ambition or the strength of the enemy. President James K. Polk's belligerent behavior toward Mexico in 1846 is a clear example of a use of force for aggression. Nations exert their ambitions, territorial or political, through armed power. A use of force for aggression is the bold, even unprovoked, initiation of hostilities to satisfy entirely selfish ambitions or aggrandizements.

Force can also be used for *subjugation*, which goes beyond the military defeat of another people to incorporate them into the victor's empire. It entails the destruction of the enemy and the absorption of its territory and wealth (though not necessarily its people) into the victor's empire. The treatment of the American Indians clearly illustrates this type of force. It is total war waged to its ultimate end. The use of force for subjugation is a violent effort to vanquish an opponent into subservience.

On numerous occasions, force has been used for *salvation*, that is, to rescue individual citizens or groups of citizens somehow imperilled in foreign lands. Its purpose is to save someone at risk, to pull them out of harm's way. During the turn-of-the-century Boxer Rebellion in China, the United States joined forces with the major European powers to dispatch an international expedition to rescue their nationals from the xenophobic Chinese. Eighty years later President Jimmy Carter tried, unsuccessfully, to rescue over a hundred Americans held hostage in Iran. A use of force for salvation is an armed rescue mission.

And force can also be used for *preservation*, which is the reliance on arms to maintain the status quo. It is violent resistance to change. President Abraham Lincoln's forceful refusal to allow the Southern states to leave the

Union exemplified this use of force. A use of force for preservation is a forcible act of conservation.

The point, of course, is that force has a wide range of applications. Each use is defined by the purposes and policies motivating a nation's leadership to resort to arms. Labeling those uses according to specific, clearly defined terms helps clarify what the uses of force are and how they are integrated into a nation's foreign policy. Defining force in all its guises simply means understanding the uses of force.

APPLYING THE VOCABULARY OF FORCE

Defining a vocabulary of force offers three major benefits to the study of war and peace. First, it allows a closer examination of the particulars of any single intervention by providing a lexicon to describe in detail complex, interconnected events. Because the terms are defined by the policies being pursued, the descriptions focus on the objectives controlling—or attempting to control—the action. For example, a vocabulary of force provides an intelligible way to describe the Punitive Expedition as initially a use of force for retribution. When that objective remained out of reach, the expedition was redefined as a use of force for protection—an effort to prevent future attacks on U.S. territory. As Carranza became increasingly hostile, Wilson saw a way to introduce himself to negotiations with the Mexicans. While Carranza wanted to talk only of the expedition's withdrawal, Wilson's envoys, blinded by their own optimism, obliviously recited the Wilsonian prescription for reforming Mexico in the American image. Analyzed thus, the vocabulary of force allows fairly concise summaries of complex events.

America's entry into World War I, to use another example, was initiated by Wilson's determination to punish Germany for its unrestricted deployment of U-boats. The use of force for retribution brought Wilson before the Congress asking for a declaration of war, but with a typically grander vision he looked beyond simple punishment to a better world. Other uses of force—for introduction and association—helped him gain the dream. By April 1917, Wilson had come to understand that American participation in any peace conference would have to be purchased in American blood. War would introduce him to the negotiations. As the United States mobilized and began dispatching its soldiers eastward across the Atlantic, Wilson saw several opportunities to associate them with the Entente powers, further cementing an international kinship that could be drawn upon to design the League of Nations. This use of force for association—in Wilson's mind, at least—portended the future international system.

Interestingly, despite a wartime rhetoric calling for the use of force for the solution of German militarism and aggression, Wilson in the end refrained from consummating this type of force. He saw, instead, the use of force for association as the world's best hope. Germany was allowed to negotiate an armistice and withdraw within its borders, bloodied and beaten, but seemingly unvanquished. By allowing Germany to retire from the field rather than flee it, Wilson found himself in the curious position during the peace conference of constantly diluting the victors' demands for stringent punishments and complicated reassurances of future German passivity. This aspect of the negotiations diverted his efforts to design the league.

The second benefit of a vocabulary for force is that it provides a way to discuss force across space. Highlighting the common purposes among Wilson's resorts to force gives greater insight into why he used force and how he used it. It also offers another perspective for assessing the strengths and weaknesses of armed power. Different interventions can be compared by the common purposes motivating them and the goals they achieved. Using general terms to discuss the several interventions allows similarities and patterns to be identified among them.

The use of force for retribution appeared during the occupation of Veracruz, the Punitive Expedition, and America's entry into World War I. Wilson used force for solution in Haiti and the Dominican Republic. He turned to force for introduction during the occupation of Veracruz, the Punitive Expedition, and World War I. Force for association ran as a common thread throughout the several interventions—Wilson consistently sought some internal group with which to associate—but was most prominent during World War I and the twin interventions in northern Russia and Siberia.

Analyzed according to these components, the uses of force can be described from comparable perspectives. Wilson used force for retribution to exact satisfaction for a petty insult, but also to avenge an unprovoked attack on American territory. He turned to force against Germany to punish its transgressions against international law. There was justice and false pride, flimsy excuses and high ideals, in these resorts to force, but withal there was little satisfaction. In none of these resorts to force did Wilson obtain the reparation he originally sought. As each intervention progressed, other opportunities and new situations developed. Wilson lost interest in vengeance as other opportunities entailing other uses of force opened for him. The pressing need to punish diminished, then dwindled away. Wilson was easily aggrieved, but rarely satisfied.

During each of his interventions, Wilson at some point used protection to justify his actions. When it became clear that the Punitive Expedition would not catch up with Villa, Wilson redefined it as an effort to protect the U.S.

border from further attack. The occupation of Veracruz, though initiated as a use of force for retribution, was prompted to protect U.S. forces by stopping the arms of the *Ypiranga*. It ended in an effort to protect those Mexicans who had worked for the American military government. The occupations of Haiti and the Dominican Republic were intended to protect the Haitians and the Dominicans from their chronic revolutions. War against Germany was a war to protect democracy, while the intervention in Siberia was excused as an effort to protect the Czech legion. The intervention in northern Russia was intended to protect the war supplies stockpiled there. Because protection seemed the most legitimate of motives, Wilson sought always to invoke it, even though it cloaked his true purposes and his actual uses of force.

But by identifying when force for protection was a dominant motive, it is possible to see certain characteristic elements. Protection appealed most to Wilson when he could protect other peoples from themselves, from their own violence and revolutions. He applied it thusly in Haiti and the Dominican Republic before expanding his vision to protect the world from itself during World War I. Like the Christian crusaders of old, Wilson seldom had selfish interests to promote. He was not particularly intent on using force to advance American material interests but instead its ideals and, when the situation demanded it, its citizens and soldiers. For Wilson, force for protection meant protecting other people from themselves.

That style of protection led to the use of force for solution. Once ashore in Haiti and the Dominican Republic, U.S. Marines quickly quelched each nation's chronic revolutions, thus assuring some measure of governmental stability. But Wilson could not leave it at that. He determined to go beyond protection to the solution of Haitian and Dominican turmoil. The marines became harsh tutors, their cane whips ever close to hand, determined to teach each country American-style democracy and capitalism.

What was most intriguing about the combined uses of force for protection and solution in Haiti and the Dominican Republic was their dismal failure over the long-term. Protection works in the short-term but loses its effectiveness over any extended period of time. The occupation of Veracruz disrupted the off-loading of the *Ypiranga*'s arms and spared the Navy from taking on a resupplied Mexican army. Extending the occupation worked as effectively in gaining Carranza's promise not to punish those Mexicans who had helped the occupation forces. For the moment the occupations of Haiti and the Dominican Republic effectively ended the revolutions constantly brewing in each country. But the American troops proved poor tutors, their example more potent than their preaching. In both nations the people learned that a strong reliance on force was far more effective than any trust in the vote. Dictatorship, not democracy, was Wilson's ultimate legacy on the isle of Hispaniola.

Third, a vocabulary for force provides a way to compare instances of force across time. The recent Persian Gulf War provides an example of how uses of force beyond the Wilson era can be described in the same terms. During the Gulf War, President George Bush combined uses of force for protection, retribution, and association against Iraq to thwart what was seen as Iraqi President Saddam Hussein's use of force for aggression.

On 2 August 1990, Saddam Hussein invaded neighboring Kuwait, quickly taking the small, largely defenseless country and annexing it as a province of Iraq. The United States may have unwittingly acquiesced to Saddam's aggressive plans by earlier indicating that it had "no opinion" about his dispute with his neighbor. As U.S. ambassador to Iraq April Glaspie confessed, "We foolishly did not realize that he was stupid." Despite that mistake, President Bush immediately formed an opinion of the invasion itself. From the first Bush determined that "this will not stand. This will not stand—the aggression against Kuwait."[1]

Bush was further discomfited by analyses from the Central Intelligence Agency (CIA) that the invasion of Kuwait was but a brief stopover on Saddam's way to Saudi Arabia. At a meeting of the National Security Council on 3 August, CIA director William Webster reported the agency's conclusion that Saddam intended to take over Saudi Arabia's eastern oilfields. Bush was convinced. That conviction underlay his initial decision to impose economic sanctions on Iraq, establish a worldwide association of nations against the Iraqi dictator, and dispatch a quarter of a million troops to bolster Saudi defenses.[2]

It also underlay his subsequent determination to increase the expeditionary force to half a million men and then to use force to push Saddam out of Iraq. "For me," Bush told his closest advisers in one of those poignantly Wilsonian moments that cropped up throughout the Persian Gulf War, "it boils down to a very moral case of good versus evil, black versus white." If he had to fight, he continued, "it's not going to matter to me if there isn't one congressman who supports this, or what happens to public opinion. If it's right, it's gotta be done." Like Wilson before him, Bush was ever-ready to stand alone if the fight was right or the cause just. Again like Wilson, Bush reserved to himself the definition of right and justice.[3]

Throughout the crisis Bush acted with Wilsonian purpose and with considerable Wilsonian restraint. The rhetoric of the war attacked Saddam's aggression and pledged the protection of the Gulf region. Working through the United Nations, Bush and Secretary of State James A. Baker III for the first time offered the world a glimpse of how the UN can work once relieved of its Cold War divisions. The effort would have done Wilson proud. It was precisely what he had envisioned for his beloved league: the nations of the world united against evil.

In that unity the other nations learned firsthand of the benign restraints of international association. Although repeatedly attacked by Iraqi missiles, neutral Israel held back from its normal policy of taking retribution because of intense pressures from Bush and Baker, who believed that any Israeli response would threaten the coalition. For the first time, several of the Arab states, particularly Syria, publicly recognized Israel's right to self-defense. It was a startling acceptance made palatable by the broad association of nations arrayed against Saddam, the first post–Cold War leader the whole world loved to hate.

In the language of force, Bush used force against Iraq for the protection of Saudi Arabia, in retribution for the invasion of Kuwait, and in practically unanimous association with the international community. By ending the war as soon as Saddam agreed to withdraw his forces from Kuwait, Bush also showed a Wilsonian insight into the limits of force. As Wilson well understood, the thirst for retribution could be better quenched with other uses of force. It may well have been that forcing Saddam from power would have been at the cost of Bush's international associates. Thus, Bush may have abandoned retribution to preserve his use of force for association. Wilson would have empathized.

Perhaps the only thing different that Wilson might have done would have been to protect those internal Iraqi elements, namely, the Kurds, who rose in rebellion at Bush's invitation and who lost, now to face alone Saddam's considerable wrath. But it may be that helping the Kurds also would have been at the cost of Bush's international associates, a price even Wilson would have shied from paying. For all its benefits, using force for association costs a significant loss of freedom of independent action.

Although hostilities have ended, the Persian Gulf War has yet to play itself all the way out. Clearly Bush used the war to introduce the United States to a broader resolution of the problems long besetting the Mideast. Just as clearly, the outcome of the war presents a number of opportunities for imaginative leadership. Exploiting those openings is a test of Wilsonian magnitude.

With the Persian Gulf War, it is possible to illustrate the broad applicability of developing a vocabulary of force. Such a lexicon provides a concise way to study in detail instances of force and to compare them with the details of other instances across space and time. In short, defining the uses of force allows a greater understanding of how force is used. It can then be seen as not only a simple contest of arms but also as an aspect of power. Defined by the political objectives controlling it, force is placed within a broad context of the many types of power available to nations in their dealings with one another.

ABUSES OF FORCE

Understanding force is even more compelling now than in Wilson's day. On 6 August 1945, technology outpaced the politics of war. Because nuclear war meant world destruction, it became all the more important to control the uses of force, tying them as tightly as possible to the objectives of policy while restraining them from getting out of hand. Sophisticated communications and incredibly complicated weapons systems have improved a leader's ability to control force, but the political determination of why force is used and what it is used for has not shared a similar evolution. The methods of force have improved, but not the uses of force.

One of the most fascinating side effects of the Cold War has been the enhanced ability to calibrate force to policy. Unfortunately there has been no equivalent improvement in the ability to define precisely that policy. The ease with which force is applied in the modern world does not equate with using force wisely. All too often during the Cold War the United States seemed to stumble blindly into a military intervention without any clearly defined purpose or objective, without, that is, a wise use of force.

The Vietnam War is the classic case. For the first time technology allowed the precise integration of the military within the president's policy. Tragically, none of the several presidents who oversaw the war ever had a consistent or lucid policy to apply. At lunch every Tuesday, President Lyndon Johnson met with his advisers—civilian and military—to determine that week's bombing targets in Vietnam. Throughout the war, Johnson held as a fundamental article of faith that his military's technical superiority—the precision of its bombing and the equipage of its soldiers—could compel North Vietnam to settle for terms. Unfortunately those terms were never really defined. Johnson prayed for that one bomb that would somehow break North Vietnam's implacable will. Those Tuesday lunches symbolized the ultimate misunderstanding of the Clausewitzian dictum.

When that bomb never exploded, Johnson began to order periodic bombing halts in forlorn gestures of peace. He never seemed to realize that in the midst of what was, for one side at least, full-scale war, relatively minor escalations and deescalations could hardly have much persuasive effect. The Vietminh were fighting for their country and their ideals; the South Vietnamese were battling for, and among, themselves. The Americans were fighting for some inconclusive game of dominoes, some vague cry of freedom.[4]

Johnson's search for the persuasive bomb showed the abuses of force more than its realistic uses. The biggest problem during the Vietnam War was the failure of the United States to articulate clearly its fundamental policy. Without a coherent understanding of its purpose, it could hardly use force to any intelligent effect. Force could not be integrated into policy because there was no policy to embrace it. The United States had, in other words, no particular use of force to apply.

American officials put forth an array of arguments to justify the war. They proffered a supermarket of policies from which one could choose the one best suited to the argument of the moment. Lacking a clear purpose, U.S. policymakers had no intelligible way to incorporate force into their overall strategy. The United States believed it was protecting the world from the expansion of communism, although there was slender evidence to support that theory. The United States was punishing North Vietnam, but never with any steely conviction of just what its crimes were. It was attempting to solve the turmoil in South Vietnam by sponsoring democracy, although bloody coups were condoned, even sponsored. It was trying to introduce itself to negotiations with North Vietnam, but only sporadically, and never with any realistic counterproposals to North Vietnam's objectives. It was associating itself with internal and external groups, but never with any clear program of what those associations entailed. Consequently, whereas the North Vietnamese fought with Wilsonian singlemindedness, the Americans stumbled blindly along, uncertain and unconvinced, yet determined to accomplish something—even if that something remained ill-defined and ever out-of-reach. Ultimately U.S. officials reduced themselves to some inchoate formula of war for peace.

Throughout the war and across three presidential administrations, American policymakers skipped desperately from one use of force to another, hardly pausing to measure the effect of any single use, rarely glancing back to observe any emerging trends, seldom looking forward to obtain a better perspective. Few seemed to comprehend that the uses of force depend on defining the policies under pursuit. The more precise the definition, the more controlled the uses of force and the more adept the incorporation of armed power into the pursuit of those policies. Without a clear enunciation of purpose, armed power is simply a bludgeon, as effective as using a sledgehammer to tune a grand piano. Its destructiveness is unmatched by any balancing constructiveness.

But there was no precision to American policy in Vietnam. Because the Americans were never quite able to define what they were fighting for, they were never able to adjust the fight to their purposes. Instead they just fought and hoped that somehow their advanced technology and superior weaponry would substitute for the lack of policy. Few understood that fighting is neither self-contained nor sui generis. Its purpose must derive from policy. Otherwise, it is meaningless—destruction gratis destruction. The essence of using force has never been so simple a question as to bomb or not to bomb. Ultimately, and perhaps unavoidably, the massacre of Vietnamese civilians at My Lai incarnated the existential absurdity of fighting for peace.

As the Vietnam War amply illustrated, compounding the problem posed by the inability to define policy clearly is the amazing ease and exactitude with which force can now be applied. Technology and communications have outpaced policy, making force quick and precise, transforming it from a ruffian's mugging into a surgeon's incision. The technology of war has become so exacting that political leaders can now refine force to meticulous objectives, even targeting particular individuals. In April 1986 President Ronald Reagan ordered a use of force for retribution against Libya for its sponsorship of terrorist activity. The U.S. Air Force picked among its targets several of the homes where they hoped Libyan leader Muammar al-Quadafi might be staying. That he survived the bombing was more a failure of intelligence to locate his position than of inaccuracy of the bombs.

Within the ease and convenience of resorting to force inhere the abuses of force. Battles too easily consume the politicians. War's technical precision has become too tempting for many national leaders. Rather than set policy, like Johnson they spend their time selecting individual targets. If war, as Georges Clemenceau said, is too important to be left to the generals, it serves little purpose if political leaders assume upon themselves the responsibilities of those generals. War may well be a politician's game, but fighting it is a soldier's.

In the spring of 1980, President Jimmy Carter dispatched a small, elite force to invade Iran and rescue American citizens held hostage in Tehran—a use of force for salvation. Throughout the mission, Carter was in moment-to-moment communications with the unit officers. With the mission sanded down in the Iranian desert, Carter was compelled to order the forces home. Not since Washington took the field against the Whiskey Rebels in 1794 have presidents acted as both commander in chief and field commander. It was not a good combination.

Although the rescue mission was clearly tied to Carter's overriding political goal of effecting, by diplomacy or force, the release of the hostages, the process that allowed him to be commander in chief and field commander was flawed. It also seemed typical of how force is used in modern times. Presidents are able to immerse themselves in the minutia of the battle, thus losing sight of any overall political context. Because the resort to force has become technologically more facile does not mean that its uses have become more intelligible.

Since World War II, U.S. foreign policy has mouthed Wilsonian ideals even as its actions have stripped those fundamentally American precepts of their true meaning. Although Wilson was a force for change in his world, innovative and creative, the United States since World War II has been a force for conservation, reactionary and dull. Like a policeman too long on the beat, American policymakers have become largely negative, generally opposed to any change, to anything new. Their uses of force have expressed tragic stagnation.

Anticommunism replaced proselytizing the American dream as fundamental policy. The United States reacted to the slightest whisper that a neighboring state was flirting with the Soviet Union. Foreign governments were violently toppled and smaller nations invaded because the technology of war made it easier to bring down Salvador Allende in Chile or to send U.S. troops into the Dominican Republic or Grenada. The Shah of Iran was supported long past the time his people had rejected him. Sophisticated weapons were traded for hostages, unsuccessfully, and the profits were used to buy other weapons for "freedom fighters" in Nicaragua. Little thought seems to have been given to the repercussions of these policies. Communism may well have been bankrupted, but at the cost of an indelible bitterness toward the United States and its abuses of force.

Nor does the abrupt demise of the Soviet Union necessarily mean peace on earth, much less the end of history. Although the Soviets were long identified as the major enemy of the United States, they were never the *direct* enemy in any use of force. The closest they came to actual fighting was during the Cuban missile crisis, but that was resolved through diplomatic and military power and not armed power. Instead both nations expended their armed power against smaller, weaker states in eastern Europe and Afghanistan for the Soviet Union and in the Western Hemisphere, Korea, and Vietnam for the United States. Despite the anticommunist rhetoric cloaking the American resorts to force, there is little reason for optimism that the sudden disappearance of communism will somehow make military interventions obsolete.

There are too many other reasons, from drug wars to Iraqi aggression, to call out the troops. The end of communism has considerably lessened the threat of nuclear war, at least in the short term and until other nations— China, Pakistan, Israel, and South Africa, among them—develop adequate delivery systems for their nuclear arsenals. Yet the breakup of the soviet states will have little effect on the employment of conventional forces. The uses of force against Saddam Hussein and Panamanian strongman Manuel Noriega had nothing to do with communism. Current turmoil in Haiti, also completely noncommunist, could easily lead to American intervention. The so-called "peace dividend" affects only the nuclear stockpile, not conventional arms. General Colin Powell, chairman of the joint chiefs of staff, continues to call for a large military establishment posted throughout the world even as President Bush retires significant portions of the nuclear arsenal.

As technology has made force too dangerous to use at one extreme, it has also made it too easy to use and control at levels below that extreme. Rather than find some resolution outside of force, it has become too easy to believe that force itself ever resolved anything. In December 1989 the United States invaded the Republic of Panama in the first of the post–Cold War, noncommunist military interventions. "Operation Just Cause" can be defined as a use of force for retribution against Panama's strongman Manuel Noriega, and a use of force for the solution of Panama's struggle to achieve democracy, as well as a use of force for the protection of the Panama Canal. The first two allowed for the third and were, therefore, the dominant motives.

President Bush pointed to several attacks on Americans in Panama, including the murder of one serviceman and Noriega's impetuous declaration of war against the United States, as sufficient reasons to punish the dictator. Attorney General Dick Thornburgh dispatched two dozen deputy U.S. Marshals to accompany the military invasion. Their mission was to arrest Noriega under an indictment handed down several years earlier by a federal grand jury in Florida. Thornburgh also put a million-dollar reward on Noriega's head. Bush clearly wanted Noriega every bit as much as Wilson had once wanted Villa.

But Bush could have learned from Wilson and saved himself a week's embarrassment. The Punitive Expedition, though intended to "Get Villa," never had that as its official objective. As chief of staff General Hugh Scott pointed out, it was unseemly for a nation as powerful as the United States to go chasing after a single bandit. Besides, he warned Secretary of War Newton Baker, what if Villa escaped, what if he ran clear across Mexico? Consequently, the initial orders to Pershing were changed. He was simply "to locate and disperse or capture" the outlaw band that had attacked Columbus, New Mexico. When Villa did indeed escape, Wilson was still able to claim success for the Punitive Expedition. Villa's bands had been broken up. The wiley bandit no longer posed a serious threat to the United States.

By focusing the invasion on Noriega, Bush embarrassed himself when Noriega slipped through his grasp. As American troops landed in Panama, then spread across the country, Noriega's reign of outlawry was over—he was no longer an effective threat to the United States or to the peace of Panama. Yet once publicly committed to getting Noriega, it became necessary ultimately to surround the papal embassy, blast it with rock music, and wait for Noriega to surrender. The most powerful nation in the world was reduced to playing Bobby Fuller's "I Fought the Law and the Law Won" at full volume as its most potent weapon. As Scott had long ago predicted, it was indeed an unseemly spectacle.

Bush also claimed, as did Wilson before him, that he wanted to restore to Panama the benefits of democracy. By using force to solve Panamanian chaos, he succeeded beyond Wilson's best efforts in Haiti and the Dominican Republic. With a local government waiting in the wings, Bush was able to move quickly to reestablish the appearance of a democratic government. After deputy marshals screened each member appointed to the new government for allegations of prior criminal activity, democracy was seemingly restored to Panama. Once the new government was in place, U.S. troops excused their actions as support of the legitimate government. Wilson never had it so convenient.

Bush can take another lesson from Wilson's experiences in Haiti and the Dominican Republic. Forcibly imposing democracy on another nation risks teaching its people the wrong lesson. What the Haitians and Dominicans learned from American occupation was that a strong, disciplined constabulary best ensured order, not to mention the longevity of the government. They learned the forms of democracy, that is, how to hold elections, but not the substance of democracy: few of the elections were fair. It is simply not enough to force democratic forms on a country. What the Panamanians will learn has yet to be seen.

Wilson's experiences should be clear. Force opened many opportunities for him, but it never—in any of his interventions—provided him an ultimate solution to any international problem. Even the use of force for solution offers no solution. Having taken over Haiti and the Dominican Republic with armed power, Wilson still had to apply diplomatic, economic, and moral power to initiate the reforms that were the true goals of his policies. In both instances the use of force for solution was but one step—neither the first nor the last—in a very long walk. During none of his other military interventions did he expect force to resolve the problems before him. Even during World War I, although force cleared the route toward restructuring the world system according to the principles of collective security, Wilson never had any illusions that force alone could effect that grand ideal.

By recognizing the limits of force and working it in concert with other forms of power, force can be an effective method for achieving international objectives, particularly when the goals are reasonably limited, well defined, and suited to the peculiar attributes of force. Force is an effective method of protection, but only provided that the object is, indeed, defensible. It is, too, a persuasive punishment, but only if its use fits the crime. Force facilitates the introduction of other forms of power to a problem's resolution, but it cannot go beyond that to effect those other types of power or gain the settle-ment. In certain circumstances, it also offers its own solution, but only in the short run and only to the extent that violence unsettles anything. Force lends itself to cooperative associations, but at the price of opening itself to the shift-ing demands and goals that are the price of any alliance.

The crumbling of the Soviet Union and its satellite states signals the dawn of a new era. The Cold War is over. This revolutionary situation provides a number of opportunities giving room for an uncommon optimism. There is a chance that the international system will find peace in cooperation, not—as it has been since World War II—in competition between the Soviets and the United States. One can hope, too, that the United Nations will be in-vigorated, that it will actually become what Franklin Roosevelt, and before him, Woodrow Wilson, hoped collective security would provide.

But there is also enough cause for concern to tinge the jubilation. The end of the Cold War may well allow more frequent resorts to force simply because the system is now imbalanced. The United States may need have no more fear of Russia's response to its deployment of troops. It is possible that the two could act in concert, even so manipulate the United Nations to ensure a unanimous response. Without the Cold War's restraints, we have only our own intelligent trepidations to keep us from using force. Unfortunately, there is little evidence to indicate that when it comes to force, either our intelli-gence or our trepidation is particularly strong.

The public emphasis on Bush's so-called "New World Order" can easily become a reactionary resistance to any future international changes. Force in that circumstance could be just as unthinking as it was in the days when any sign of communism summoned a militant American response. The revolu-tion against Jean-Bertrand Aristade in Haiti led Bush to impose an interna-tional embargo on trade with the hapless country. There was also considerable talk of using force to reinstall the deposed president, to try again, in effect, the Wilsonian tutorial in democracy.

Yet starving Haitians, even fighting them, is not enough to overcome their traditional method of changing governments. No nation can fight the history of another nation. Haitians have always used revolutions, usually relatively bloodless, to change regimes. That this was among the first tests of Bush's "New World Order" is ironic. Should he meet it with force would be a tragic repetition of Wilsonian proselytizing at its most obnoxious.

Subduing by arms does not equate with, nor facilitate, converting a peo-ple to the intricacies of self-government. What they learn is that force is the easy way to rule, far easier than the complex, clumsy methods of democracy. Force can defeat an enemy, but it cannot reform him; it can destroy, but it cannot rebuild. Its effects are entirely destructive; it has no constructive attributes. At the conclusion of every war or military intervention lie the imposing tasks of reform and reconstruction. Other types of power—economic, diplomatic, and moral—are needed to accomplish the rebuilding. As part of this process armed power creates the opportunities to express or facilitate those other forms of power. It is not an end of itself. When the Greeks finally embarked on their homeward odyssey, they left Troy a smoldering ruin—and the gods punished them for their impudence.

Our generation manifests a greater arrogance—and risks a more terrifying punishment. The means of controlling force, the systems and process, the technology and equipment, are well in place. What we lack is the reasoned ability to define force strictly by the policies under pursuit and to apply force only when those policies are better served in no other way. In some ways we have become too habituated to the uses of force without learning how to apply those uses practically. By treating armed power as substantially different from other types of power we exalt force beyond its capabilities. As potent as force is, it is an implementation only, not a consummation. It is a means among many to an end, but it is never the end.

The uses of force are simply the execution of policy, in substance little different from the exercise of economic or diplomatic power. If we can begin to understand them as nothing more than that, if we can distinguish force solely by the policies enlivening it, then we chance imposing greater controls on the resorts to force. Defining those uses is a first step to gaining that control. The uses of force need not be synonymous with the abuses of force; they become so only as they are abused by our insolence.

NOTES

1. THE USES OF FORCE IN WILSONIAN DIPLOMACY

1. Frederick S. Calhoun, *Power and Principle: Armed Intervention in Wilsonian Foreign Policy* (Kent, Ohio: Kent State Univ. Press, 1986), 250–67.
2. Woodrow Wilson, "A Commencement Address," 5 June 1914, in Arthur Link, ed., *The Papers of Woodrow Wilson* (Princeton, N.J.: Princeton Univ. Press, 1979), 30:146; see also Wilson, "Address to the Graduating Class of the United States Naval Academy," 5 June 1914, in James Brown Scott, ed., *President Wilson's Foreign Policy: Messages, Addresses, Papers* (New York: Oxford Univ. Press, 1918), 53, 52; Calhoun, *Power and Principle*, 251.
3. Calhoun, *Power and Principle*, 34–51.
4. Ibid., 51–67.
5. Ibid., 69–113.
6. Ibid., 114–84.
7. Ibid., 185–218.
8. Adm. Bradley Fiske, Diary entry, 27 Oct. 1914, Bradley A. Fiske Papers, Library of Congress Manuscript Division, Washington, D.C. (hereafter cited as Fiske Papers); William S. Graves, *America's Siberian Adventure, 1918–1920* (New York: J. Cape and H. Smith, 1931), 343.
9. Gen. Tasker H. Bliss to Hamilton Holt, 11 Oct. 1918, Papers of Gen. Tasker H. Bliss, Library of Congress Manuscript Division, Washington, D.C. (hereafter cited as Bliss Papers); Bliss to Sec. of State Robert Lansing, 19 Apr. 1919, Bliss Papers.
10. Gen. Bliss to Nellie Bliss, 25 Mar. 1919; Bliss to Seward Prosser, 6 Mar. 1919, all in Bliss Papers.
11. Woodrow Wilson, "Address at Peace Conference," 14 Feb. 1919, quoted in Donald Day, *Woodrow Wilson's Own Story* (Boston: Little, Brown, 1952), 322.
12. Woodrow Wilson, "A Speech Accepting a Statue of Philip Kearney," 11 Nov. 1914, in Link, ed., *Papers of Woodrow Wilson* (Princeton, N.J.: Princeton Univ. Press, 1979), 31:562; Wilson, "Address to Seventh Annual Dinner of Railway Business Association," 27 Jan. 1916, in Ray S. Baker and William E. Dodd, *The Public Papers of Woodrow Wilson, The New Democracy* (New York: Harper and Bros., 1926), 2:8–9; Harley Notter, *The Origins of the Foreign Policy of Woodrow Wilson* (Baltimore, Md.: Johns Hopkins Univ. Press, 1937), 186; Wilson, "Bible and Progress," 7 May 1911, quoted in Baker and Dodd, *The Public Papers of Woodrow Wilson, College and State* (New York: Harper and Bros., 1925), 2:294.
13. Wilson, "Address to National Press Club," 15 May 1916, in Baker and Dodd, *New Democracy* 2:171; Wilson, "Address at Soldiers Hall, Pittsburgh," in Baker and Dodd, *New Democracy* 2:26.

14. Wilson, "Speech at Cincinnati," in Baker and Dodd, *New Democracy* 2:380; Wilson, "Address before Salesmanship Congress, Detroit," 10 July 1916, in Baker and Dodd, *New Democracy* 2:229; "Speech at Omaha," in Baker and Dodd, *New Democracy* 2:348.

15. Calhoun, *Power and Principle*, 34–68.

2. FORCE FOR PROTECTION

1. Frederick S. Calhoun, *Power and Principle*, 39–44.

2. For the facts leading to the occupation, see Adm. Frank Fletcher to Sec. of the Navy, 9 Apr. 1914, RG 45, U.S. Navy Records, WE-5, Despatches File, NA (hereafter cited as RG 45, WE-5, Despatches); William Canada to Sec. of State, 12 Apr. 1914, RG 59, U.S. Dept. of State Records Relating to Mexico, 812.00 / 11478, NA (hereafter cited as RG 59); Fletcher to Sec. of the Navy, 13 Apr. 1914, RG 45, WE-5, Despatches; Leonard Wood, Diary entry, 20 Apr. 1914, Papers of General Leonard Wood, Library of Congress Manuscript Division (hereafter cited as Wood Papers). The best secondary accounts are Robert Quirk, *An Affair of Honor: Woodrow Wilson and the Occupation of Veracruz* (Lexington: Univ. of Kentucky Press, 1962); Jack Sweetman, *The Landing at Veracruz: 1914* (Annapolis, Md.: United States Naval Institute Press, 1968); Richard Challener, *Admirals, Generals, and American Foreign Policy, 1898–1914* (Princeton, N.J.: Princeton Univ. Press, 1973), 379–97; Arthur Link, *Wilson: The New Freedom* (Princeton, N.J.: Princeton Univ. Press, 1956), 394–416; and Calhoun, *Power and Principle*, 39–51.

3. Josephus Daniels, *The Life of Woodrow Wilson* (Westport, Conn.: Greenwood Press, 1971), 183.

4. Canada to Dept. of State, 18 Apr. 1914, RG 59, 812.00 / 11547; Canada to Sec. of State, "Subject: Report. Occupation of the Port of Veracruz by the American Forces, April 21st and 22nd, 1914," RG 94, U.S. Department of the Army, Records of the Adjutant General's Office, AGO 2202145, Inclosure 2, NA (hereafter cited as RG 94, AGO).

5. Henry Breckinridge Diary entries, 19 Apr. and 29 May 1914, Papers of Henry Breckinridge, Library of Congress Manuscript Division, Washington, D.C. (hereafter cited as Breckinridge Papers).

6. Daniels to Adm. Frank F. Fletcher, 1 A.M., 20 Apr. 1914, Papers of Josephus Daniels, Library of Congress Manuscript Division, Washington, D.C. (hereafter cited as Daniels Papers), Subject File 536; D. F. Malone to William Jennings Bryan, 20 April 1914, Papers of Woodrow Wilson, Ser. 2, Library of Congress Manuscript Division (hereafter cited as Wilson Papers); Fletcher to Daniels, 11 P.M., 20 Apr. 1914, RG 45, WE-5, Despatches.

7. Michael Meyer, "The Arms of the *Ypiranga*," *Hispanic American Historical Review* 50 (Aug. 1970):551–52; Quirk, *An Affair of Honor*, 69–70; Daniels to Fletcher, 5 P.M. and midnight, 20 Apr. 1914; Rough Notes and Information by Lt. Col. A. Morano, 20 Apr. 1914, all in RG 45, WE-5, Despatches; Wood Diary entry, 20 Apr. 1914, Wood Papers.

8. Wood Diary entry, 20 Apr. 1914, Wood Papers; Daniels to Fletcher, 5:50 A.M., 21 Apr. 1914; Report of Adm. F. F. Fletcher, "Seizure and Occupation of Vera Cruz April 21–April 30th, 1914," both in RG 45, WE-5, Despatches.

9. Adm. Charles Badger to Sec. of the Navy, 24 Apr. 1914, Fletcher to Secy. of the Navy, 25 Apr. 1914, both in RG 45, WE-5, Despatches; Bryan to German Ambassador, 29 Apr. 1914, RG 59, 812.00 / 11922a; Bryan to American Commissioners, 6 June 1914, RG 59, 812.00 / 12631 1 / 2; Badger to Daniels, "Report on Operations of Atlantic Fleet, East Coast of Mexico, May 16–31, 1914," 13 July 1914, RG 45, U.S. Navy Department Records, Area File, Caribbean, Box 158, NA (hereafter cited as RG 45, Area File C); Lindley Garrison to Bryan, 26 May

1914, Wilson Papers, Ser. 2; Gen. Frederick Funston to AGO, 26 May 1914, War Diary, U.S. Expeditionary Forces, Galveston, Texas, to Veracruz, Mexico, 1914, RG 94, AGO 2228507, Inclosure 38 (hereafter cited as War Diary); Bryan to American Commissioners, 6 June 1914, RG 59, 812.00 / 12164 1 / 2.

10. Funston to AGO, 22 Sept. 1914, RG 94, AGO 2211488BCC, filed with 2149991; Garrison to Wilson, 22 Sept. 1914, Wilson Papers, Ser. 2.

11. Bryan to Garrison, 8 June 1914, RG 94, AGO 2171826A.

12. Garrison to Funston, 15 Sept. 1914, RG 94, AGO 2209440, filed with 2149991.

13. Funston to AGO, 17 Sept. 1914, RG 94, AGO 2209440A, filed with 2149991, and 20 Sept. 1914, RG 94, AGO 2210809, filed with 2149991.

14. Garrison to Bryan, 21 Sept. 1914, RG 94, AGO 2211572; Garrison to Wilson, 21 Sept. 1914, RG 94, AGO 2214383, filed with 2149991.

15. Garrison to Wilson, 22 Sept. 1914, RG 94, AGO 2212892, filed with 2149991; Robert Lansing to Brazilian Minister, 22 Sept. 1914, RG 59, 812.00 / 13384.

16. Wilson to Bryan, 2 Oct. 1914, RG 59, 812.00 / 13407.

17. Gen. W. W. Wotherspoon to Gen. Tasker H. Bliss, 10 Oct. 1914, Bliss Papers; Funston to AGO, 15 Oct. 1914, RG 94, AGO 2219800A, filed with 2149991.

18. Wotherspoon to Bliss, 3 Nov. 1914, Bliss Papers; Lansing to Brazilian Minister, 1 Nov. 1914, RG 59, 812.00 / 13610; James Silliman to Bryan, 9 Nov. 1914, RG 59, 812.00 / 13728, 10 Nov. 1914, RG 59, 812.00 / 13730 and 10 Nov. 1914, RG 59, 812.00 / 13732 (two letters).

19. Garrison to Daniels, 14 Nov. 1914, RG 94, AGO 2228507, filed with 2149991; Funston to AGO, 23 Nov. 1914, RG 94, AGO 2228507E, filed with 2149991; Funston to AGO, 3 Dec. 1914, RG 94, AGO 2228507G, filed with 2149991.

20. Blanchard to Bryan, 24 Feb. 1915, RG 59, Dept. of State, Records Relating to Internal Affairs of Haiti, 838.00 / 1119, NA; Blanchard to Bryan, 27 Feb. 1915, RG 59, 838.00 / 1122.

21. Calhoun, *Power and Principle*, 89.

22. Boaz Long to Bryan, 23 Jan. 1914, Wilson Papers, Ser. 2; Lemuel W. Livingston to Secy. of State, 19 Dec. 1914, RG 59, 838.00 / 1072.

23. Memo by unknown author, USS *Washington*, ca. Jan. 1915, RG 45, WA-7; Campaign Order No. 1 by Comdr. R. C. Moody, USS *Wheeling*, 31 Jan. 1915, RG 45, Area File C; Rear Adm. William B. Caperton, "History of U.S. Naval Operations under the Command of Rear Admiral William B. Caperton, U.S.N., commencing January 5, 1915, ending April 30, 1919," RG 45, Subject File 1911–27, ZN, Box 802, pp. 14, 2–3, (hereafter cited as Caperton Report); Caperton to Comdr. J. H. Y. Blakely, 19 Feb. 1914, RG 45, Area File C.

24. Wilson to John F. Fort, 2 Aug. 1915, Wilson Papers, Ser. 4; Bryan to Blanchard for Fort, 27 Feb. 1915, RG 59, 838.00 / 1382; Wilson to Bryan, 13 Jan. 1915, Wilson Papers, Ser. 3.

25. Adm. George Dewey to Secy. of the Navy John D. Long, 10 Dec. 1900, RG 45, U.S. Navy Department Records, Letters of the General Board, NA (hereafter cited as RG 45); Testimony of Adm. William Caperton, U.S. Congress, Senate, *Inquiry into the Occupation and Administration of Haiti and the Dominican Republic*, Report No. 794. 67th Cong., 2d sess., 1922 (hereafter cited as Senate Inquiry), 295; Bryan to Wilson, 21 Jan. 1914, RG 59, Dept. of State Records, Correspondence between Woodrow Wilson and Secy. of State William Jennings Bryan, NA (hereafter cited as Wilson-Bryan Correspondence).

26. Bryan to Wilson, 14 June 1913, RG 59, Wilson-Bryan Correspondence; Adm. Caperton to Secy. of the Navy, 23 Nov. 1915, RG 94, Records of the General Board; Challener, *Admirals, Generals*, 45, 379–81; Arthur Link, *Wilson: The Struggle for Neutrality*, (Princeton, N.J.: Princeton Univ. Press, 1960), 517; Jordon Stabler to Bryan, 3 Feb. 1914, Wilson Papers, Ser. 2; Memo, unsigned, 14 May 1914, RG 59, 838.00 / -; Hans Schmidt, *The United States Occu-*

pation of Haiti, 1915–1934 (New Brunswick, N.J.: Rutgers Univ. Press, 1971), 56, 59; Lansing to Senator McCormick, 4 May 1922, Senate Inquiry, 32–34.

27. Boaz Long to William Phillips, 16 May 1914, RG 59, 838.00 / 1669; Memo to Senator McCormick from Maj. Edwin N. McClellan, USMC, Senate Inquiry, 63; U.S. Dept. of the Navy, *Annual Report of the Department of the Navy, Fiscal Year 1914*, 469.

28. Schmidt, *Occupation of Haiti*, 54; Calhoun, *Power and Principle*, 90–91.

29. Bryan to Wilson, 18 Dec. 1914, Wilson Papers, Ser. 4; Bryan to Blanchard, 12 Dec. 1914, RG 59, 838.51 / 379; Bryan to Bernstorff, 16 Sept. 1914, RG 59, 838.51 / 354.

30. Bryan to Blanchard, 19 Dec. 1914, RG 59, 838.00 / 1065, and 12 Dec. 1914, RG 59, 838.51 / 379; Unsigned State Dept. memo, 25 June 1914, RG 59, 838.00 / -; Bryan to Blanchard, 2 July 1914, RG 59, 838.51 / 341a.

31. Bryan to Wilson, 7 Jan. and Apr. 2, 1915, RG 59, Wilson-Bryan Correspondence; Wilson to Bryan, 26 Mar. 1914, Wilson Papers; Bryan to Daniels, 10 July 1914, RG 59, 838.00 / 954; Press Notice on Marines Sent to Haiti, 13 July 1914, RG 59, 838.00 / -; Wilson, "Remarks at a Press Conference," 23 July 1914, in Link, *Papers of Woodrow Wilson*, 30:296; Lansing to Daniels, 20, 28 Oct. 1914, RG 59, 838.00 / 1059a and 1059b; Lansing to Wilson, 28 Oct. 1914, RG 59, 838.00 / 1078a; Lansing to American Legation, Haiti, 30 Oct. 1914, RG 59, 838.00 / 1006; Plan of Occupation, Fifth Regiment, USMC, 9 Nov. 1914, RG 45, WA-7, Attachés Reports, Dept. of the Navy Records, NA (hereafter cited as RG 45, WA-7, Attachés Reports); Caperton to Commanding Officer, *Descartes*, 2 July 1915, RG 45, Area File C.

32. Caperton testimony, Senate Inquiry, 307; Lansing to Daniels, 28 July 1915, RG 59, 838.00 / 1220; Caperton Report, 47.

33. Wilson to Daniels, 31 July 1915, Daniels Papers.

34. Lansing to Wilson, 3 Aug. 1915, RG 59, 838.00 / 1275b; Wilson to Lansing, 4 Aug. 1915, RG 59, 838.00 / 1418; Wilson to Daniels, 4 Aug. 1915, Wilson Papers.

35. Lansing to McCormick, Senate Inquiry, Appendix B, 37.

36. Ibid.

37. Bryan to Wilson, 8 July 1914, Wilson Papers; "San Domingo. Proposed Memorandum," Wilson Papers, Ser. 2.

38. Bryan to James M. Sullivan, 9 Sept. 1913, RG 59, Dept. of State Records Relating to the Internal Affairs of Santo Domingo, 839.00 / 912a, NA; Bryan to Sullivan, 4 Apr. 1914, RG 59, 839.00 / 1136; Bryan to Wilson, 26 Feb. 1914, RG 59, Wilson-Bryan Correspondence.

39. Calhoun, *Power and Principle*, 76–80.

40. Lansing to Bryan, 30 May 1914, RG 59, 839.00 / 1520; Bryan to Sullivan, 28 May 1914, RG 59, 839.00 / 1245; Bryan to Wilson, 2 July 1914, Wilson Papers.

41. Calhoun, *Power and Principle*, 84–86.

42. Capt. E. W. Eberle to Commanding Officers in San Domingo, 8 Oct. 1914, RG 45, WA-7; Bryan to Sullivan, 14 Nov. 1914, RG 59, 839.00 / 1608.

43. J. W. Wright to Lansing, 24 Jan. 1916, RG 59, 839.00 / 1781; Gen. Frank McIntyre to Clarence Baxter, 4 June 1915, RG 139, Dept. of the Army, Records of the Dominican Customs Receivership, DCR 58, NA (hereafter cited as RG 139, DCR).

44. Bryan to Wilson, 15 Jan. 1915, RG 59, Wilson-Bryan Correspondence; Bryan to Sullivan, 12 Jan. 1915, RG 59, 839.00 / 1660a, 13 Feb. 1915, RG 59, 839.00 / 1678, 2 Feb. 1915, RG 59, 839.00 / 1668, 9 Apr. 1915, 839.00 / 1684, and 20 Apr. 1915, RG 59, 839.00 / 1687.

45. Calhoun, *Power and Principle*, 105–6.

46. Johnson to Secy. of State, 5 Sept. 1915, RG 59, 839.00 / 1749; 9 Sept. 1915, RG 59, 839.00 / 1765 1 / 2, and 4 Sept. 1915, RG 59, 839.00 / 1747.

47. Wilson to William W. Russell, 31 July 1915, Papers of Ray Stannard Baker, Library of Congress Manuscript Division (hereafter cited as R. S. Baker Papers); Lansing to Russell, 17 Sept. 1915, RG 59, 839.51 / 1633a.

48. Long to Wright, 18 Nov. 1915, RG 59, 839.00 / 1715.

49. Lansing to Wilson, 24 Nov. 1915, RG 59, 839.00 / 1776; Lansing to Russell, 2 Dec. 1915, RG 59, 839.00 / 1651.

50. Calhoun, *Power and Principle*, 108–9; Lansing to American Legation, 29 Apr. 1916, RG 59, 839.00 / 1806; Lansing to Daniels, 29 Apr. 1916, RG 49, WA-7.

51. Russell to Secy. of State, 5 May 1916, RG 59, 839.00 / 1814 and 1817; Daniels to Lansing, 3 May 1916, RG 49, WA-7, 2781824-152; Caperton to Adm. William S. Benson, 5 May 1916, Papers of Adm. William Caperton, Library of Congress Manuscript Division (hereafter cited as Caperton Papers); Benson to Caperton, 5 May 1916; Caperton to Secy. of the Navy, 6 May 1916 (two letters) all in RG 127, U.S.M.C., Records of the Office of the Commandant, NA, MC 1975-70 / 5-2:52655 (hereafter cited as RG 127, MC).

52. Caperton to Secy. of the Navy, 6 May 1915, RG 127, MC 9:25a and RG 49, Area File C.

53. Calhoun, *Power and Principle*, 109–10; Lansing to Russell, 7 May 1916, RG 59, 839.00 / 1818; Benson to Caperton, 6 May 1916, RG 45, WA-7.

54. Campaign Order No. 2, 21 May 1916, RG 45, Area File C; Russell to Secy. of State, 5 June 1919, RG 59, 839.00 / 2123; C. S. Freeman to Secy. of the Navy, 10 Nov. 1920, RG 45, Secy. of the Navy 16870-561.

55. Memo to Scott from Baker, 19 Apr. 1916, Scott Papers; Adj. Gen. to Scott and Funston, 26 Apr. 1916, RG 94, AGO 2394312A14.

56. Lansing to all Central and South American Missions, 21 June 1916, RG 59, 812.00 / 18534a; Lansing to Wilson, 21 June 1916, RG 59, 812.00 / 18533a.

3. FORCE FOR RETRIBUTION

1. William Bishop, *International Law: Cases and Materials* (Boston, Mass.: Little, Brown, 1971), 902–5.

2. Memo, unsigned but probably by Robert Lansing, 14 April 1914, RG 59, 812.00 / 11510 1 / 2.

3. For Wilson's descriptions of his policies, see Link, *Papers of Woodrow Wilson*, 29:468–70, 488, 493, and 452–53; Daniel M. Smith, *Robert Lansing and American Neutrality 1914–1917* (New York: DaCapo Press, 1972), 13–14; James Brown Scott, *President Wilson's Foreign Policy*, 37.

4. Josephus Daniels to Adm. Frank F. Fletcher, 21 Apr. 1914, Daniels Papers, Subject File 136; William Jennings Bryan to Judge Charles Douglas, undated, RG 59, 812.00 / 12631 1 / 2; Bryan to Carothers, 21 Apr. 1914, RG 59, 812.00 / 11637a; Lindley Garrison to Gen. Frederick Funston, 14 May 1914, RG 94, AGO 2160103, filed with 2149991; Judge Adv. Gen. to Chief of Staff, 22 Oct. 1914, RG 94, AGO 2218767A.

5. L. F. L. Oppenheim, *International Law: War and Neutrality*, 2d ed. (New York: Longman's Green, 1912), 39, 44; William E. Hall, *A Treatise on International Law*, ed. J. B. Atlay, 5th ed. (London: Clarendon Press, 1904), 367–68; Henry Wheaton, *Elements of International Law*, ed. Richard H. Dana, Jr., 8th ed. (Boston: Little, Brown, 1866), 336; John B. Moore, *A Digest of International Law* (Washington, D.C.: GPO, 1906), 3:120.

6. Link, ed., *Papers of Woodrow Wilson*, 29:441; Daniels to R. S. Baker, ca. 13 Apr. 1929, R. S. Baker Papers; James Brown Scott, ed., *Foreign Policy*, 33–36, 38.

7. "The Tampico Incident," undated, unsigned but marginal notation indicates Adm. Victor Blue as author, Daniels Papers, Subject File 537; Frederick S. Calhoun, *Power and Principle*, 42–47.

8. Daniels to Fletcher, 21 April 1914, 1 A.M. and 5:50 A.M., RG 45, Subject File, WE-5, Despatches; N. P. Moore to Fletcher, 22 April 1914, RG 45, Area Files C, Box 157; Charles Badger intercept of State Dept. telegram to American Consul, Puerto México, 22 Apr. 1914, RG 45, Subject File, WE-5; Navy Dept. Bulletin No. 29, 23 April 1914, RG 45, Area Files C, Box 157; Robert Quirk, *An Affair of Honor*, 103.

9. Bryan to James Carothers, 22 Apr. 1914, RG 59, 812.00 / 11634d, specified that the action was directed against Huerta alone. Wilson made the same point in his speech to Congress on 20 Apr. 1914 (see Scott, *Foreign Policy*, 33–36).

10. Henry Dodge to Bryan, 20 May 1914, RG 59, 812.00 / 12136, and 12 June 1914, RG 59, 812.00 / 12239; Protocol No. 4, 24 June 1914, in Dodge to Bryan, 3 July 1914, RG 59, 812.00 / 12421.

11. Zachary N. Cobb to Secy. of State, 9 Mar. 1916, RG 59, 812.00 / 17385.

12. Annual Report, Fiscal Year 1916, by Funston, undated, RG 94, AGO 2480591. The best histories of the Punitive Expedition are Frank Tompkins, *Chasing Villa: The Story Behind the Story of Pershing's Expedition into Mexico* (Harrisburg, Pa: Military Service Publishing, 1934) and Donald Smythe, *Guerrilla Warrior: The Early Life of General John J. Pershing* (New York: Charles Scribner's Sons, 1973).

13. Secy. of State to Charles Paerk, representing American interests in Mexico City, 9 Mar. 1916, RG 59, 812.00 / 17377; Funston to Adj. Gen., 9 Mar. 1916, RG 94, AGO 2377335G, and 10 Mar. 1916, RG 94, AGO 2377335J, both filed with 2212358.

14. Memo, Secy. of the Navy Josephus Daniels, 14 Mar. 1916, Daniels Papers; Joseph Tumulty to Wilson, 15 Mar. 1916, Papers of Joseph Tumulty, Library of Congress Manuscript Division (hereafter cited as Tumulty Papers); Funston to AGO, 17 Mar. 1916, RG 94, AGO 2380672, and 4 Apr. 1916, RG 94, AGO 2379201, Add 68, both filed with 2377632; Franklin K. Lane to Wilson, 13 Mar. 1916, Wilson Papers, Ser. 2.

15. Gen. Tasker Bliss to AGO, 10 Mar. 1916, RG 94, AGO 2377632A; Gen. Hugh Scott to W. E. Wilder, 22 July 1916, Papers of Hugh S. Scott, Library of Congress Manuscript Division, Washington, D.C. (hereafter cited as Scott Papers); Hugh L. Scott, *Some Memories of a Soldier* (New York: Appleton Century, 1928), 519–20; Memo for Chief of Staff from Newton D. Baker, 10 Mar. 1916, RG 94, AGO 2377632, Add B 1 / 2; Baker to Wilson, 10 Mar. 1916, Wilson Papers, Ser. 2.

16. Bliss to AGO, 10 Mar. 1916, RG 94, AGO 2377632A; White House Announcement, *New York Times*, 11 Mar. 1916; Robert Lansing to All American Consular Officers in Mexico, 10 Mar. 1916, RG 59, 812.00 / 17426a; Baker to Wilson, 10 Mar. 1916, Wilson Papers, Ser. 2; Scott to AGO, 10 Mar. 1916, RG 94, AGO 2377632; Scott to George Carothers, 17 Mar. 1916, Scott Papers; AGO to Funston, no date, RG 94, AGO 2377632, O; Scott to Leonard Wood, 11 Mar. 1916, Scott Papers.

17. Scott to M. M. Parker, 18 Mar. 1916, RG 94, AGO 2381631; Scott to James Garfield, 17 Apr. 1916, Scott Papers; Memo for the Chief of Staff from Baker, 16 Mar. 1916, RG 94, AGO 2378799B; Lansing to James L. Rodgers, 14 Apr. 1916, RG 43, Rodgers File.

18. Wilson to Lansing, 13 Mar. 1916, RG 59, 812.00 / 17743.

19. Handwritten notes inscribed "Prepared to use with Prest.," by Lansing, ca. 22 June 1916, RG 59, 812.00 / 18534 1 / 2.

20. Leon J. Canova to Lansing, 19 June 1916, RG 59, 812.00 / 20525; Lansing to Wilson, 21 June 1916, RG 59, 812.00 / 18533a.

21. Wilson to Lansing, 21 June 1916, RG 59, 812.00 / 18533 1 / 2; Wilson to Louis Wiley, 22 June 1916, Wilson Papers, Ser. 2; Wilson to House, 22 June 1916, R. S. Baker Papers.

22. Memo of a Conversation with Mr. Arredondo by Lansing, 9 Mar. 1916, RG 59, 812.00 / 17510 1 / 2.

23. James Silliman to Secy. of State, 11 Mar. 1916, RG 59, 812.00 / 17415.

24. Lansing to Silliman, 13 Mar. 1916, RG 94, AGO 2378907, and RG 59, 812.00 / 17415.

25. Acting Secy. of State Frank Polk to All American Consular Officers in Mexico, 14 Mar. 1916, RG 59, 812.00 / 17455; Polk to John W. Belt, 15 Mar. 1916, RG 59, 812.00 / 1752 4a; Silliman to Secy. of State, 15 Mar. 1916, RG 59, 812.00 / 17491.

26. Bliss to Scott, 13 Mar. 1916, Bliss Papers; Calhoun, *Power and Principle*, 53–55.

27. Licenciado E. Arredondo to Secy. of State, 18 Mar. 1916, RG 59, 812.00 / 17920; Memo of conversation with Arredondo by Polk, 18 Mar. 1916, RG 59, 812.00 / 24290.

28. Arredondo to Polk, 19 Mar. 1916, RG 59, 812.00 / 18481, and 812.00 / 17593; Rodgers to Secy. of State, 19 Mar. 1916, and Polk to Rodgers, 20 Mar. 1916, RG 59, 812.00 / 17529; Lansing to Arredondo, 4 Apr. 1916, RG 59, 812.00 / 17650 1 / 2; Arredondo to Lansing, 13 Apr. 1916, RG 59, 812.00 / 17867.

29. Scott to Col. J. T. Dickman, 8 Apr. 1916, Scott Papers.

30. Funston to AGO, quoting Gen. John J. Pershing, 1238, 14 Apr. 1916, RG 94, AGO 2379210A107; Funston to AGO, quoting Funston to Pershing, 19 May 1916, RG 94, AGO 2379210A194; Funston to Scott, 30 May 1916 and Funston to James Parker, 27 May 1916, both in Funston Papers; Pershing to Theodore Roosevelt, 24 May 1916; Pershing to Bird McGuire, 15 June 1916, Pershing to Frank P. Holm, 19 June 1916, Pershing to Charles R. Cameron, 15 June 1916, all in Papers of Gen. John J. Pershing, Library of Congress Manuscript Division (hereafter cited as Pershing Papers).

31. Memo to Scott from Baker, 19 Apr. 1916, Scott Papers.

32. Lansing to Baker, 22 Apr. 1916, RG 59, 812.00 / 24290a; AGO to Scott and Funston, 26 Apr. 1916, RG 94, AGO 2394312A14. For a discussion of the Scott-Obregón conference, see Calhoun, *Power and Principle*, 60–62.

33. Secy. of Foreign Relations, Mexico, to Lansing, 22 May 1916, in U.S. Dept. of State, *Foreign Relations of the United States, 1916* (Washington, D.C.: GPO, 1928); Polk to Wilson, 31 May and 1 June 1916, both in Wilson Papers.

34. Pershing to Frederick Palmer, 23 Oct. 1916, Pershing Papers.

35. Wilson, "Flag Day Address," 14 June 1917, in Ray S. Baker and William E. Dodd, *The Public Papers of Woodrow Wilson: War and Peace* (New York: Harper and Brothers, 1927), 1:61.

36. Wilson, "Speech to Congress," 2 Apr. 1917, in Baker and Dodd, *War and Peace* 1:6–11.

37. Ibid., 1:11–16.

38. Wilson, "Address Accepting Democratic Nomination," 2 Sept. 1916, in Baker and Dodd, *New Democracy* 2:282; Wilson to Congressman J. Thomas Heflin, 27 May 1917, in Baker and Dodd, *War and Peace* 1:47.

39. Unsigned memo reporting conversation with Lindley Garrison, 5 May 1915, Papers of Enoch Crowder, Western Historical Manuscripts Collection, State Historical Society of Missouri Manuscripts, Columbia, Missouri (hereafter cited as Crowder Papers).

40. Lansing to Bryan, 1 June 1915, Wilson Papers, Ser. 2.

41. Wilson to Edith Boling Galt, 19 Aug. 1915, Wilson Papers, Ser. 20.

42. Wilson, "Speech to Congress," 2 Apr. 1917, in Baker and Dodd, *War and Peace* 1:7.

4. FORCE FOR SOLUTION

1. Woodrow Wilson, "Address to National Press Club," 15 May 1916, in Ray S. Baker and William E. Dodd, *New Democracy* 2:171.

2. Wilson, "Address to Joint Session of Congress," 11 Nov. 1918, in Baker and Dodd, *War and Peace* 1:361.

3. Wilson, "Address at Rome," 3 Jan. 1919, in Baker and Dodd, *War and Peace* 1:361.

4. Gen. Smedley Butler Testimony, Senate Inquiry, 518.

5. Gen. Frederick Funston to AGO, 3 May 1914, RG 94, AGO 2155673H, filed with 2149991; Leonard Wood to E. St. Loe Strackey, 28 May 1914, Wood Papers.

6. "Memorandum in Reference to the Methods to Be Employed in the Capture and Occupation of Latin-American Cities," by Command of Brig. Gen. Funston, Bing Alvord, Acting Chief of Staff, 10 August 1914, RG 94, AGO 2228507, Enc 29, WCD 6476-61, Exhibit I.

7. Lindley Garrison to Funston, 14 May 1914, RG 94, AGO 2160103, filed with 2149991.

8. Adm. Frank F. Fletcher, Proclamation of 26 Apr. 1914, Appendix to "Report on the Military Government of Vera Cruz, Mexico," RG 94, AGO 2228507, Enc 40, WCD 6476-61; War Dept. Bulletin No. 29, 3 May 1914, RG 94, AGO 2160103A; Memo for the Chief of Staff from Brig. Gen. Joseph E. Kuhn, "Subject: Report of Occupation of Vera Cruz, Mexico," 9 Mar. 1917, RG 165, Records of the Military Intelligence Div., War College Div., WCD 6476-61, NA (hereafter cited as RG 165, WCD); Funston to AGO, 12 May 1914, RG 94, AGO 2162826, and 8 May 1914, AGO 2160103D, both filed with 2149991.

9. "Report of Operations of U.S. Expeditionary Forces at Vera Cruz Covering the Period from April 20 to June 30, 1914," submitted by Brig. Gen. Funston, 30 June 1914, RG 94, AGO 2228507, WCD 6476-60.

10. "Operations of U.S. Expeditionary Forces," Extracts from Report of Brig. Gen. Funston on the Military Occupation of Vera Cruz, Mexico, April–Nov. 1914, RG 165, Entry 282, Box 180; Robert Quirk, *An Affair of Honor*, 129–35.

11. Ibid.

12. Ibid.

13. Hans Schmidt, *Occupation of Haiti*, 74.

14. Wilson to Edith B. Galt, 15 Aug. 1915, Wilson Papers, Ser. 20; Wilson to Galt, 30 and 23 Aug. 1915, Wilson Papers, Ser. 12.

15. Wilson to Galt, 15 Aug. 1915, Wilson Papers, Ser. 20, 9 Sept. 1915, Wilson Papers, Ser. 2; Wilson to John F. Fort, 2 Aug. 1915, Wilson Papers, Ser. 4, CF612, Haiti.

16. Robert Lansing to Col. Edward M. House, 15 Aug. 1915, in U.S. Dept. of State, *Papers Relating to the Foreign Relations of the United States: The Lansing Papers* (Washington, D.C.: GPO, 1920) 1:129; Lansing to Wilson, 13 Aug. 1915, RG 59, 711.38 / 24A.

17. Lansing to Wilson, 3 Aug. 1915, RG 59, 838.00 / 1275B, and 2 Aug. 1915, Wilson Papers, Ser. 2.

18. Wilson to Lansing, 4 Aug. 1915, RG 59, 838.00 / 1418; Wilson to Galt, 15 Aug. 1915, Wilson Papers, Ser. 20.

19. Lansing to Am. Legation, Haiti, 10 Aug. 1915, RG 59, 838.00 / 1246a; William B. Caperton to Secy. of the Navy, "Report of Operations of Commander, Cruiser Squadron in Haitien Waters from 1 August to 6 August, 1915," 8 Aug. 1915, RG 45, WA-7 Attachés Reports, 1911–27.

20. Caperton Testimony, Senate Inquiry, 312–14; Caperton to Secy. of the Navy, "Report of Operations," 13 Aug. 1915, RG 45, WA-7 Attachés Reports, 1911–27; William S. Benson to Josephus Daniels, 8 Aug. 1915, RG 45, Area File C, 1911–27.

21. Caperton, "History of U.S. Naval Operations Under Command of Rear Admiral W. B. Caperton, USN, Commencing January 5, 1915, Ending April 30, 1919," RG 45, Subject File, 1911–27, ZN, pp. 55, 62.

22. Lansing to Am. Legation, Haiti, 10 Aug. 1915, RG 59, 838.00 / 1246a; Lansing to Wilson, 10 Aug. 1915, RG 59, 838.00 / 1275 1 / 2.

23. Caperton to Secy. of the Navy, "Report of Operations," 13 Aug. 1915, RG 45, WA-7 Attachés Reports, 1911–27.

24. Lansing to Wilson, 13 Aug. 1915, RG 59, 711.38 / 24A.

25. Caperton to Secy. of the Navy, "Report of Operations," 21 Aug. and 20 Sept. 1915, RG 45, WA-7 Attachés Reports, 1911–27.

26. Ibid.

27. Caperton to Secy. of the Navy, "Report of Operations," 28 Aug. 1915, RG 45, WA-7 Attachés Reports 1911–27.

28. Wilson to Galt, 23 Aug. 1915, Wilson Papers, Ser. 12; Lansing to Am. Legation, Haiti, 22 Aug. 1915, RG 59, 711.38 / 25a.

29. Caperton, "Report of Operations," 28 Aug. 1915, RG 45, WA-7 Attachés Reports, 1911–27.

30. Secy. of the Navy to Caperton, and Caperton to Secy. of the Navy, 19 Aug. 1915, both quoted in Caperton to Secy. of the Navy, "Report of Operations," 21 Aug. 1915, RG 45, WA-7 Attachés Reports, 1911–27.

31. Caperton Report, 56; Caperton to Secy. of the Navy, 3 Aug. 1915, RG 45, Area File C; Lansing to Am. Legation, Haiti, 24 Aug. 1915, RG 59, 711.38 / 24.

32. Caperton to Secy. of the Navy, "Report of Operations," 6 Sept. 1915, RG 45, WA-7 Attachés Reports, 1911–27.

33. Wilson to Galt, 30 Aug. 1915, Wilson Papers, Ser. 12; Caperton to Benson, 31 Aug. 1915, RG 45, WA-7, SD Military Political Financial and Economic Situation.

34. Caperton to Benson, 3 Sept. 1915, Caperton Papers; Caperton to USS *Connecticut*, 8 Sept. 1915, RG 45, Area File C, 1911–27; Wilson to Galt, 9 Sept. 1915, Wilson Papers, Ser. 2; Caperton to Secy. of the Navy, "Report of Operations," 14 Sept. 1915, RG 45, WA-7 Attachés Reports, 1911–27.

35. Caperton to Secy. of the Navy, "Report of Operations," 20 Sept. 1915, RG 45, WA-7 Attachés Reports, 1911–27.

36. Ibid.

37. Caperton to Benson, 24 Sept. 1915, Caperton Papers; Caperton to Secy. of the Navy, "Report of Operations," 18 Oct. 1915, RG 45, WA-7 Attachés Reports, 1911–27.

38. Caperton to Secy. of the Navy, "Report of Operations," 26 Oct. 1915, RG 45, WA-7 Attachés Reports, 1911–27.

39. Caperton, "History of Operations," 100; Caperton to Benson, 26 Oct. 1915, Caperton Papers.

40. Caperton to Secy. of the Navy, "Report of Operations," 27 Oct. 1915, RG 45, WA-7 Attachés Reports, 1911–27.

41. Ibid., 8 Nov. 1915, RG 45, WA-7 Attachés Reports, 1911–27.

42. Ibid., 20 Nov. 1915, RG 45, WA-7 Attachés Reports, 1911–27.

43. Ibid.

44. Daniels to Caperton, 10 Nov. 1915, quoted in Caperton to Secy. of the Navy, "Report of Operations," 20 Nov. 1915, RG 45, WA-7 Attachés Reports, 1911–27.

45. Ibid.

46. Caperton Report, 217–18.

47. Gen. Littleton Waller to his sons, 28 Nov. 1915, Papers of Gen. Littleton Waller, PC 224, Marine Corps Historical Center, Collections Branch, Navy Yard, Washington, D.C. (hereafter cited as Waller Papers); Schmidt, *Occupation of Haiti*, 68; Butler Testimony, Senate Inquiry, 516.

48. General Smedley Butler to Expeditionary Comdr., 16 Aug. 1915, Papers of Smedley Darlington Butler, Marine Corps Historical Center, Collections Branch, Navy Yard, Washing-

ton, D.C. (hereafter cited as Butler Papers), PC 54; Butler to Mr. Mann, 4 Apr. 1916, and Butler to Dear Colonel, 13 July 1916, Butler Papers, PC 54.

49. Benson, "Memorandum for the Secretary of the Navy," 15 Aug. 1916, Benson Papers (Hai-SD).

50. Maj. Gen. John H. Russell, "A Laboratory of Government," and Russell, "A Marine Looks Back on Haiti," ca. 1933, Papers of Maj. Gen. John H. Russell, Marine Corps Historical Center, Collections Branch, Navy Yard, Washington, D.C. (hereafter cited as Russell Papers); Marshall Morgan, "Military Control in Haiti for Establishment of Stable Government," ca. Feb. 1919, RG 59, 838.00 / 1604.

51. Rear Adm. Thomas Snowden to Russell, 14 May 1920, RG 38, Military Gov SD GC 1920, 41–43.

52. "Excerpts from Report of Court of Inquiry into Haitian Matters, 1920, Summing up of Judge Advocate; and Findings of Facts and Conclusions," 19 Oct. 1920, Papers of Maj. Gen. George Barnett, Marine Corps Historical Center, Collections Branch, Navy Yard, Washington, D.C. (hereafter cited as Barnett Papers), PC 247.

53. Caperton to Benson, 18 May 1916, RG 45, WA-7 Attachés Reports, 1911–27; Leahy Diary, Papers of Adm. William D. Leahy, Library of Congress Manuscript Division; Caperton to Secy. of the Navy, "Report of Operations," 25 May 1916, RG 45, Area File C, 1911–27.

54. Caperton to Secy. of the Navy, "Report of Operations," 25 May 1916, RG 45, Area File C, 1911–27.

55. Ibid.; Bryan to Am. Legation, Haiti, 12 Jan. 1916, RG 59, 839.00 / 1660a.

56. Russell to Secy. of State, 7 May 1916, RG 59, 839.00 / 1822, and 29 May 1916, RG 59, 839.51 / 1745.

57. Russell to Secy. of State and "W.R.," Div. of Latin American Affairs, 29 May 1916, RG 59, 839.51 / 1745; Daniels to Caperton, 17 May 1916, RG 45, WA-7 Attachés Reports; Lansing to Am. Legation, 17 May 1916, RG 59, 839.00 / 1826.

58. Russell to Secy. of State, 15 May 1916, RG 59, 839.00 / 1826.

59. Russell to Secy. of State, 18 May 1916, RG 59, 839.00 / 1830; Caperton to Secy. of the Navy, 20 May 1916, RG 127, MC 1975-70 / 5-2 SD 1817 and 1828; Russell to Secy. of State, 22 May 1916, RG 59, 839.00 / 1832; Caperton to Secy. of the Navy, 22 May 1916, RG 127, MC 1975-70 / 5-2 SD 1811; Russell to Secy of State, 23 May 1916, RG 59, 839.00 / 1833; Caperton to Secy. of the Navy, 24 May 1916, RG 127, MC 1975-70 / 5-2 SD 1845; Caperton to Secy. of the Navy, 25 May 1916, "Report of Operations," RG 45, Area File C, 1911–27.

60. Daniels to Caperton, 24 May 1916, RG 127, MC 1975-70 / 5-2 SD 1846; Russell to Secy. of State, 25 May 1916, RG 59, 839.00 / 1840; Caperton to Benson, 29 May 1916, and Caperton to Secy. of the Navy, 30 May 1916, RG 127, MC 1975-70 / 5-2 SD 1866; Russell to Secy. of State, 2 June 1916, RG 59, 839.00 / 1846.

61. Russell to Secy. of State, 2 June 1916, RG 59, 839.00 / 1847; Frank Henry (U.S. consul at Puerto Plata) to Secy. of State, 3 June 1916, RG 59, 839.00 / 1860.

62. Frank Polk to Wilson, 3 June 1916, Wilson Papers, Ser. 2; Polk to Am. Legation, SD, 3 June 1916, RG 59, 839.00 / 1847; Daniels to Caperton, 3 June 1916, RG 127, MC 1975-70 / 5-2 SD 1883.

63. "Dominican Republic," by Lansing, 3 July 1916, RG 59, 839.00 / 1891 1 / 2.

64. Caperton to Secy. of the Navy, 3 June 1916, RG 127, MC 1975-70 / 5-2 / SD 1884, and 4 June 1916, RG 127, MC 1975-70 / 5-2 / SD 1889; Russell to Secy. of State, 4 June 1916, 839.00 / 1851; Caperton to Secy. of Navy, 5 June 1916, RG 127, MC 1975-70 / 5-2 / SD 1879 and 1896; Russell to Secy. of State, 5 June 1916, RG 59, 839.00 / 1853; Caperton to Secy. of

the Navy, 10 June 1916, MC 1975-70 / 5-2 SD 1910; Russell to Secy. of State, 14 June 1916, RG 59, 839.00 / 1861, 17 June 1916, RG 59, 839.00 / 1883, and 13 July 1916, RG 59, 839.00 / 1899.

65. Caperton to Benson, 7, 15 June 1916, Caperton Papers.

66. Caperton to Secy. of the Navy, "Report of Operations," 8 July 1916, RG 45, Area File C, 1911–27; Russell to Secy. of State, 20 June 1916, RG 59, 839.00 / 1884, and 7 July 1916, RG 59, 839.00 / 1891, and 3 June 1916, RG 59, 839.00 / 1849; Col. T. P. Kane to Caperton, 5 June 1916, RG 45, Area File C, 1911–27; Kane, "To the People of Monte Cristi," 7 June 1916, RG 45, Area File C, 1911–27; Col. Joseph Pendleton to All officers of the forces, 24 June 1916, Papers of General Joseph H. Pendleton, Marine Corps Historical Center, Collections Branch, Navy Yard, Washington, D.C. (hereafter cited as Pendleton Papers); Caperton to Pendleton, 11 July 1916, RG 45, WA-7 Attachés Reports; Caperton to Secy. of the Navy, "Report of Operations," 18 July 1916, RG 45, Area File C, 1911–27.

67. Clarence Baxter to Frank McIntyre, 10 June 1916, RG 139, DCR 58; Russell to Secy. of State, 6 June 1916, RG 59, 839.00 / 1856, and 17 June 1916, RG 59, 839.51 / 1753; Baxter to Minister of Finance José Manuel Jimines, 18 June 1916, and Baxter to McIntyre, 26 June 1916, RG 139, DCR 54; Baxter to Reed Paige Clark, 19 July 1916, RG 139, DCR 311; Caperton to Secy. of the Navy, "Report of Operations," 22 June 1916, RG 45, Area File C, 1911–27.

68. Russell to Secy. of State, 26 June 1916, RG 59, 839.00 / 1892; Adee to Charles Fuller, 5 July 1916, RG 59, 839.00 / 1747.

69. Russell to Secy. of State, 25 July 1916, RG 59, 839.00 / 1900, 10 Aug. 1916, RG 59, 839.00 / 1905, and 4 Aug. 1916, RG 59, 839.00 / 1904.

70. Russell to Secy. of State, 14 Aug. 1916, and Lansing to Russell, 16 Aug. 1916, RG 59, 839.00 / 1780; Baxter to McIntyre, 11 Sept. 1916, RG 127, DCR 313; Russell to Secy. of State, 18 Aug. 1916, RG 59, 839.00 / 1783.

71. Adm. Charles F. Pond to Secy. of the Navy, 2 Aug. 1916, RG 127, MC 1975-70 / 5-2 SD; Colonel Kane, "Special Order No. 45," 2 Aug. 1916, RG 45, WA-7 Attachés Reports, 1911–27; Benson to Beach, 5 Aug. 1916, Papers of Adm. William S. Benson, Library of Congress Manuscript Division (hereafter cited as Benson Papers); Daniels to Pond, 16 Aug. 1916, MC 1975-70 / 5-2 SC 2115; Pond to Secy. of the Navy, 23 Aug. 1916, RG 45, Area File C, 1911–27.

72. Russell to Secy. of State, 25 Aug. 1916, RG 59, 839.00 / 1914, and 26 Aug. 1916, RG 59, 839.00 / 1915; Lansing to Am. Legation, SD, 26 Aug. 1916, RG 59, 839.00 / 1912, and 29 Aug. 1916, RG 59, 839.00 / 1915.

73. Jordon Stabler to Lansing, 28 Aug. 1916, RG 59, 839.00 / 1915; Russell to Secy. of State, 5 Sept. 1916, and Lansing to Am. Legation, SD, 8 Sept. 1916, both in RG 59, 839.00 / 1923; Russell to Secy. of State, 14 Sept. 1916, RG 59, 839.00 / 1925, and 25 Sept. 1916, RG 59, 839.00 / 1915; Stabler to Lansing, 8 Sept. 1916, RG 59, 839.00 / 1922.

74. Baxter to McIntyre, 29 Sept. 1916, RG 127, DCR 72; Russell to Secy. of State, 27 Oct. 1916, RG 59, 839.00 / 1941.

75. Pond to Secy. of the Navy, 25 Oct. 1916, RG 127, MC 1975-70 / 5-2 SD 2251; Brewer to Secy. of State, 24 Oct. 1916, RG 59, 839.00 / 1933, and 24 Oct. 1916, RG 59, 839.00 / 1934; Barnett to Marine Corps, 26 Oct. 1916, RG 127, MC 1975-70 / 5-2 SD 52655; Brewer to Secy. of State, 25 Oct. 1916, RG 59, 839.00 / 1935, and 26 Oct. 1916, RG 59, 839.00 / 1937; Stabler to Lansing, 27 Oct. 1916, RG 59, 839.00 / 1939; Brewer to Secy. of State, 30 Oct. 1916, RG 59, 839.00 / 1939; Benson to Pond, 1 Nov. 1916, RG 127, MC 1975-70 / 5-2 SD 2275.

76. Stabler to Polk, 31 Oct. 1916, RG 59, 839.00 / 1952.

77. Russell to Secy. of State, 9 Nov. 1916, RG 59, 839.00 / 1952; Lansing to Am. Legation, SD, 14 Nov. 1916, RG 59, 839.00 / 1958; Brewer to Secy. of State, 20 Nov. 1916, RG 59, 839.00 / 1948; Stabler to Lansing, 21 Nov. 1916, RG 59, 839.00 / 1952; Lansing to Wilson, 22 Nov. 1916, in Papers of Robert Lansing, Library of Congress Manuscript Division, Washington, D.C. (hereafter cited as Lansing Papers).

78. Capt. H. S. Knapp to Benson, 23 Nov. 1916, RG 45, Area File C, 1911–27; Knapp to Navy Operations, 24 Nov. 1916, RG 127, MC 1975-70 / 5-2 SD 2345.

79. Wilson to Lansing, 26 Nov. 1916, RG 59, 839.00 / 1951a; Lansing to Daniels, 27 Nov. 1916, RG 59, 839.00 / 1952; Lansing to Am. Legation, SD, 27 Nov. 1916, RG 59, 839.00 / 1951a; Brewer to Secy. of State, 29 Nov. 1916, RG 59, 839.00 / 1951.

80. Knapp to Secy. of the Navy, ca. Dec. 1916, RG 45, Bureau of Navigation 5266-503; Knapp to Secy. of the Navy, 17 Dec. 1916, RG 45, WA-7 Attachés Reports, 27923-347.

81. Pendleton to Barnett, 18 Dec. 1916, Pendleton Papers; Knapp to Secy. of the Navy, 14 Jan. 1917, RG 45, WA-7 Attachés Reports, SD 1917.

82. Baxter to McIntyre, 4 Jan. 1917, RG 350, DCR 61; Knapp to Benson, 21 Jan. 1917, Benson Papers; F. Mayer to Latin American Div., 25 Feb. 1918, RG 59, 839.00 / 2075.

83. Interview with Adm. Snowden, 27 Jan. 1921, Hearings before the General Board of the Navy, 1921, vol. 2, RG 139, DCR.

84. Wilson, "Address to the Graduating Class of the U.S. Naval Academy," 5 June 1914, quoted in James Brown Scott, ed., Foreign Policy, 52.

5. FORCE FOR INTRODUCTION

1. Carl von Clausewitz, On War, ed. Michael Howard and Peter Paret (Princeton, N.J.: Princeton Univ. Press, 1976), 87–88.

2. Ibid., 595, 75, 90, 604.

3. Ibid., 603, 606–7.

4. Ibid., 606–8.

5. Woodrow Wilson, "An Address to the Officers of the Atlantic Fleet," in Arthur Link, Papers of Woodrow Wilson 43:428. For a more detailed discussion of Wilson's relations with the military, see Frederick S. Calhoun, Power and Principle, 34–69, passim.

6. Wilson, "A Speech Accepting a Statue of Phillip Kearney," 11 Nov. 1914, in Link, Papers of Woodrow Wilson 31:562; Wilson, "A Memorial Address," 11 May 1914, in Link, Papers of Woodrow Wilson 30:14.

7. Woodrow Wilson to Henry Van Dyke, 27 Apr. 1914, Wilson Papers, Ser. 2; Wilson to Lindley Garrison, 8 Aug. 1914, Wilson Papers, Ser. 3; Wilson, "Remarks at Press Conference," 24 Nov. 1914, in Link, Papers of Woodrow Wilson 31:351–52.

8. Wilson to Sir William Tyrrell, 22 Nov. 1913, RG 59, 812.00 / 1260 1 / 2.

9. John Lind to William Jennings Bryan, 13 Oct. 1914, RG 59, 812.00 / 11437; Calhoun, Power and Principle, 40–42; Lind to Bryan, 1 Apr. 1914, RG 59, 812.00 / 11371.

10. Bryan to George Carothers, 21 Apr. 1914, RG 59, 812.00 / 11608a.

11. Wilson to Oswald Garrison Villard, and Wilson to Charles A. D. Burk, 24 Apr. 1914, Wilson Papers; Josephus Daniels to William E. Dodd, 27 Apr. 1914, and Daniels to E. A. Alderman, 1 May 1914, Daniels Papers; Josephus Daniels, Life of Woodrow Wilson, 183–84.

12. Robert Quirk, An Affair of Honor, 124.

13. Wood Diaries, 26 and 29 Apr. 1914, Wood Papers record Wood's conversations with the French ambassador, Jules Jusserand, during which the latter discussed his participation in arranging the mediation. The British believed that Wilson had suggested mediation by the ABC

powers—see Kenneth L. Grieb, *The United States and Huerta* (Lincoln: Univ. of Nebraska Press, 1969), 159. The British ambassador told Henry Cabot Lodge on 25 April that "Jusserand had hinted to Brazil, Argentina, and Chile to move." See Henry Cabot Lodge, *The Senate and the League of Nations* (New York: Charles Scribner's Sons, 1925), 20. An American aid to the Mexican delegation to the ABC conference wrote Emilio Rabasa, a member of the delegation, on 24 April that the ABC powers "offered their services on account of an insinuation from Bryan." See Berta Ulloa, *La Revolucion Intervenida* (Buanajuato: El Colegio de Mexico, 1971), 188. See also Rose to Bryan, 29 May 1914, Bryan Papers; Lorillard to Secy. of State, 27 Apr. 1914, RG 59, 812.00 / 11737, and 29 Apr. 1914, RG 59, 812.00 / 12096; Mediators to Secy. of State, 25 Apr. 1914, RG 59, 812.00 / 11744c.

14. Mediators to Secy. of State, 25 Apr. 1914, RG 59, 812.00 / 11744c.

15. Bryan to Mediators, 25 Apr. 1914, RG 59, 812.00 / 11744c; Wilson, "Confidential Memorandum to Mediators," 25 Apr. 1914, Wilson Papers; Lansing to Bryan, 1 May 1914, RG 59, 812.00 / 11800 1 / 2; Wilson to George L. Record, 1 June 1914, Wilson Papers, Ser. 4, Case File 95.

16. Wilson to Walter Hines Page, 1 June 1914, Wilson Papers; Wilson to Page, 30 June 1914, in Link, *Papers of Woodrow Wilson* 30:230; Wilson to Page, 4 June 1914, Wilson Papers; Wilson, "Fourth of July Address at Philadelphia," 4 July 1914, in Link, *Papers of Woodrow Wilson* 30:252.

17. Mediators to Bryan, 2 May 1914, RG 59, 812.00 / 23425; Bryan, circular telegram, 29 Apr. 1914, RG 59, 812.00 / 11776a; Bryan to Wilson, attaching correspondence between Mediators and Carranza, 4 May 1914, Wilson Papers; Consul Letcher to Secy. of State, 23 Apr. 1914, RG 59, 812.00 / 11651; Bryan to Judge Douglas, ca. 30 Apr. 1914, Wilson Papers; Bryan to Lind, ca. May 1914, Lind Papers; Consul Letcher to Secy. of State, 30 Apr. 1914, RG 59, 812.00 / 11782.

18. Am. Commissioners to Bryan, 23 May 1914, Bryan Papers, and 30 May 1914, RG 59, 812.00 / 12631 1 / 2.

19. Bryan to Am. Commissioners, 27, 29 May, 1 June 1914, RG 59, 812.00 / 12631 1 / 2; Bryan to Wilson, 30, 31 May 1914, Wilson Papers; Bryan to Wilson ca. 31 May 1914, Wilson Papers.

20. Bryan to Am. Commissioners, 2, 3, 4 June 1914, RG 59, 812.00 / 12631 1 / 2.

21. Am. Commissioners to Secy. of State, 21, 26 May 1914, RG 59, 812.00 / 12631 1 / 2, and 29 May 1914, RG 59, 812.00 / 12631 1 / 2; Bryan to Am. Commissioners, 30 May 1914, RG 59, 812.00 / 12631 1 / 2; Am. Commissioners to Secy. of State, 31 May 1914, RG 59, 812.00 / 12631 1 / 2. See Grieb, *United States and Huerta*, 165–77; Link, *New Freedom*, 409–13; Larry D. Hill, *Emissaries to a Revolution: Woodrow Wilson's Executive Agents in Mexico* (Baton Rouge: Louisiana State Univ. Press, 1973), 182–5.

22. Mediators to Bryan, 5 May 1914, RG 59, 812.00 / 11849; Lansing to Bryan, 1 May 1914, RG 59, 812.00 / 11800; Bryan, circular telegram, 11 May 1914, RG 59, 812.00 / 11902a; Bryan to Wilson, 14, 15 May 1914, Wilson Papers.

23. Bryan to Wilson, enclosing Long to Bryan, 9 May 1914, Wilson Papers.

24. "A News Report," *New York World*, 18 May 1914, in Link, *Papers of Woodrow Wilson* 30:39; Unsigned, "The Mexican Situation," 4 May 1914, RG 59, 812.00 / 11984 1 / 2.

25. Bryan to Am. Embassy, London, 9 May 1914, Wilson Papers.

26. Henry Dodge to Secy. of State, 20 May 1914, RG 59, 812.00 / 12136; Bryan to Am. Commissioners, 20 May 1914, RG 59, 812.00 / 234526.

27. Am. Commissioners to Bryan, 21 May 1914, RG 59, 812.00 / 12631 1 / 2; Bryan to Am. Commissioners, 21 May 1914, Tumulty Papers.

28. Am. Commissioners to Bryan, 21 May 1914, RG 59, 812.00 / 12631 1 / 2; Bryan to Am. Commissioners, 21 May 1914, Tumulty Papers; Dodge to Bryan, 22 May 1914, RG 59, 812.00 / 12048; Am. Commissioners to Secy. of State, 22 May 1914, RG 59, 812.00 / 12631 1 / 2, and 23 May 1914, Wilson Papers.

29. Bryan to Am. Commissioners, 24 May 1914, Tumulty Papers.

30. Wilson Memo, 26 May 1914, Wilson Papers.

31. Bryan to Am. Commissioners, 26, 27, 29 May 1914, RG 59, 812.00 / 12631 1 / 2; Am. Commissioners to Secy. of State, 26, 28 May, 13 June 1914, RG 59, 812.00 / 12631 1 / 2; Wilson Memo, 26 May 1914, Wilson Papers; Bryan to Wilson, 30 May 1914, RG 59, 812.00 / 23452H; Am. Commissioners to Secy. of State, 31 May 1914, RG 59, 812.00 / 12130; Lansing, "Memorandum on report of Special Commission of the President near the Mediators," 3 June 1914, RG 59, 812.00 / 24265; Am. Commissioners to Bryan, and Dodge to Bryan, 9 June 1914, RG 59, 812.00 / 12631 1 / 2; Am. Commissioners to Secy. of State, 10 June 1914, RG 59, 812.00 / 23466; Am. Commissioners to Bryan, 11 June 1914, RG 59, 812.00 / 23469; Unsigned memo for president, 11 June 1914, RG 59, Wilson-Bryan Correspondence; Joseph Lamar to Secy. of State, and Bryan to Am. Commissioners, 12 June 1914, RG 59, 812.00 / 12631 1 / 2; Dodge to Bryan, 12 June 1914, RG 59, 812.00 / 12239; Frederick Lehman to Secy. of State, 13 June 1914, RG 59, 812.00 / 12241; Bryan to Am. Commissioners, and Bryan to Lamar, 15 June 1914, RG 59, 812.00 / 12631 1 / 2; Dodge to Secy. of State, 16 June 1914, RG 59, 812.00 / 12288.

32. Bryan to Am. Commissioners, 27 May 1914, RG 59, 812.00 / 12631 1 / 2.

33. Am. Commissioners to Secy. of State, 16, 18, 19 June 1914, RG 59, 812.00 / 12631 1 / 2; Memo of telephone conversation, and Bryan to Am. Commissioners, 19 June 1914, RG 59, 812.00 / 12631 1 / 2.

34. Bryan to Lind, 4 July 1914, Lind Papers; Bryan to Am. Commissioners, and Am. Commissioners to Secy. of State, 19 June 1914, RG 59, 812.00 / 12631 1 / 2; Dodge to Bryan, 20 June 1914, RG 59, 812.00 / 12314; Am. Commissioners to Bryan, 21 June 1914, RG 59, 812.00 / 12631 1 / 2; Wilson to House, 22 June 1914, Wilson Papers; Am. Commissioners to Secy. of State, 22, 24, 25, 26 June 1914, RG 59, 812.00 / 12631 1 / 2; Bryan to Am. Commissioners, 23, 24 June, 1 July 1914, RG 59, 812.00 / 12631 1 / 2; "Handed to Commissioners by Mediators," 24 June 1914, RG 59, 812.00 / 12631 1 / 2; Dodge to Bryan, 25 June 1914, RG 59, 812.00 / 12363; Bryan to Carothers, 30 June 1914, RG 59, 812.00 / 12381a; Dodge to Bryan, 3 July 1914, RG 59, 812.00 / 12411 and 12429; Leon J. Canova to Secy. of State, 6 July 1914, RG 59, 812.00 / 12429; Bryan, telephone conversation with Wilson, 10 July 1914, Wilson Papers.

35. Wilson to Page, 4 June 1914, and Wilson to William R. Kent, 29 June 1914, Wilson Papers; Calhoun, *Power and Principle*, 52.

36. Calhoun, *Power and Principle*, 52.

37. McCain to Gen. Hugh L. Scott, 23 Apr. 1916, Scott Papers; Newton Baker to Scott, 22 Apr. 1916, RG 94, AGO 2394312; McCain to Scott, 22, 24 Apr. 1916, RG 94, AGO 2394312; General Tasker H. Bliss to Scott, 27 Apr. 1916, RG 94, AGO 2394312A 14; Scott to Mary Scott, 24, 26 Apr. 1916, Scott Papers.

38. McCain to Scott, 26, 30 Apr. 1916, RG 94, AGO 2394312A 14; Baker to Scott, 30 Apr. 1916, RG 94, AGO 2394312A 14; Baker to Scott, 1 May 1916, Scott Papers; McCain to Scott, 1 May 1916, RG 94, AGO 2394312.

39. Scott and Gen. Frederick Funston to Secy. of War, 29 Apr. 1916, Scott Papers; Scott and Funston to Secy. of War, 2 May 1916, RG 94, AGO 2394312A 14 and, AGO 2394312M; Scott and Funston to Secy. of War, 3 May 1916, Scott Papers.

40. Baker to Chief of Staff, 4 May 1916, RG 94, AGO 2394312Q; Scott to Secy. of War, 8 May 1916, RG 94, AGO 2394312A 14; Scott and Funston to Secy. of War, 8 May 1916, RG 94, AGO 2394312X.

41. Scott to Secy. of War, 8 May 1916, RG 94, AGO 2394312A 14; Scott and Funston to Secy. of War, 8 May 1916, RG 94, AGO 2394312X; McCain to Funston, 9 May 1916, RG 94, AGO 2394312A 14; Memo to AGO from Bliss, 9 May 1916, RG 94, AGO 2394312Y; Baker to Gov. George W. P. Hunt, 9 May 1916, RG 165, WCD 6474-379; Scott and Funston to Secy. of War, 9 May 1916, RG 94, AGO 2394312a 14; "Description of the Scott-Obregón Conference of May 8 and 9, 1916," Scott Papers; Scott and Funston to Secy. of War, 11 May 1916, RG 94, AGO 2394312A 16 and 8; Scott, "Border Conference with General Obregón," 12 May 1916, Bliss Papers.

42. Donald Smythe, *Guerilla Warrior*, 258–59; Cobb to Secy. of State, 21 June 1916, RG 59, 812.00 / 18524; Rodgers to Secy. of State, 21 June 1916, RG 59, 812.00 / 18525; Robert Lansing to W. C. Steubens, 22 June 1916, Lansing Papers.

43. Canova to Secy. of State, 22 June 1916, RG 43, Gray-Lane Files, NA, Washington, D.C. (herafter cited as RG 43 Gray-Lane Files); R. L. Rowe to Wilson, 23 June 1916, Wilson Papers; Lansing to James Linn Rodgers, 25 June 1916, RG 59, 812.00 / 18574; Baker to Wilson, 26 June 1916, Wilson Papers; James Silliman to Secy. of State, 26 June 1916, RG 59, 812.00 / 18582; Canova to Secy. of State, 26 June 1916, RG 59, 812.00 / 18681 1 / 2; State Dept. memo, "Attitude on Mediation in Mexican Controversy," 26 June 1916, RG 59, 812.00 / 18607 1 / 2; Lansing to Am. Minister, Honduras, 1 July 1916, RG 59, 812.00 / 18610.

44. Wilson to Louis Wiley, 22 June 1916, Wilson Papers; Lansing to Wilson, 21 June 1916, RG 59, 812.00 / 18533a; Wilson to Lansing, 21 June 1916, RG 59, 812.00 / 18533 1 / 2; Lansing to Wilson, 21 June 1916, RG 59, 812.00 / 18534 1 / 2; Baker to Wilson, 1 July 1916, Wilson Papers.

45. Funston to AGO, quoting Pershing, 25 June 1916, RG 94, AGO 24161720; Lansing to Wilson, 3 July 1916, RG 59, 812.00 / 17714 1 / 2.

46. Lansing to Wilson, 3 July 1916, RG 59, 812.00 / 17714 1 / 2.

47. Licenciado E. Arredondo to Lansing, 4 July 1916, RG 59, 812.00 / 17715 1 / 2; Lansing to Wilson, 5 July 1916, Wilson Papers; Rodgers to Lansing, 6 July 1916, RG 59, 812.00 / 18664.

48. Rodgers to Secy. of State, 7 July 1916, RG 59, 812.00 / 18670; Wilson to S. H. Church, 6 July 1916, Wilson Papers; Lansing to Charles E. Holbrook, 7 July 1916, Lansing Papers.

49. Rodgers to Secy. of State, 8 July 1916, RG 59, 812.00 / 18674; Arredondo to Frank Polk, 12 July 1916, RG 59, 812.00 / 19039.

50. Polk to Wilson, 12 July 1916, Wilson Papers.

51. Rodgers to Secy. of State, 13 July 1916, RG 59, 812.00 / 18723; Polk to Wilson, 19 July 1916, RG 59, 812.00 / 18790 1 / 2; Polk to Rodgers, 20 July 1916, RG 59, 812.00 / 18749; Lansing to Polk, 14 July 1916, RG 59, 812.00 / 18790 1 / 2; Rodgers to Secy. of State, 21 July 1916, RG 59, 812.00 / 18767; Polk to Lansing, 21 July 1916, RG 59, 812.00 / 18791 1 / 2.

52. Lansing to Polk, 21 July 1916, RG 59, 812.00 / 18792 1 / 2; Polk to Wilson, 21 July 1916, RG 59, 812.00 / 18791 1 / 2; Polk to Rodgers, 21 July 1916, RG 43, Telegrams of J. L. Rodgers, NA, Washington, D.C. (hereafter cited as Rodgers Telegrams); Rodgers to Secy. of State, 22 July 1916, RG 59, 812.00 / 18768.

53. Polk to Lansing, 25 July 1916, Lansing Papers; Rodgers to Secy. of State, 25 July 1916, RG 59, 812.00 / 18792; Polk to Rodgers, 28 July 1916, RG 59, 812.00 / 19039.

54. Polk to Lansing, 28 July, 3 Aug. 1916, Lansing Papers; Rodgers to Secy. of State, 29 July 1916, RG 59, 812.00 / 18822; Polk to Rodgers, 1 Aug. 1916, RG 59, 812.00 / 19039; Rodgers to Secy. of State, 3 Aug. 1916, RG 59, 812.00 / 18851.

55. Polk to Lansing, 4 Aug. 1916, RG 59, 812.00 / 24297; Arredondo to Lansing, 4 Aug. 1916, RG 59, 812.00 / 18980; Polk to Wilson, 8, 9 Aug. 1916, Wilson Papers; Wilson to Polk, 10 Aug. 1916, Wilson Papers.

56. Lansing to Richard Olney, 15 Aug. 1916, RG 59, 812.00 / 24300; Lansing to Wilson, 4 May 1916, Wilson Papers; Wilson to Lansing, 26 Aug. 1916, RG 59, 812.00 / 24302.

57. Lansing to Rodgers, 15 Aug. 1916, RG 59, 812.00 / 18949a; "Interview with Frank Polk," 9 Feb. 1926, R.S. Baker Papers; Lansing to Rodgers, 23 Aug. 1916, RG 59, 812.00 / 18995a. The text of the opening speeches are in R. L. Rowe, "Report on the Proceedings of the Commission with Accompanying Papers," 26 Apr. 1917, RG 59, 812.00 / 20849.

58. "Opening Remarks by Arredondo," 4 Sept. 1916, RG 59, 812.00 / 19178; "Opening Remarks by Cabrera," 4 Sept. 1916, RG 59, 812.00 / 19819; Lansing to House, 5 Sept. 1916, RG 59, 812.00 / 19156C; Lansing to John W. Foster, 6 Sept. 1916, Lansing Papers.

59. Anne W. Lane and Louise H. Wall, *The Letters of Franklin K. Lane, Personal and Political* (Boston, Mass.: Houghton Mifflin, 1922), 225; "Opening Remarks of Lane," 4 Sept. 1916, RG 59, 812.00 / 19138; Lane to Wilson, 6 Sept. 1916, Wilson Papers; Lane to Lansing, 6 Sept. 1916, RG 59, 812.00 / 19093; Gray to Lane, 8 Sept. 1916, Box 1, Memo 2, RG 43, Gray-Lane Files; Lane to Lansing, 8 Sept. 1916, RG 59, 812.00 / 19105.

60. Lansing to Lane, 8 Sept. 1916, RG 59, 812.00 / 19101a; Lane to Lansing, 9 Sept. 1916, RG 59, 812.00 / 19117, and 10 Sept. 1916, RG 59, 812.00 / 19160 1 / 2; and 11 Sept. 1916, RG 59, 812.00 / 19137.

61. Lane to Secy. of State, 14 Sept. 1916, RG 59, 812.00 / 19177; Bliss to AGO, 14 Sept. 1916, Bliss Papers; Lansing to Lane, 15 Sept. 1916, RG 59, 812.00 / 19160 1 / 2; Johnson to Canova, 15 Sept. 1916, RG 59, 812.00 / 19156; Bliss to AGO, ca. 14 Sept. 1916, Bliss Papers; Bliss Memo, ca. 15 Sept. 1916, RG 43, Gray-Lane Files.

62. Lane to Secy. of State, 15 Sept. 1916, 812.00 / 19188, and 17 Sept. 1916, RG 59, 812.00 / 19319 1 / 2, and 18 Sept. 1916, RG 59, 812.00 / 19213.

63. Lane to Lansing, 17 Sept. 1916, RG 59, 812.00 / 19319 1 / 2.

64. Lane to Secy. of State, 20 Sept. 1916, RG 59, 812.00 / 19241; Am. Commissioners to Mex. Commissioners, 22 Sept. 1916, RG 59, 812.00 / 19861; Rowe to Secy. of State, 22 Sept. 1916, RG 59, 812.00 / 19277.

65. Lane to Secy. of State, 22 Sept. 1916, RG 59, 812.00 / 19265; Rowe to Secy. of State, 23 Sept. 1916, RG 59, 812.00 / 19413 1 / 2, and 26 Sept. 1916, RG 59, 812.00 / 19328; Baker to Wilson, enclosing memo from Bliss, 23 Sept. 1916, Papers of Newton D. Baker, Library of Congress Manuscript Division (hereafter cited as N. D. Baker Papers).

66. Lane to Frederick J. Lane, 29 Sept. 1916, quoted in Lane, *Letters of Lane*, 227; Lane to Alexander Vogelsang, 29 Sept. 1916, quoted in Lane, *Letters of Lane*, 226; Lane to Lansing, 29 Sept. 1916, RG 59, 812.00 / 19416 1 / 2.

67. Lane to Secy. of State, 29 Sept. 1916, RG 59, 812.00 / 19416 1 / 2, 2 Oct. 1916, RG 59, 812.00 / 19389, and 3 Oct. 1916, RG 59, 812.00 / 19401.

68. Lane to Secy. of State, 13 Oct. 1916, RG 59, 812.00 / 19523, and 19 Oct. 1916, RG 59, 812.00 / 19582.

69. Bliss to Col. Henry T. Allen, 23 Oct. 1916, Bliss Papers; Rowe to Lansing, 12 Nov. 1916, RG 59, 812.00 / 24314; Lane to Benjamin Ide Wheeler, 14 Nov. 1916, in Lane, *Letters of Lane*, 230; Bliss to Polk, 15 Nov. 1916, Bliss Papers; Wilson to Lane, 5 Dec. 1916, Wilson Papers, Ser. 4, CF 3448; Mex. Commissioners to Am. Commissioners, 27 Dec. 1916, RG 59, 812.00 / 19861 1 / 2.

70. Rowe to Lansing, 16 Jan. 1917, RG 59, 812.00 / 20383.

71. Wilson, "Remarks at a Press Conference," 3 Aug. 1914, in Link, *Papers of Woodrow Wilson* 30:332; Wilson, "Address Accepting Democratic Nomination," 2 Sept. 1916, in Baker

and Dodd, *New Democracy* 2:282; Wilson, "Address in Des Moines," 1 Feb. 1916, in Baker and Dodd, *New Democracy* 2:75; Wilson, "Address to DAR," 11 Oct. 1915, in Baker and Dodd, *New Democracy* 1:378.

72. Wilson, "Address Accepting the Democratic Nomination," 2 Sept. 1916, in Baker and Dodd, *New Democracy* 2:282; Wilson to Thomas Nelson Page, 28 Jan. 1915, Wilson Papers, Ser. 3.

73. Wilson to House, 21 Aug. 1915, R. S. Baker Papers; Wilson, "Speech to Congress," 2 Apr. 1917, in Baker and Dodd, *War and Peace* 1:11–16.

74. Wilson to Associated Press, 29 Apr. 1915, in Ray S. Baker, *Woodrow Wilson, Life and Letters: Neutrality* (Westport, Conn.: Greenwood Press, 1968), 269.

75. Wilson to House, 17, Jan., 18, 20 May 1915, Wilson Papers, Ser. 2; Wilson, letter of introduction for House, 18 Jan. 1915, Wilson Papers, Ser. 3; House to Wilson, 11, 15 Feb., 20, 26 Mar., 18 Apr., 11, 5, 7, 18, 19, 20, 27, 28 May 1915, Wilson Papers, Ser. 2; House to Wilson, 22 May 1915, quoted in Charles Seymour, *The Intimate Papers of Colonel House* (Boston, Mass.: Houghton Mifflin, 1926), 1:285; Daniel M. Smith, *Lansing and American Neutrality*, 79, 146; E. H. Buehrig, *Woodrow Wilson and the Balance of Power* (Bloomington: Univ. of Indiana Press), 201–2.

76. House to Wilson, 16 June 1915, Wilson Papers, Ser. 2; House to Wilson, 29 May 1915, quoted in Seymour, *Intimate Papers of Colonel House* 1:249, 469–70.

77. Wilson to House, 24 Dec. 1915, Wilson Papers, Ser. 2.

78. House to Wilson, 8, 11, 15, 16 Jan., 3, 9 (two letters), 11 Feb. 1916, Wilson Papers, Ser. 2; Wilson to House, 9 Jan. 1916, R. S. Baker Papers; Wilson to House, 12 Feb. 1916, and House to Wilson, 16 Feb. 1916, Wilson Papers, Ser. 2; Seymour, *Intimate Papers of Colonel House* 2:85–86; 90–91, 118, 120, 163–65, 171, 472; James W. Gerard, *My Four Years in Germany* (New York: Grossett and Dunlap, 1917), ix–x.

79. Calhoun, *Power and Principle*, 148–50.

80. Wilson, "Speech to Congress," 2 Apr. 1917, in Baker and Dodd, *War and Peace* 1:11–16; Calhoun, *Power and Principle*, 182–83.

81. Arthur Walworth, *America's Moment: 1918* (New York: W. W. Norton, 1977), 18–19, 25–30; Arthur Link, *Woodrow Wilson: Revolution, War, and Peace* (Arlington Heights, Ill.: A. H. M. Publishing, 1979), 87; Calhoun, *Power and Principle*, 182–83.

82. "President's Response to Senate Resolution as to the Reason for Retaining American Troops in Siberia," 25 July 1919, Papers of Breckinridge Long, Library of Congress Manuscript Division (hereafter cited as Long Papers); Calhoun, *Power and Principle*, 235–36.

83. Calhoun, *Power and Principle*, 236–49.

6. FORCE FOR ASSOCIATION

1. Woodrow Wilson, "The Ideals of America," Dec. 1902, in Ray S. Baker and William E. Dodd, *College and State* 1:441; Wilson, "Democracy and Efficiency," Mar. 1901, in Baker and Dodd, *College and State* 1:414.

2. Wilson, "Bible and Progress," 7 May 1911, in Baker and Dodd, *College and State* 2:294; Wilson, "A Commencement Address," 5 June 1914, in Arthur Link, *Papers of Woodrow Wilson* 30:146.

3. Frederick S. Calhoun, *Power and Principle*, 174–75.

4. Calhoun, *The Lawmen: United States Marshals and Their Deputies, 1789–1989* (Washington, D.C.: Smithsonian Institution Press, 1990), 221–27.

5. Wilson, "Speech to Gathering of College Presidents," 5 May 1917, quoted in Newton Baker, *Frontiers of Freedom* (New York: Doran, 1918), 30; Wilson, "Speech to Southern Society Banquet," 12 Dec. 1917, quoted in Josephus Daniels, *The Navy and Nation* (New York: Doran, 1919), 86–87.

6. Woodrow Wilson to Edward M. House, 1 Dec. 1917, Wilson Papers, Ser. 2.

7. Newton Baker to Gen. John J. Pershing, 26 May 1917, Wilson Papers, Ser. 2; Russell Weigley, *History of the United States Army* (New York: Macmillan, 1967), 377; Louis Smith, *American Democracy and Military Power* (Chicago: Univ. of Chicago Press, 1951), 49–50; Maurice Matloff, *American Military History* (Washington, D.C.: Office of Center for Military History, U.S. Army, 1969), 381.

8. Joseph Bernardo and Eugene H. Bacon, *American Military Policy: Its Development Since 1775* (Harrisburg, Penn.: Military Publishing Service, 1955), 361; Wilson to House, 2 Nov. 1917, and Wilson, "Note," ca. 15 Nov. 1917, Wilson Papers, Ser. 2; House to Wilson, 25 Nov. 1917, quoted in Seymour, *Intimate Papers of Colonel House* 3:281; Lansing to Wilson, 29 June 1918, Lansing Papers.

9. Calhoun, *Power and Principle*, 178–79.

10. Josephus Daniels to Adm. William S. Sims, 18 July 1918, Papers of Adm. William S. Sims, Library of Congress Manuscript Division (hereafter cited as Sims Papers); David F. Trask, *Captains and Cabinets: Anglo-American Naval Relations, 1917–1918* (Columbia, Mo.: Univ. of Missouri Press, 1972); Calhoun, *Power and Principle*, 179–81.

11. Wilson, "Speech to Alliance for Labor and Democracy," 22 Feb. 1918, quoted in Daniels, *Navy and Nation*, 127–28.

12. House Diary entries, 22 and 30 Apr. 1917, quoted in Seymour, *Intimate Papers of Colonel House* 3:37–38, 54.

13. Calhoun, *Power and Principle*, 194.

14. Betty Miller Unterberger, *The United States, Revolutionary Russia, and the Rise of Czechoslovakia* (Chapel Hill: Univ. of North Carolina Press, 1989).

15. Wilson to Mrs. H. H. Dyer Dermott, 20 Sept. 1918, Wilson Papers, Ser. 2.

16. Gen. Tasker H. Bliss to Gen. Hugh L. Scott, 31 Mar. 1917, Bliss Papers.

17. Weigley, *History of the United States Army*, 355–56; Bliss to Scott, 25 May 1917, Bliss Papers; Baker to Wilson, 2 May 1917, Wilson Papers, Ser. 2; Wilson to Baker, 3 May 1917, and Baker to Wilson, 8 May 1917, N. D. Baker Papers; Frederick Palmer, *Bliss, Peacemaker: The Life and Letters of General Tasker Howard Bliss* (New York: Dodd, Mead, 1934), 151.

18. Baker, "America's Duty," *National Geographic* 31 (May 1917): 453; Russell Weigley, *The American Way of War: A History of U.S. Military Strategy and Policy* (New York: Macmillan, 1973), 202.

19. "A Note for the year 1918," Lansing Diary, 31 Dec. 1917, Lansing Papers.

20. In *Power and Principle*, 185–218, I explored in some detail the theory that wartime cooperation and the need to prove the value of collective security eventually convinced Wilson to take part in the twin interventions. Consequently, I will only summarize that argument here.

21. Baker to Mrs. Casserly, 15 Nov. 1924, N. D. Baker Papers; see also Baker, "Foreword," in William S. Graves, *America's Siberian Adventure*, ix–xii.

22. Wilson, "Notes for Aide-Memoir," ca. 17 July 1918, Wilson Papers, Ser. 2; Gen. Peyton March to Bliss, 23 July 1918, Bliss Papers; "Draft Statement to Press," 3 Aug. 1918, R. S. Baker Papers; Wilson to Thomas Masaryk, 7 Aug. 1918, Wilson Papers, Ser. 2; Breckinridge Long, Diary entry, 5 Sept. 1918, Long Papers; Wilson notes on assurances to Russia, ca. 3 Aug. 1918, and Polk to Wilson, 20 July 1918, Wilson Papers, Ser. 2; Unterberger, *America's Siberian Expedition, 1918–1920* (Durham, N.C.: Duke Univ. Press, 1956), 88, 232; and Unterberger, *United States, Revolutionary Russia*, 216–42.

23. Permanent Military Reps. to the Supreme War Council, Joint Note No. 5, 23 Dec. 1917, Bliss Papers.

24. "Memo on the Russian Situation," Lansing Diary, 7 Dec. 1917, Lansing Papers; see also Lansing to Wilson, 10 Dec. 1917, Lansing Papers.

25. Permanent Military Reps. to the Supreme War Council, Joint Note No. 16, 19 Feb. 1918, Bliss Papers.

26. Arthur Balfour to Wilson, 18 Mar. 1918, and Jules Jusserand to Wilson, 13 Mar. 1918, Wilson Papers, Ser. 2; Roland Morris to Secy. of State, 19 Mar. 1918, Lansing Papers.

27. Lansing to Daniels, 3 Jan. 1918, Daniels to Comdr. in Chief, Asiatic Fleet, 3 Jan. 1918, Lord Reading to Wilson, 27 Feb. 1918, and Balfour to House, 7 Mar. 1918, all in Wilson Papers, Ser. 5A; Balfour to U.S. Government, 16 Mar. 1918, Bliss Papers; Balfour to Wilson, 18 Mar. 1918, Wilson Papers, Ser. 2.

28. Wilson to Herbert Bayard Swope, 2 Apr. 1918, Wilson Papers, Ser. 2; Lansing to Wilson, 29 Apr. 1918, Wilson Papers, Ser. 5A; George Kennan, *The Decision to Intervene* (Princeton, N.J.: Princeton Univ. Press, 1958), 50–52; 123–29; Note by Permanent Military Reps. to the Supreme War Council, Inter–Allied Naval Council, 20, 23 Mar. 1918, "Note by Allied Naval Council," 20 Mar. 1918, and "Note by Allied Naval Council," 23 Mar 1918, all in Bliss Papers.

29. Breckinridge Long, Diary entry, 26 Feb. 1918, Long Papers.

30. Wilson to Breckinridge Long, 2 Mar. 1918, and Wilson to Long, 14 Mar. 1918, Long Papers; Long Diary, 26 Feb. 1918, Long Papers; Kennan, *Decision to Intervene*, 99-100; Permanent Military Reps. to the Supreme War Council, Joint Note No. 20, 8 Apr. 1918, Bliss Papers.

31. Unterberger, *United States, Revolutionary Russia*, 133–216.

32. Permanent Military Reps. to the Supreme War Council, Joint Note No. 25, 27 Apr. 1918, Bliss Papers.

33. Lansing to Wilson, 11 May 1918, Wilson Papers, Ser. 2.

34. Bliss to Permanent Military Reps. to the Supreme War Council, 1 June 1918, Bliss Papers.

35. Permanent Military Reps. to the Supreme War Council, Joint Note No. 31, 3 June 1918, Bliss Papers.

36. Breckinridge Long, Diary entry, 31 May 1918, Long Papers.

37. Minutes of Third Meeting of Sixth Session of Supreme War Council, 3 June 1918, Bliss to AGO, 3 June 1918, Bliss to Newton Baker, 4 June 1918, all in Bliss Papers.

38. Bliss to AGO, 2 July 1918, Bliss Papers; Kennan, *Decision to Intervene*, 389–90; Unterberger, *United States, Revolutionary Russia*, 231.

39. Lansing to Wilson, 28 June 1918, Wilson Papers, Ser. 2; Bliss to AGO, 2 July 1918, Bliss Papers; Kennan, *Decision to Intervene*, 391–94; Unterberger, *America's Siberian Expedition*, 60, 66; Unterberger, *United States, Revolutionary Russia*, 235.

40. "Memo on Siberian Situation," Lansing Diary entry, 4 July 1918, and "Memo for a Conference at the White House in Reference to the Siberian Situation," 6 July 1918, Lansing Papers; Wilson to House, 8 July 1918, R. S. Baker Papers; Lansing to Wilson, 8, 9 July 1918, Wilson Papers, Ser. 2; Unterberger, *United States, Revolutionary Russia*, 235.

41. Gen. Tom Molesworth Bridges to Baker, 25 July 1918, N. D. Baker Papers.

42. Wilson to Lansing, 23 Aug. 1918, *Lansing Papers* 2:378–79; Calhoun, *Power and Principle*, 219–49.

43. Wilson to Joseph Tumulty, ca. 23 Apr. 1919, Wilson Papers, Ser. 5B.

44. Wilson comments, 5th Plenary Sess., 28 Apr. 1919, Wilson Papers, Ser. 5B.

45. Wilson, "Presenting Report on League," 14 Feb. 1919, in Woodrow Wilson, *The Messages and Papers of Woodrow Wilson* (New York: Review of Reviews, 1924) 2:618, 621.

46. Wilson, "Address before the Senate," 10 July 1919, in *Messages and Papers* 2:709, 710–11, 712; Wilson to Tumulty, 23 June 1919, Wilson Papers, Ser. 5B.

7. THE ABUSES OF FORCE

1. Russell Watson, Margaret Garrard Warner, and Thomas M. DeFrank, "Was Ambassador Glaspie Too Gentle With Saddam?" *Newsweek*, 1 Apr. 1991, 17; Tom Mathews, "The Road to War," *Newsweek*, 28 Jan. 1991, 59.

2. Mathews, "Road to War," *Newsweek*, 28 Jan. 1991, 58.

3. Ibid., 65.

4. Lyndon Johnson, *The Vantage Point: Perspectives of the Presidency, 1963–1969* (New York: Popular Library Edition, 1971), 250, 579–91.

NOTE ON SOURCES

Some excellent scholarship has been published on Woodrow Wilson and his various military interventions since The Kent State University Press published *Power and Principle: Armed Intervention in Wilsonian Foreign Policy* in 1986. Yet rather than repeat the lengthy bibliography at its conclusion, I will mention the most recent works here and simply refer those readers interested in the sources I used to that earlier work.

Scholars of American diplomatic history continue to show an unflagging interest in Woodrow Wilson and his legacies. Hardly a meeting of the Society of Historians of American Foreign Relations convenes without at least one session devoted to Wilson. The summer 1991 meeting heard three. Scholars continue to debate Wilson's health, his Russian policies, and his status as realist or idealist. Wilson is attributed with defining best the American vision of liberal international captialism, a vision that continues to motivate much of U.S. foreign policy. Akira Iriye—and who could know better?—claims that understanding Wilson is "essential for a better understanding of twentieth-century U.S. foreign policy" ("Exceptionalism Revisited," *Reviews in American History*, June 1988).

Much of recent scholarship on Wilson has focused on the latter years of Wilson's presidency, particularly his efforts at the Paris Peace Conference. In 1986 Arthur Walworth published *Wilson and His Peacemakers: American Diplomacy at the Paris Peace Conference, 1919* (New York: W. W. Norton), thus concluding his series on Wilson. Klaus Schwabe's *Woodrow Wilson, Revolutionary Germany, and Peacemaking, 1918–1919* (Chapel Hill: Univ. of North Carolina Press, 1985) is equally useful. Lloyd E. Ambrosius has written a particularly fine study of Wilson's troubles with the treaty, titled *Woodrow Wilson and the American Diplomatic Tradition: The Treaty Fight in Perspective* (Cambridge: Cambridge Univ. Press, 1987).

Relations with Russia have attracted almost as many studies. Linda Killen's *The Russian Bureau* (Lexington: Univ. Press of Kentucky, 1983) is the best account of U.S. efforts to help revolutionary Russia. Betty Miller Unterberger's recent book, *The United States, Revolutionary Russia, and the Rise of Czechoslovakia* (Chapel Hill: Univ. of North Carolina Press, 1989) provides refreshing views on Wilson's clumsy interventions in Russia.

Robert H. Ferrell offered a new look at the American entry into World War I in *Woodrow Wilson and World War I: 1917–21* (New York: Harper and Row, 1985). In 1987, Kendrick Clements published a very good study of Wilson titled *Woodrow Wilson, World Statesman* (Boston: Twayne, 1987).

No one with any interest in Woodrow Wilson can ignore the tireless work of Arthur Link and his fellow editors in the *Papers of Woodrow Wilson* (Princeton, N.J.: Princeton Univ. Press). The series is indispensable for any study of the Wilson era and will stand as the model by which all other editions of personal papers are measured.

Although these works and those I cited in *Power and Principle* were crucial to my understanding of Wilson and his uses of force, as the reference notes in this volume testify, I relied first and foremost on a range of primary sources. The huge collection of Wilson's papers stored at the Library of Congress Manuscript Division was fundamental. So too were the records of the State Department, War Department, Navy Department, Marine Corps, and Bureau of Insular Affairs maintained at the National Archives. The papers of Newton D. Baker, Tasker Howard Bliss, William Jennings Bryan, Josephus Daniels, Robert Lansing, John J. Pershing, Hugh L. Scott, Leonard Wood, and a score of other collections, most again—fortunately—at the Library of Congress Manuscript Division, were also essential to the study.

Unfortunately, and somewhat surprisingly given the pressing importance of the topic, the uses of force have not received nearly as much scholarly treatment. There is, of course, a considerable body of literature addressing issues of war and peace, with particular emphasis on finding a way to replace the former with the latter. Especially interesting is the curious book by Francis D. Wormuth and Edwin B. Firmage titled *To Chain the Dog of War: The War Power of Congress in History and Law*, 2d ed. (Urbana: Univ. of Illinois Press, 1989). Wormuth and Firmage would strip the presidency of most of its powers, including the power to deploy troops, giving Congress the power to make such basic decisions. Throughout their book the authors strenuously insist that the congressional power to declare war actually encompasses control over all those acts, political and diplomatic, that might *initiate* hostilities. How their plan could be of much advantage was never adequately explained. There is much that can be done to reform presidential abilities to resort to force, but using some peculiar constitutional interpretation to transfer that power to Congress hardly gives cause for optimism.

If *The Uses of Force* accomplishes anything, I hope that it encourages the objective study of force, stripping it of reactionary emotionalism that distorts much more than it enlightens. Force is only as good or bad—however defined, whether morally, ideally, practically, or realistically—as the purposes controlling it. Until we fully understand those purposes, we have little reason to hope that future uses of force will be any better controlled or more intelligently applied than they have been in the past. The first step toward understanding, it seems to me, is to define the subject at hand.

INDEX

ABC Conference, 39, 82–88, 107–8
Abuses of force: defined, 128; in Cold
War, 136; in Vietnam War, 136–38;
during rescue mission to Iran, 138; since
WWII, 139–40; in Panama, 140–41
Aggression, 130
Aguilar, Candido, 16
Allende, Salvador, 139
Allied Naval Council, 111
American Expeditionary Force, 114
Arabic, 50, 101
Archangel, 118–23
Argentina: and ABC conference, 82–88
Arias, Desiderio, 30–31, 69, 72, 73
Aristade, Jean-Bertrand, 142
Armistice, 103–4
Arms control, 101
Arredondo, Licenciado Elisso: and Punitive
Expedition, 43–44; and establishment of
Joint Mexican-American Commission,
92–94
Association, use of force as: defined, 9;
role in twin Russian interventions, 33–
34; as applied by Wilson, 106–9; during
WWI, 109–13; during twin Russian in-
terventions, 113–23; as part of League
of Nations, 123–26; mentioned, 131,
132; in Persian Gulf War, 134–35; limits
of, 142
Austria-Hungary, 110, 122

Báez, Ramón, 28–29
Baker, James A., 134–35
Baker, Newton: and Punitive Expedition,
32, 41–47, 91; orders to Pershing, 110;

wartime strategy of, 114; twin interven-
tions in Russia, 115, 122; mentioned,
140
Balfour, Arthur, 116
Baxter, Clarence, 71, 73, 75
Beach, Edward, 59
Belt, John W., 44
Benson, William S.: and occupation of
Haiti, 64, 66; and occupation of Do-
minican Republic, 68, 71, 73
Bliss, Tasker H.: disillusionment with
Wilsonianism, 4; mentioned, 17; and
Punitive Expedition, 44; and Joint
Mexican-American Commission, 95–99;
sent to Europe, 110; on Supreme War
Council, 110–13; and WWI strategy,
113–14; and twin Russian interventions,
116, 119
Blue, Victor, 38
Bobo, Rosalvo, 23, 58–59
Bolsheviks, 33, 103
Bolshevik Revolution, 103, 111, 114–16
Bonilles, Ignacio, 95–99
Boquillas, Tex., 90
Bordas Valdés, José, 26–28
Boxer Rebellion, 130
Boyd, Charles T., 91
Brazil: and ABC conference, 82–88
Breckinridge, Henry, 13–14
Brest-Litovsk, Treaty of, 114
Bridges, Tom Molesworth, 121–22
Bryan, William Jennings: and occupation
of Veracruz, 13–15; and protection of
Mexican employees, 16–18; and occupa-
tion of Haiti, 20–25; and occupation of
Dominican Republic, 26–29; and force

166

USES OF FORCE

was composed in 10/12 Electra
on a Xyvision system with Linotronic output
by BookMasters, Inc.;
printed by sheet-fed offset
on 50-pound Glatfelter Natural acid-free stock,
notch bound in signatures,
and wrapped with paper covers printed in two
colors on 12-point C1S stock with film lamination
by Braun-Brumfield, Inc.;
text designed by Diana Gordy;
cover designed by Will Underwood;
and published by

The Kent State University Press

KENT, OHIO 44242